Kesva an Taves Kernewe...
The Cornish Language Board

Reversing Language Shift:
The Case of Cornish

Ute Wimmer

The published version of a doctoral thesis
successfully submitted in 2006 to
Karl Franzens University, Graz, Austria

Kynsa Dyllans mis Meurth 2010

First Edition March 2010

Dyllys gans Kesva an Taves Kernewek
Published by the Cornish Language Board

Pryntys gans Redborne Printers, Rysrudh, Kernow
Printed by Redborne Printers, Redruth, Cornwall

ISBN 978-1-902917-59-7

Foreword

The present work, in fact the slightly modified version of my doctoral thesis submitted to the Faculty of the Humanities at Karl-Franzens-University Graz, Austria, in March 2006, aims to assess the highly interesting sociolinguistic situation of Cornish in an international context. Both its title and theoretical framework rely on Joshua Fishman's model (1991).

I would especially like to thank Prof. Annemarie Peltzer-Karpf for kindly supporting me through all the years. She has always encouraged my interest in research, being the motivating force behind my activities abroad. I also wish to thank Prof. Alwin Fill for being my second supervisor and for opening up an ecolinguistic perspective on my topic.

In Cornwall, I am greatly obliged to Dr. Ken George, Head of the Cornish Language Board vocabulary and grammar committee and representative of the 'European Bureau for Lesser Used Languages' Cornish sub-committee, for his valuable advice and for establishing useful contacts. Moreover, I am very grateful to Prof. Philip Payton, Director of the Institute of Cornish Studies, for providing me with free material and to Jenefer Lowe from Cornwall County Council for giving two extensive interviews. Further thanks go to the Cornish speakers/teachers John Parker, Gary Retallick, Malou George, Tony Hak, Pol Hodge, Ray and Denise Chubb, Deborah Griggs from Hayle Community School and Daniel Prohaska-Ryan.

During my several stays in Cornwall, I have also made friends among the non-Cornish-speaking population, and I am particularly indebted to Paul Stevens and the families Weldon and Stephens for making me feel welcome in their homes when I was faced with a lack of accommodation (especially in summer, when Cornwall attracts huge numbers of tourists).

In addition, I would like to thank my sister-in-law, Dr. Susan Collins, for her considerate assistance and my friend, Dr. Georg Marko, for his practical advice and help with the layout. Last but not least, I want to say thank you to my family for their support and above all, to my husband Michael, whose generosity and understanding made this project possible at all.

Kesva an Taves Kernewek / The Cornish Language Board

Table of Contents

0   Introduction

> Obviously we must do some serious rethinking of our priorities, lest linguistics go down in history as the only science that presided obliviously over the disappearance of 90 percent of the very field to which it is dedicated. (Krauss 1992:10)

Since completing my Master's Thesis on *Language Death and Revival: A Sociolinguistic Investigation of Cornish and Welsh* (Hirner 1997), I have observed an enormous rise in publications, surveys, conferences, Internet platforms and newsletters on endangered languages. Linguists and organizations worldwide are trying to raise awareness of the alarming situation which witnesses the death of one language roughly every fortnight (Crystal 2004:47). According to Broderick (1999:1), the development cannot be stopped. These shocking statistics made me take a closer look at the facts related to the sad phenomenon and compare figures from different sources to arrive at a somewhat reliable estimate, if that is possible at all.

Chapter 1 is dedicated to language death, providing a survey of the tragic trend world-wide and reviewing studies and theories. Interestingly, research into the Celtic languages has contributed considerably to the establishment of the field, e.g. Breton (Dressler 1972), Scottish Gaelic (Dorian 1981) or Manx (Broderick 1999). The main subject of this paper, however, will be Cornish, another Celtic language, which was virtually extinct throughout the 19th century and had not been given much attention until the beginning of the 20th century. Thus, the history of Cornish will be outlined by applying it to a theoretical framework of language death after Sasse (1992).

The problem of diverging realities will be taken up again when it comes to determining the present state of Revived Cornish whose existence, after a remarkable revival, still seems to be ignored by a number of sources. Since the spread of English has been responsible for the decline of Cornish and many other languages, its dangerous but also beneficial potential as a global language will be examined.

In the ensuing chapter, which is devoted to language revival, the issue of multilingualism will be discussed and arguments in favour of linguistic diversity will be presented. The relatively new discipline of ecolinguistics draws parallels between linguistic and biological diversity and pleads for the preservation of both. In recent years, the protection of minority languages as part of a human rights awareness has been provided by several international agreements but whether they are put into practice still depends on the policies of the respective governments. Although linguists can support language communities to maintain their indigenous languages, the attitude of the community itself has been identified as the crucial factor.

In order to evaluate the success of language restoration, Fishman (1991) has created the theoretical model of 'Reversing Language Shift' (RLS) which has also lent its name to this dissertation. The theory hinges upon several stages that small endangered language communities may pass on the way towards revitalization with the ultimate goal of intergenerational transmission. Consequently, the position of Cornish will be assessed against the background of selected reports of other minority languages which have already undergone RLS efforts. In this context, the role of new communication technologies, above all the Internet, will be considered. Obviously, electronic dissemination of information (e.g. through newsletters) has made it easier to organize projects and conferences which give moribund language communities a platform and also the Cornish movement has been able to benefit.

Chapter 3 will introduce a number of institutions linked to the European Union which specifically promote Europe's 'lesser-used' languages and contribute to the principle of cultural diversity. Especially the 'European Charter for Regional or Minority Languages' protects and encourages historical regional or minority languages in Europe and in 2002, the British Government finally recognized Cornish as an official minority language by including it in the Charter. Paradoxically, the Cornish people themselves still do not count as a national minority despite a proven distinct culture and identity. However, official recognition of the language opens up new possibilities. For the first time ever, the language movement can expect funding and a strategy paper is supposed to implement the objectives of the Charter. On the successful models of Hebrew, sister language Welsh and cousin Manx, the priority is to integrate Cornish into the (pre-) school system.

As will be demonstrated in chapter 4, Revived Cornish, which has in the past been criticized as artificial, is capable of expressing modern concepts but the existence of four language varieties complicates the situation. Despite its enhanced status, there are several other obstacles, such as the changing population structure, lack of learners' motivation or negative attitudes, which may prevent the development of Cornish into a community language. Accordingly, hypotheses concerning the consequences of official recognition will include positive expectations and future challenges.

The fieldwork in Cornwall was undertaken in the course of four stays (January/February 1997, August/September 2000, August 2002, March 2005) over a nine-year period of observation. Methods to obtain authentic data involved interviews with speakers and learners of Cornish, attendances at social and cultural events, visits of several institutions and the study of local newspapers, magazines and electronic newsletters. The empirical survey of language attitudes was carried out by means of questionnaires during the most recent stay which was financed by a research grant from the Central Office of the Faculty of the Humanities at Karl-Franzens-University Graz. In addition, I was inspired by the participation at the IX. International Conference on Minority Languages in Kiruna, Sweden, in June 2003, which was kindly sponsored by the *Österreichische Forschungsgemeinschaft* and the *Steirische Landesregierung*.

The following chapters will present subjects, material, methods and results of the questionnaire investigation which was supposed to find out about attitudes, habits and motivational factors of three different target groups: Cornish speakers/learners, pupils who have received Cornish lessons at a pilot school and a sample from the non-Cornish-speaking population. Besides, individual comments of the respondents will be given ample room to complete the picture. In the overall discussion (chapter 10), where findings will be compared according to the hypotheses established, implications of Fishman's model will be reviewed as well.

It has been fascinating to observe how a 'sleeping language' has been recalled to life. While writing, conditions for Cornish have improved again but as will be described in chapter 11 ("Conclusion and Perspectives"), setbacks still have to be faced. Another long-term study might be needed in order to keep track of this dynamic process.

1   Language Death as a Worldwide Phenomenon

1.1   Preliminary remarks

The extinction of a language is an integral part of the loss of identity of a tribe, people or nation. Peoples and their languages have always died out throughout history. What is new and so alarming about the current situation is the "breathtaking" **speed** at which this loss takes place (Wuketits 2003:19,171). Also Trudgill (2000:191f.) stresses the extraordinary pace and extent of this universal development since the last years of the 20th century. Haarmann (2001:51) thinks that our progressive society has used its technological knowledge to exploit nature which consequently threatens the habitats of small communities.

The first chapter tries to explore both the theoretical aspects and practical consequences that the loss of languages entails. In order to illustrate the mechanisms of the phenomenon, the history of Cornish, the actual language of interest in this book, will be reviewed.

1.2   Definitions, types and theory

The concept of *language death*, actually the metaphorical name of language extinction, only became established as an independent field of study within historical linguistics in the second half of the 20th century (1957). Since then it has been applied to different contexts so that it seems useful to comment on various definitions and expressions connected to the phenomenon. One of the first who applied the term in sociolinguistic studies of Breton was the Austrian Dressler (1972a/b):

> Language death may include such an extinction of a minority language due to language shift, physical liquidation (genocide) of all speakers of a language or brutally enforced assimilation to a majority language (linguacide) or rapid extinction of a language without intermediate bilingualism (multilingualism). (Dressler 1981:5)

Broderick (1999:1) who has been investigating the death of another Celtic language, Manx, comes up with the following interpretation:

> Though somewhat macabre in formulation, the notion of 'language death' would adequately describe the endpoint of a sociolinguistic development affecting minority languages in competition with a dominant language or languages, during which process the cultural traditions attached to the dying language and the sociocultural and perhaps the ethnic distinctiveness of the group that speaks it may perish together with it.

Whereas Aitchison (1993:198-209) distinguishes between the terms *suicide* and *murder*,[1] Campbell and Muntzel (1989:182f.) have introduced *sudden death* as opposed

---

[1] In the more dramatic version of language murder, languages may disappear at the worst "by the destruction of the habitats of their speakers, as well as by genocide, forced assimilation and assimilatory

to a *gradual* one. A similar approach has been adopted by Haarmann (2001:53-58) who identifies three types:

a. **Gradual language death**, the most frequent type, occurs when a dominant language slowly undermines more and more functional domains of the weaker language. Typically, the young generation first switches over to a more prestigious language.

b. **Abrupt language death** is a collective event, caused by an external, often violent, impact, such as genocide, natural disasters or epidemic diseases (cf. footnote 1).[2] Brasil, where ethnocide is still being practised because of economic interests, represents a sad, current example.

c. **Language death as a consequence of a functional weakening process** mostly takes place in a certain direction: from formal to informal and from specialized to general functions, e.g. a language first loses its status as a regional official language, then as a medium of instruction, next in the workplace, then among friends and finally within the family. The second subtype, "from the bottom to the top", occurs less frequently, namely when public and private functions get lost and only special (symbolic) functions remain, as in the case of ritual languages.

Haarmann (2001:58) points out that the three types may overlap, for instance a minority language belonging to category a.) may develop into type b.). Type c.) can be considered a preliminary stage of type a).

Jones (1998:4f.) defines language death as the "end-point of *language obsolescence*" allowing varying rapidity from 2 generations to hundreds of years. If the death of a language is extremely rapid, it may happen that the last speakers are fully fluent. For instance, Swadesh (1948) reports in his history of the extinction of Yahi, a northern Californian Indian language, that Yahi died in a period of only 60 years. Fishman (1991, see below chapter 2.6) and Trudgill (2000:191) use the term *language shift* (defined as "the change from the habitual use of one language to that of another" by Weinreich 1968:106-110) which, similar to *language obsolescence* (see below), carries the meaning of 'gradually abandoning or disappearing'. The shift of language use is normally understood to move "toward loss of the indigenous [...] language in favour of national and world languages" (Dauenhauer and Dauenhauer 1998:60f.).

For Haarmann (2002b:189), language death as the extreme case of *language conflict* occurs when a dominant language exerts too much situational, functional and prestigious pressure on the minority language until it declines at all levels. Phillipson (2003:145) holds economic interests and government policies responsible if "less powerful languages [...] become victims of *linguicide*". Also Grenoble and Whaley (1998a:52f.) claim that economics may be decisive in determining the fate of a threatened language as the pressure to assimilate to an economically dominant culture is

---

education, [...] and bombardment by electronic media, which Krauss calls 'cultural nerve gas'." (Pinker 1994:260). For a summary of Aitchison's distinction, see Hirner 1999:16f.

[2] Crystal (2004:52) mentions natural disasters, among them – highly topical – tsunamis, as frequent causes for the decimation of small, isolated communities. The consequences of the tragic flood from December 2004 in south-east Asia may have destroyed the infrastructure of entire communities and thus affect the ecolinguistic balance in the long run.

huge. Naturally, triggers have changed in the course of time as colonisation and expansion and the formation of national states have been replaced by advanced mobility and communication technology, which "reach and penetrate even the remotest corners of the world" (Broderick 1999:1).[3]

Nancy Dorian (1981),[4] whose fieldwork on Scottish Gaelic is considered one of the major contributions to the establishment of the field, has coined the term linguistic *tip*:

> In terms of possible routes toward language death it would seem that a language which has been demographically highly stable for several centuries may experience a sudden "tip" after which the demographic tide flows strongly in favor of some other language. (Dorian 1981:51)

In the case of language *obsolescence*, the number of speakers of a language is declining and gradually, the language is being used in fewer and fewer contexts. A frequent pattern is the diminishing competence of younger community members and the only remaining elderly fluent speakers. The generation of (mostly middle-aged) imperfect speakers whose communicative ability is limited is called *semi-speakers* (cf. Dorian 1981, Bradley 2002:6). Their speech is typically characterized by extensive lexical borrowing from the intruding language, historically inappropriate forms and a reduction of morphological complexity.[5]

However, studies have also revealed that the decay in certain parts of the system may be compensated by an enrichment of structures in others (Dorian 1981:153-155, Aitchison 1993:206f., Bradley 2002:7). Aikhenvald (2002a:31, 2002b:144) even asserts that endangered languages may become "innovative in that they develop new categories and new terms". A problem could be an extremely rapid change so that younger people might end up speaking a completely different language (Dorian 1994).

At this point, the frequently claimed parallel between language death as "the end-point [...] of a possible linguistic life-cycle" (Jones 1998:40) and the processes of pidginization and creolization, in fact "creolization in reverse" should be mentioned (Trudgill 1976 and Mühlhäusler 1980:21, cf. also Menn 1989:335, Dressler and Wodak-Leodolter 1977:37, cit. in Jones 1998:40). In Dressler and Wodak-Leodolter's (1977) view, the simplifications in a dying language are not systematic but random, which means that the language undergoes a process of pidginization. In accordance with Mougeon and Beniak (1991:15), Jones (1993:9) demonstrates that despite several sociolinguistic similarities, the simplifications taking place in pidgin languages are far more massive than those arising during obsolescence (details in Jones 1998:40-43).

---

[3] Other causes for language death are discussed in Baker (1993:42f.) and Crystal (2004:52-56).

[4] For a synopsis of Dorian's study, cf. Hirner (1997:10-12).

[5] Hagen and de Bot (1990) and Jones (1998:249-257) describe structural changes in dying languages in detail. Tsitsipis (1989) and Sasse (1992b:61) propose a continuum of imperfect speakers ranging from *rusty speakers* who are not fluent due to a lack of practice but have a sound basic knowledge, to competent semi-speakers and finally to *rememberers* (cf. Jones 1998:246). Dressler's (1981:6f.) categorization of such speakers is even more elaborate. However, none of these categories can be applied to Cornish as living speakers with different degrees of linguistic competence were not available to interview, let alone to record.

From a purely formal approach, language death is defined as the final stage of "the decay of linguistic structure a minority language undergoes on the way to total language shift" (Dressler 1981:5). However, the irregular simplification on the one hand and a continuation of complex systems on the other hand, made Dorian (1981:154) conclude that

> Sociolinguistic rather than purely linguistic features distinguish change in 'healthy' languages from change in dying ones. The types of changes in formal language structures are not notably different from those well established in the study of language change in general. But the timespan for change seems to be compressed and the amount of change seems relatively large.

1.2.1 Sasse's model

Since the study of language death as a linguistic branch in its own right has come into existence relatively recently, suitable models are only in the process of being created (Broderick 1999:4). Currently, the most comprehensive theoretical schema is that of Sasse (1992a), where he generally sets out three forces occurring in a chain reaction which typically lead to language death (cf. Jones 1998:240, Broderick 1999:7-11 and Bowden 2002:115f.):

a.   The External Setting (ES) triggers the entire process. Extralinguistic – cultural, sociological, ethnohistorical and economic – factors put so much pressure on a speech community that it has to abandon its language.

b.   Speech Behaviour (SB) and attitudes change due to ES (see below 1.3 loss of balance in *diglossia*).

c.   Structural Consequences (SC) are the formal linguistic changes in phonology, morphology, syntax and the lexicon of the endangered language as a result of SB change (see above 1.2).

Figure 1 illustrates the phased-displaced appearance of the forces:

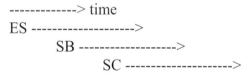

Figure 1: Continually operating factors leading to language death (after Sasse 1992a:13)

There are divergent opinions on when to declare a language extinct: some linguists consider a language already extinct if it is used only passively. Others think that a language is alive when some record of it exists (cf. Broderick 1999:9f., Crystal 2000:11-19, Dalby 2002:220f. and Wuketits 2003:168-170). According to Sasse (1992b), the final point of language death is reached when regular communication within a speech community has stopped. Yet also a dead language may survive as a ritual language (see above 1.2c) or as in the case of Manx, leave a substratum in the lexicon of the Manx-English dialect (Sasse 1992a:18).

Following Broderick's study of Manx (1999:7-11), the model will now be applied to the decline of Cornish.

Photo taken in Mousehole, Cornwall (January 1997)

1.2.1.1 The death of Cornish

The history of Cornish is usually divided into four phases (George 1993a:410):

1.   **Primitive Cornish:** about AD 600 to 800 (no written records)
2.   **Old Cornish:** 800 to 1200
3.   **Middle Cornish:** 1200 to 1575
4.   **Late Cornish:** 1575 to 1800

When Cornwall was under Norman influence after 1066, the progress of English was halted because the ruling Normans spoke Norman-French among themselves and used Cornish to communicate with the mass of population (Berresford Ellis 1974:30f.). In addition, not only Bretons who had arrived with the army of William the Conqueror and who soon held higher positions in Cornwall, but also Breton workers came to Cornwall as the wages were higher than at home (George 1993a:413). Since Cornish and Breton are sister languages, one can suppose that this close contact must have had a beneficial effect on the communicative status of both languages.

Although during the period between 1300 and 1500, Cornish literature, especially miracle plays, was flourishing (for details cf. Berresford Ellis 1998:10f. and Payton 2002c:18), the percentage of Cornish speakers decreased continuously from 95% in 1050, 61% in 1400, 26% in 1600 to only 5% in 1700 (George 1993a:415). Still, in 1542 Andrew Borde witnessed the existence of Cornish monoglots (Berresford Ellis 1998:12, Payton 2002c:17):

> In Cornwall is two speeches; the one is naughty Englyshe, and the other Cornyshe speche. And there may be many men and women the which cannot speake one word of Englyshe, but all Cornyshe.

Despite the geographical remoteness of the peninsula, situated in the southwest corner of the British Isles and surrounded by sea, the Cornish language receded further and further west (see Spriggs 2003).

Map 1: Cornwall's geographical position

Ad a.): The process of decline was set in motion by the following historical developments (External Setting):

- During the Wars of the Roses (1455-1485), many of Cornwall's gentry were killed and new families moved into the county. Cornish speakers were regarded as being inferior and the language a rural dialect (Berresford Ellis 1998:11).

- Tudor Centralism and the Reformation: The first Act of Uniformity of 1549 introduced English in all church services in England, Cornwall and Wales. As a consequence, Cornwall rose in arms and the leaders of the insurrection demanded, "We, the Cornishmen, whereof certain of us understand no English, utterly refuse this new English," but in vain (Berresford Ellis 1985:137). The Prayer Book rebellion, regarded as 'The Cornish Holocaust', claimed 11% of the Cornish population (MacKinnon 2004:269).

  George (1993a:413) considers the Reformation as main cause of the decline of Cornish because it additionally stopped the intensive Cornish-Breton relationship. As a consequence, the Bible and prayer book were not translated into Cornish as it had been into Welsh. Pool (²1982:7) even thinks that Cornish would not have died out if it had got its own Bible.

Due to the pressure, Cornish became increasingly irrelevant, which also weakened the national consciousness, created a negative attitude among the Cornish people themselves and finally led to the decision to abandon Cornish in favour of English. Lyon (2001:20f.) reports:

> [...] those who spoke Cornish were looked upon as second-class citizens, and that if one was to be recognised at all in this Anglo-centric world, he or she had no option but to forget anything that smacked of Cornishness; and replace it by English – speech, thinking and mannerisms.

Ad b.):

As a result, Speech Behaviour was affected: Parents stopped transmitting the Cornish language to their children so that they would not be "handicapped" (Berresford Ellis 1998:17). The domains which kept Cornish alive longest were fishing and tin mining. One of the last speakers, who had learned Cornish as a second language, noticed in 1776 (George 1993a:414):

> *Nag es moye vel pager po pemp en dreau nye ell clapia Cornoack leben, poble coath pager egance blouth, Cornoack ewe all neceaves gen poble younk.*

> There are no more than four or five in our village who can speak Cornish now, old folk of fourscore years. Cornish is all forgotten by young people.

Ad c.):

In addition, structural consequences were triggered by the change in speech behaviour. So William Scawen in his '*Antiquitas Cornu-Britannia*' (around 1680) and the great Welsh Celticist Edward Lhuyd, who observed Cornish just after 1700, clearly commented on its corruption (Brown and Sandercock 1994:14).

Also the literature of Late Cornish shows signs of decay: English words, assimilated to Cornish phonotactics, and English word order intrude, verbal particles are left out and initial mutations are not used according to the grammatical rules (Pool ²1982:13; see below 4.3.3 and cf. also Jones's chapter on linguistic phenomena in obsolescent Cornish 1998:334f.).[6]

Although name and death year (1777) of the reputedly last native speaker, Dolly Pentreath, are typically cited in many books (cf. photo 1.2.1), there is disagreement about when exactly Cornish completely died out as a spoken language. Berresford Ellis (1998:20) claims that the last native speakers died only one hundred years later, Lyon (2001:20f.) even gives detailed evidence that "a certain working knowledge of the traditional language was carried right through into the 20th century".

Undoubtedly, Cornish has survived in over 500 dialect and loan words which are still known nowadays in the Cornish variety of English (e.g. 'clunk' = to swallow, from Cornish *collenky)*, in thousands of place names (e.g. 'Penzance' from Cornish *penn* = head, end)[7] and personal surnames (see 9.2; Pool ²1982:29 and Dalby 2002:219). According to Dalby (2002:230), Cornish also left traces on the standard English lexicon ('mort', 'bludgeon', 'bugaboo' and technical terms in tin-mining).

Another example of the continued effect of Cornish on the local dialect is the use of the of the word *mis* ('month') in combination with the actual name of the month. So it is still common to hear 'January month' (*mis Genver* = January) or 'May month' (*mis Me)* in the Cornish dialect of English.

---

[6] Mutations, the most remarkable feature which Cornish shares with the other Celtic languages, are systematic changes affecting the initial consonant of words in certain grammatical situations, see below 4.3.1. For a detailed description of Cornish word order cf. Brown (²1993) and Page (1993b).

[7] Over 75% of Cornwall's place names are derived from Cornish (MacKinnon 2000:14).

1.3   Why are some languages more liable to death than others?

> There are no primitive languages. The great and abstract ideas of Christianity can be discussed even by the wretched Greenlanders. (Johann Peter Suessmilch, 1756, in a paper delivered before the Prussian Academy, quoted in Fromkin and Rodman 1998:476)

> Irish will butter no bread. (Hindley 1990:179)

> Why should one want to remain Breton, backward and superstitious, when the possibility existed to become a fully-fledged member of a modern, progressive and fully-civilised French society? (Williams 1991a:6)

The cause cannot lie in the fact that there is something wrong with the dying language itself, let alone primitive according to the misconception of some 19th century "Eurocentric" colonialists (Haarmann 2001:13). Also Jones (1998:241) refers to one of the most influential linguists of the 19th century August Schleicher's view that North American Indians "are unfitted for historical life because of their endlessly complicated languages" and are therefore predetermined to "gradual extinction" (Schleicher 1856:82) as being at best naïve. Some scholars who ignore social and economic causes have supported another extreme opinion: a language can commit suicide when its structure has become too impoverished. Research results, however, have proved quite the reverse: structural changes are not the cause but the consequence of language decay. The Darwinian view does not work here because languages lack genes and are thus not apt to natural selection (cf. Dalby 2002:218).

A language's functions, inherent linguistic structure and complexity have always been sufficient for the needs of its speakers as otherwise it would not have survived so long. In addition, each language has its specific lexicon, e.g. the Sami (Lapp) languages of northern Scandinavia have several individual words to tell apart different types of English *reindeer* (Trudgill 2000:15f.). On the other hand, English definitely contains more words referring to the semantic field of computer technology. As the linguist Edward Sapir (1921:19) observed: "The lowliest South African Bushman speaks in the forms of a rich symbolic system that is in essence perfectly comparable to the speech of the cultivated Frenchman." From this follows that all languages spoken today are equally efficient (Cavalli-Sforza 2001:78), have equal status in their function as vents of cultural identity and none is more important than any other (Haarmann 2001:14).

The problem is that languages are vulnerable to social, economic and political changes and an unsteady situation often enables a more socially dominant language, usually the one which is more fashionable and has higher prestige, to take over. If a generation chooses to speak the mainstream language in order to expect a better future, one could argue that this is much more important than the maintenance of a 'superfluous' language. Quite frequently, the younger generation is simply not interested in tradition and regards the dominant language as a way to economic prosperity, modernization and social advancement (Rottland and Okombo 1992:277, Kulick 1992:249). In this case speakers "cease to nourish" their traditional language (Dalby 2002:219).

The term which describes the transitional situation is *diglossia*, where two mutually exclusive varieties are used in the same speech community.[8] Whereas the 'high' (H) variety, in language death situations equivalent to the dominant language, is used in

---

[8] It is the mutual exclusiveness that distinguishes diglossia from bilingualism.

official domains such as administration, education and the media, the 'low' variety (L), the language in decline, is primarily spoken in familiar surroundings.[9] In language obsolescence, the balance is gradually being lost in favour of H, so that L has to give up more and more functions.

As the decline of Cornish has demonstrated, the process may be accompanied by feelings of inferiority (see 1.2.1.1) and even turn to hate towards the minority language which could be seen as the reason for economic hardship suffered by its speakers, as it was the case with Irish.

Dalby (2002:84) reports that before the 20th century the general attitude of majority language speakers towards speakers of minority languages was biased in the sense of "unlucky, backward or […] under-developed". In addition, numerous cases of obsolescent languages that were outlawed in the classroom have been reported, e.g. Sorbian (see Bott-Bodenhausen 1996b:136-139), Welsh and the notorious "Welsh Not" or the equivalent Breton *symbole*.[10]

1.4   Language death from a chaotic perspective

According to Haarmann (2001:15f.,59), although the interplay of variables causing language death are chaotic in nature, it doesn't mean that the course is in disorder. What is more, language demise is an extremely complex and dynamic phenomenon. Recent chaos theory research has confirmed that all complex systems function along chaotic principles of organization (cf. Lightfoot 1999 and Peltzer-Karpf 2006). This also applies to the chaotic interaction of ecolinguistic factors whose framework is so many-sided that predictions about developmental trends are hardly possible. Population size, bilingualism, urbanization, modernization, migration, industrialization and speaker attitudes have different impacts on different societies and interact in dynamic ways. A language that looks healthy now could become moribund within ten years and reversely, languages which once were in danger have quite recovered.

Latin seems to have had everything that most languages can only dream of: formal institutions, large numbers of speakers and enormous prestige. Dorian (1981:2) mentions a few of the now well-established European languages: for example, Finnish was threatened by Swedish, German was under French pressure in the seventeenth century and even English, now impending over many minority languages, was at risk in the two centuries after the Norman conquest. Haarmann (2001:59f.) gives the example of Rapa Nui, the native name for the Easter Island which also denotes its language.

---

[9] Diglossia also occurs in normal stable language situations, e.g. Swiss German and Faroese are not endangered (Romaine 1989:39).

[10] In 1847 a report on the state of education in Wales emphasized the gap between the English-speaking wealthy and the Welsh monoglot poorer classes in blaming the Welsh language for the often inadequate state of schools and for all other negative, including moral, conditions. The report also revealed how Welsh-speaking children were treated in many schools: "My attention was attracted to a piece of wood suspended by a string round a boy's neck, and on the wood were the words 'Welsh…[not]'. This, I was told, was a stigma for speaking Welsh. But, in fact, his only alternative was to speak Welsh or say nothing. He did not understand English and there is no system in exercise of interpretation." (Berresford Ellis 1985:81)

Wars, diseases and slave trade heavily decimated the number of speakers in the 1860s and 1870s. It seemed as if Rapa Nui was doomed to die by the end of the 19th century. Now the language is still widely spoken on the island as it has been resistant to the dangerous impacts and successfully adapted to the conditions of a changing world. Undoubtedly, the huge geographical distance from American mainland (3,760 km) has contributed to the unity of the small language community.

To sum up, obsolescence does not necessarily lead to the extinction of languages (Brenzinger and Dimmendaal 1992:3, Mougeon and Beniak 1991:43). As this study aims to show, the process may be hindered and languages, in particular Cornish, may be actively revived.

Before that, it seems useful to take a look at the international linguistic situation.

1.5   Facts and figures

Crystal (2000:10) warns that "estimates about the number of languages in the world [...] must be treated with caution", let alone translating percentages of threatened languages into absolute figures. Before one can grasp the real scope of the linguistic "crisis" (Krauss 1992), it is necessary to relate figures of moribund languages to an overall number. Since recent estimates vary enormously, some reasons for such inaccuracy will be discussed first. In order to gain a detailed insight into this problematic matter, the reader should consult Crystal (2000:2-10).

1.5.1 How many languages are there?

> And the whole earth was of one language, and of one speech.
>
> Let us go down, and there confound their language, that they may not understand one another's speech. (Genesis 11:1,7 quoted in Fromkin and Rodman 1998:476)

Never before has there been such a high amount of data on language diversity as today. Although in the past ten years information seems to have exploded, there are still languages whose existence is uncertain, e.g. Iapama in Brasil (Haarmann 2001:21).

What makes answering this question accurately even more difficult is the sometimes vague distinction between dialects from languages in their own right (Trudgill 2000:3-5,191).[11] When it comes to determining an exact number, a further problem arises due to the existence of different names for one and the same language. Hence as many as 22,000 distinct terms have been collected (cf. Crystal 1995) and the 'Language Name Index' of the *Ethnologue*[12] (Grimes 2000) even lists 41,806 alternate names.

---

[11] Dialect death is a distinct field of study (see Jones 1998 and Fromkin and Rodman 1998:472f.).

[12] <http://www.sil.org/ethnologue> The Ethnologue database is probably the most comprehensive survey which updates information on the world's languages every four years. It has included research results from thousands of linguists for more than 50 years and on the other hand provides them with other current language data.

Consequently, the reader is faced with extremely divergent representations ranging from fewer than 3,000 to 10,000 languages (Wuketits 2003:165; Fromkin and Rodman (1998:483) give 4,000 to 8,000, Gibbs (2002:64) 5,000 to 7,000 and Fill (1993:19) 3,000-5,000). Bodmer (1955), Berlitz (1982), Winkler and Schweikhardt (1982) and Décsy (quoted in Fill 1993:19) put the number at around 2,800, which definitely seems too low from the present state of the art. Most linguists agree that there must be at least 4,000 languages which can be classified into 20 language families (cf. Wuketits 2003:165). Viereck, Viereck and Ramisch (2002:37) state that linguists and archeologists had investigated 6,760 languages till the 1980s, of which 3,964 have already died out.

The most commonly mentioned figure is the average of "6,000 or so" (e.g. Krauss 1992:5, Crystal 2004:47). Whereas Haarmann (2001:21, 2002a) offers the most exact number of 6,417, Trudgill's estimate (2000:191), "It is not too inaccurate to say [...] that there are about 6,000 languages in the world today." is more guarded. In addition, DoBeS, the German acronym[13] which represents a programme for the 'Documentation of Endangered Languages', counts approximately 6,500 languages, and the 'Foundation for Endangered Languages' homepage[14] 6,800. An article from the German weekly quality newspaper *Die Zeit* (28 February 2002) quotes UNESCO's *Atlas of the World's Languages in Danger of Disappearing* (Wurm 2001) with 6,000 "idioms". The Austrian newspaper *Salzburger Nachrichten* (7 September 2004, p.11) refers to an estimate of 6,500 by the *Volkswagenstiftung*, a German charity foundation promoting the documentation of moribund languages. In another article (2 August 2005, p.19), around 7,000 languages are reported based on a publication by the German Max-Planck-Institute of Evolutionary Anthropology in Leipzig. Whereas the web version of the *Ethnologue* (Grimes 2000) has registered 6,809 languages spoken in the world, Gibbs (2002:64) refers to its latest edition listing 7,202 languages worldwide. After citing various other sources and their estimates, such as Dixon (1997:143) or Grenoble and Whaley (1998), Crystal (2000:10f.) decides to take the range of 5,000 to 7,000 as lower and upper limits.

In accordance with the mean figures listed above as well as for the sake of simplicity, percentages will relate to the average of 6,000, if not stated otherwise.

1.5.2 How are they distributed?

According to Haarmann (2001, 2002a, cit. in Wuketits 2003:165f.), there are 1,906 languages in Asia, 1821 in Africa, 1268 in the Pacific Ocean area, 1013 in America, 266 in Australia and 143 in Europe.

Figure 2 illustrates the distribution across continents (percentages are rounded off to integers):

---

[13] DoBeS = **Do**kumentation **Be**drohter **S**prachen, <http://www.mpi.nl/DOBES/introduction.html>

[14] <http://www.ogmios.org/176.htm>, quoting the Worldwatch Institute, Washington (AP), June 19, 2001.

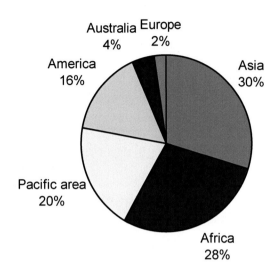

Figure 2: Distribution of languages across continents

Again, numerical data vary, so e.g. Crystal (1995) considers Africa, not Asia, the richest continent in terms of languages (Wuketits 2003:166). What linguists agree on, however, is the "poorest" position of Europe in this ranking despite a rich history and cultural diversity. On the other hand, Wuketits (ibid.) stresses the enormous concentration of languages on the small Pacific islands, above all the republic of Vanuatu with the official languages English and French plus 80 languages scattered over 15,000 square kilometres and 170,000 inhabitants.

Yet the most outstanding example is Papua New Guinea with 800 (826 according to Haarmann 2001:212) mostly unrelated languages dispersed over 500,000 square kilometres and 5 million inhabitants (Wuketits 2003:160f.). Due to their isolation, archipelagos tend to be natural language barriers and therefore provide favourable conditions for the development of distinct tongues.

Nevertheless, like their natural counterparts, animals and plants, insular languages tend to be particularly endangered. The reason is simple if you look at the proportions of number of languages to the number of speakers. Statistically speaking, in Papua New Guinea each language is spoken by fewer than 7,000 people. So many of these insular languages with a maximum of 1,000 speakers are defined as *Kleinsprachen*, so-called "dwarf languages"[15] (cf. Haarmann 2001:13).

The credit for the documentation of the world's 1,982 small languages which are equivalent to 30.8% of the total of languages goes to the linguist Harald Haarmann (2001). A majority of 64.8% accounts for "*Kleinere Sprachen*" ('smaller languages'), spoken by more than 1,000 but fewer than 1 million speakers (Haarmann 2001:211).[16] In contrast to that, only 4.2% (n=273) of the world's languages are classified as "*Millionensprachen*", spoken by at least 1 million people which also includes the

---

[15] Since this not politically correct term evokes negative associations, it is frequently avoided. For the time being Haarmann's term *Kleinsprachen* ('small languages', minority languages) seems to denote the category best. For a presentation of different terminology in use see chapter 3.1.1.

[16] Another comparative value was mentioned in the Austrian weekly scientific TV programme 'Modern Times' (broadcast on 14 January 2005): 90% of all languages are spoken by fewer than 5,000 people.

category of "*Großsprachen*" with over 100 million speakers (Haarmann 2002a, cit. in Wuketits 2003:167). Languages of this category include (in increasing order concerning number of speakers) Mandarin Chinese, English, Hindi, Spanish, Russian, Arabic, Bengali, Portuguese, Indonesian, French, Japanese and German (for details cf. Haarmann 2002a).

Not all of these *Großsprachen* are considered 'world languages' as this status implies supraregional influence (cf. Wuketits 2003:167). Crystal (2000:14) only counts 8 languages over 100 million, excluding Arabic (209 million speakers according to Haarmann 2002a), Indonesian (175 million, ibid.), French (131 million, ibid.) and German (101 million, ibid.). This statistical deviation appears odd since Wuketits (2003:166f.) even ranks Arabic and Indonesian with the category 'world languages'.

Summarizing Crystal's statistical observations (2000:14f.), the 8 languages over 100 million are spoken by nearly 2.4 billion people and further, the top 20 languages are shared among 3.2 billion people who constitute more than half of the world's population.[17] An analysis downwards leads to the astonishing deduction that 96% of the total population speak only 4% of the world's languages or if this calculation is turned upside down: the remaining 4% of the population speak 96% of the world's languages (see also Crystal 2004:50). Beyond doubt, the trend is towards *Großsprachen*.

The following subsection will examine the distribution of *Kleinsprachen* in more detail.

1.5.2.1   Kleinsprachen (minority languages)

It is a fact that an abundance of languages concentrated in an area implies a large portion of 'small languages'. Crystal (2000) and Haarmann (2001) also obtain different results in terms of percentages in the category of languages with fewer than 1,000 speakers. Whereas Haarmann counts more than 30% of the languages among this category (see above 1.5.2), Crystal's estimate arrives at 25%. Although their figures vary, both agree that the percentages are too high to be ignored even if the overall number of speakers may be small. Multilingual states with the highest portions of *Kleinsprachen* are Papua New Guinea (n = 459 ≅ 55.6%), Australia (n = 255 ≅ 93.4%), Indonesia (n = 207 ≅ 28.8%), USA (n = 158 ≅ 74.2%), and Brasil (n = 151 ≅ 64%) followed by Vanuatu (see above 1.5.2, 74.5%). Haarmann (2001) provides many more interesting data which would go beyond the scope of the actual topic.

Finally, the proportion of *Kleinsprachen* to the total number of languages across continents in Table 1 (source: Haarmann 2001:212) should point out the discrepant situation in comparison to Figure 2 above (n = number of):

---

[17] 6 billion is a widely accepted approximate value for the world's population.

Continent/area	n languages	n *Kleinsprachen*	portion of *Kleinsprachen*
World	6,417	1,982	30,8%
Asia	1,906	231	12,1%
Africa	1,821	122	6,7%
Pacific area	1,268	775	61,1%
America	1,013	575	56,7%
Australia	273	255	93,4%
Europe	143	15	10,5%

Table 1: Proportion of *Kleinsprachen* to the total number of languages across continents

1.5.3 Classification of languages according to the level of danger

In order to assess the future of *Kleinsprachen* and compare degrees of endangerment in all parts of the world, the need for a general classification arises. Three levels are widely accepted: **safe**, **endangered** and **extinct** (Crystal 2000:20).

In addition, Krauss (1992:4) has introduced the notion **moribund**, which describes languages that are no longer transmitted from one generation to the next. Moreover, a five-level system is in use that makes a finer distinction between the two extreme levels: **viable**, **viable but small** (isolated or strongly organized communities with more than 1,000 speakers), **endangered**, **nearly extinct** (spoken by a few old people) and **extinct** languages (cf. Kincade 1991:160-163).

Another one subdivides the level 'endangered' into **potentially endangered, endangered, seriously endangered, moribund** (equivalent to Kincade's 'nearly extinct') and **extinct** (for a detailed description of the terms see Wurm 1998:192).

Linguist Leanne Hinton (2001b:413) of Berkeley University California prefers the "less final metaphor" of **silent** or **sleeping** languages, which obviously applies to the case of Cornish.

The process of classification gets even more complicated when one compares the different interpretations of 'safe'. In fact, the absolute number of speakers is not necessarily expressive concerning vitality or sociocultural developments. Rather the age of speakers and their social contact behaviour are crucial. Krauss (cit. in Pinker 1994:259) assumes that only about 600 languages are safe by means of a minimum of 100,000 speakers and this is even optimistic since the sheer number of 100,000 does not guarantee survival (cf. Crystal 2004:51).[18]

1.5.4 Languages on the way to extinction

In the past 100 years, 600 languages have fallen out of use. Sometimes, the exact year of death is given, namely that of the last speaker. Wuketits (2003:158f., adopted from

---

[18] The UNESCO holds that at least 100,000 speakers are necessary to ensure intergenerational transmission.

Haarmann 2002b) lists a few recent cases, such as Tillamook (Oregon, †1970), Manx Gaelic (Isle of Man, †1974), Homa (Sudan, †1975), Yamana (south Chile and Argentina, †1978) or Suryoyo (Syria, †1998).

In the 1970s and 1980s, many languages were spoken by just one or two speakers, which implies that some of them must already be extinct today.[19] Both Wuketits (2003:163f.) and Haarmann (2001:15f.) regard the sadly famous example of Ainu[20], the native language of the Japanese people which now only few old people are having a passive knowledge of, typical of a language in its final stages.

Moreover, Haarmann (ibid.) states that most of the 105 "dwarf languages" with one (n = 47; in 1999 the figure was still 51 according to a 1999 survey by the Summer Institute of Linguistics organization Ethnologue), two (n = 36) or three speakers (n = 22) alive, are prevalent in Australia and Brasil.

Wuketits (2003:174) even goes as far as to call the USA, Brasil, Colombia and the Australian continent, which have witnessed an accumulation of deaths, "language cemeteries."[21]

Of the hundreds of Indian languages in North and South America, which have died out since the arrival of the Europeans, most names are not known (cf. also Trudgill 2000:192).

In Africa, most expired languages have not left any traces so that nothing can be said about the causes of their demise.

More favourable conditions for linguists can be found in Asia. The continent once housed a majority of the old civilized languages which were able pass on their ideas to posterity, e.g. Sumerian culture was transmitted via the Old Testament (e.g. the division of the week into seven days). Although more than 20 Asian languages have become extinct in the last few decades and many of the *Kleinsprachen* spoken in Siberia have just got few speakers left, the overall situation in Asia (apart from Indonesia and Malaysia) is not as dramatic as in America and Australia (Wuketits 2003:175).

The same applies to Europe which will be treated separately (see below 1.5.6). Similarly, the dead languages Old Greek and Latin have survived at schools and universities exerting enormous influence on other cultures and languages.

In 2000, a third of the world's languages had not been recorded yet (Crystal 2004:49). In addition, the problem of conservation and documentation of languages which have only been orally transmitted easily raises prejudice towards 'primitive' languages (see above 1.3). Wuketits (2003:176) argues that those peoples who are unable to write tend to be threatened physically as well so that many might have become extinct by the end of this century.

---

[19] Wuketits (2003:169, adopted from Haarmann 2001) presents a non-exhaustive list of 27 languages distributed over different continents that had fewer than 100 speakers in the 1980s.

[20] Ainu, like e.g. Basque, is an isolated language which means that it is not related to any other one (cf. Cavalli-Sforza 2001).

[21] However, extinct aboriginal languages have survived in hundreds of loanwords for typical Australian terms, e.g. *kangaroo* and *boomerang* (Dixon et al. 1990).

1.5.5 How many languages are threatened?

Since a language does not expire from one day to the next, it is quite difficult to determine when a language is dead. Similarly, scholars come up with divergent interpretations concerning the initial stages of decline. Some believe that a language is already threatened when it is not passed on to all members of the following generation, others think that in order to survive a language must be taught at school, regardless of the number of speakers.

Haarmann (2001:17f.) stresses the fact that it is not possible to categorize the languages of the world according to their level of "vitality" without hesitation. Even experts can be mistaken when it comes to assessing a language's chances of survival. One reason for this may be that minorities and their languages are often neglected in national census forms and researchers rely a lot on official statistics if speakers of small languages are scattered geographically, a situation that applies to Cornish as well.

Also the Welsh language has been object of two sharply differing speculations: in 1880, it was predicted that the number of speakers would grow to 3 million within 100 years.[22] 80 years later, another estimate foresaw the death of Welsh by the year 2000 – the reality is more than half a million speakers (2001 Census figure: 582,368, excluding speakers aged under 3).

Haarmann (ibid.) also raises the issue of "winner and loser languages" throughout history. Whereas information on majority languages abounds, the documentation of minority languages was rather scanty in the past.

In 1992, the linguist Michael Krauss "sent a shudder through the discipline of linguistics" when he predicted that 50% of the world's languages would very likely disappear as communication tools within the next century (Gibbs 2002:64). He also warned that unless worldwide efforts were undertaken to stabilize the decay of many indigenous languages, the percentage might increase to 90%.

In concrete terms, 150 Indian languages in North America (about 80% of the existing ones, further details are provided by Fill 1993:23; for the situation in Canada consult Edwards 1994:21f.), 40 languages in Alaska and northern Siberia (90%), 160 languages in Central and South America (23%), 45 languages in Russia (70%), 225 aboriginal languages in Australia (90%, cf. also Fill 1993:24, Trudgill 2000:192 and Wuketits 2003:174) are moribund (cit. in Pinker 1994:259) and nearly 200 languages (around 11%) are endangered in Africa (Sim 1995:470). Krauss's opinion was joined by other authorities in the field (e.g. Crystal 2004:47).

According to a recent report on behalf of UNESCO (Wurm 2001), half to three quarters of the 6,000 languages are doomed or likely to disappear in the foreseeable future and also the *Volkswagenstiftung* estimates that two thirds (out of 6,500) might fall out of use within two generations.

Summing up, whereas gloomy estimates which predict the death of 90% of the world's languages seem to be a bit exaggerated, the assumption that only two thirds will survive the 21st century are realistic (Haarmann 2002a). The seriously endangered third will primarily affect *Kleinsprachen*, whose chances are minimal. The probability for a

---

[22] Today, this would roughly equal 100% of the overall population.

Kleinsprache to become a *Millionensprache* within the next 100 years is considered zero, but the probability for a majority of *Kleinsprachen* to die out is extremely high (Robins and Uhlenbeck 1991).

Finally, Crystal (2000:166) concedes that even current figures are relative because "languages are dying at an unprecedented rate." He concludes, "If the estimates I reviewed in chapter 1 are right, another six or so have gone since I started to write this book."

In the following subsection the problematic issue of categorization will be examined more closely by comparing the state of Cornish as described by different authors.

1.5.5.1   *Representation of Cornish in different sources: what is true?*

The highly interesting case of Cornish, after "virtually lying on its deathbed, had fresh life breathed into it, and rose again" (Lyon 2001:21), is frequently mentioned in sociolinguistic literature.

Due to the absence of a suitable question in recent censuses, it is hard to assess the present, actual number of speakers. Estimates range from 2,000 to 3,500 speakers with different communicative competence (semi-speakers), which does not even amount to 1% of the total population of 482,700 (*Die Zeit*, encyclopaedia, vol.3, p.161, Hamburg, 2005). Only about 10% (n ≈ 200-300) are considered to be fluent, effective speakers.[23] Nowadays, ten to a dozen families use Cornish in the home as principal medium of communication and the number of people learning the language is continuously rising.

Since publications on minority languages and language loss and maintenance are steadily on the increase (see below 2.8.2), only a selection of general sources, excluding specifically Celtic books, was taken into consideration. The range of representation has turned out to be wide: Whereas many experts stress the remarkable achievements of the revival (e.g. Crystal 2000:162), several authors have been treating Cornish, often together with Manx, as a dead language.[24]

In Wardhaugh (1987:76-78), Cornish is still listed under the heading of 'extinct languages' (along with Shetland Norn, Channel Islands French and Manx) although the author mentions that "a few hundred people claim to be able to speak and read Cornish today". In addition, he calls revived Cornish "a somewhat piecemeal and quite artificial creation of antiquaries" (Wardhaugh 1987:78).

It is astonishing that the online UNESCO *Red Book Report on Endangered Languages* (see 2.8.1) also lists Cornish as extinct (last updated in 1993), referring to only one source (Price 1984).[25]

---

[23] The UK Committee of the European Bureau for Lesser Used Languages (see 3.2) has even identified 840 fluent speakers. Details on the problematic issue of determining an exact number are given by Kennedy (2002:285f.).

[24] The last speaker of Manx reputedly died in 1974. After being revived, it now claims several hundred speakers (see below 4.6).

[25] After the publication of Professor Glanville Price's book *The Languages of Britain* (1984), which severely criticized Unified Cornish, the prevailing standard spelling system of the revivalists, an amended system of orthography was adopted (see below 4.3).

The widely acclaimed linguistic introductory course book by Fromkin and Rodman (1998:472) devotes one sentence to Cornish: "Cornish, a Celtic language akin to Breton, expired in England in the late eighteenth century". Also Trudgill's introduction to sociolinguistics (2000) only mentions the death of Cornish, withholding its revival. Mackey (1980/2001:68) simply reports that Cornish "is no longer used" in Cornwall.

Dalby's account (2002:80) also gives the impression that Cornish, "the lost Celtic language of Cornwall", has never been revived. In fact, he draws gloomy parallels with regard to the future of Gaelic and Welsh whose speakers are now almost all bilingual. Since Cornish was in a similar position in 1600, Gaelic and Welsh could suffer the same fate (Dalby 2002:84).

Whereas Haarmann's comprehensive documentation of the world's *Kleinsprachen* (2001) has been praised in 1.5.2, a critical remark must be made at this point because it simply neglects Cornish but includes Manx. This seems even more weird because Haarmann's source, the *Ethnologue* (Grimes 1996), counts Cornish among the living languages of the United Kingdom (UK). The Internet version of 2003 based on Grimes (2000) informs the visitor of a number of teenagers who have learnt Cornish from birth as their first language and reports the existence of 1,000 speakers who use Cornish as their everyday language plus 2,000 (!) who speak it fluently.

Also Payton (2000b:109) writes about a tiny number of 'native speakers' who have been raised bilingually by their parents. The majority of speakers, however, have studied Revived Cornish at evening classes.

Edwards (1991:270), although stating that "Manx and Cornish are no longer the maternal languages of anyone", pays attention to ongoing revival efforts.

Extra and Gorter (2001a:10) treat Cornish as a modern European regional minority language, estimating the number of speakers at 200.

According to Hinton (2001b:416), Cornish is learnt and spoken widely by adults as a second language. Moreover, she does not exclude the possibility of it being revived as a language of the home in the future.

Janich and Greule's handbook of language cultures in Europe (2002:126-128) gives a detailed, realistic account of the sociolinguistic status based on the independent MacKinnon Report (2000, see below 2.6.1.1). Despite the still relatively low number of effective speakers which amounts to approximately 300, the authors attest the movement a considerable growth (see Figure 3 below).

Joseph (2004:126) reports optimistically that "the highly interesting case of Cornish [...] is looking increasingly alive and well, in conjunction with the identity it corresponds".

It seems notable that the revival of Cornish is also covered in German magazines and newspapers. For example, a well-informed article in the culture section of the weekly *Rheinischer Merkur* (Nr. 16, 17 April 2003, p. 24) gives account of 3,000 people with some knowledge of the language, 300 daily users and some 20 children and teenagers who have grown up with it.

According to *Die Zeit* (28 February 2002), modern Cornish, a result of "tinkering about" with medieval texts, has hit public taste. Thousands have a command of it and infants learn it as a mother tongue.

Finally, *Spotlight*, a monthly magazine aimed at German speakers learning English, has also featured the "comeback" of Cornish (September 2003, p.20f.). 3,000 people are reported to speak some Cornish, around 200 speak it routinely.

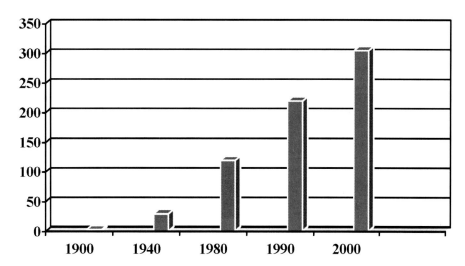

Figure 3: Increase in the number of effective Cornish speakers (see MacKinnon 2000, Appendix F)

As will be discussed later on, achievements of the contemporary Cornish revival are closely connected to its position in Europe and the European Union. Bearing this perspective in mind, the following chapter ought to set the framework.

1.5.6 Language death and multilingualism in Europe

Even though the situation in Europe does not seem as serious as in Australia or America, a number of languages have become extinct, e.g. Dalmatian in the 19th century and most notably for the purpose of this study the Celtic languages Cornish in the 18th (see above 1.2.1.1 and 1.5.5.1) and Manx in the 20th century.

Although Europe's linguistic diversity seems rather poor compared to other parts of the world (15 *Kleinsprachen* as against 44 *Millionensprachen*), it is very hard to find a strictly monolingual country without any indigenous linguistic minority speakers. The exception is Iceland with 100% native speakers of Icelandic (Trudgill 2000:120). In Romania, the most multilingual country, 15 languages are unevenly distributed among 24 million inhabitants (Trudgill 2000:122). National multilingualism in Europe, however, differs from situations on other continents in that dominant official national languages are considered linguistic minorities elsewhere, e.g. Swedish in Finland.

Trudgill (2000:121f.) lists German as an indigenous minority language in Denmark, Belgium, France, Italy, Slovenia, Serbia, Romania, Russia, Ukraine, Kazakhstan, Hungary, Czechia and Poland or, on the other hand, Danish spoken by a minority in Germany. Thus, the languages as such are not threatened by extinction.

Yet also several *regional* languages[26] have become endangered by national languages, such as the different varieties of Sami in Norway, Sweden, Finland and Russia, Frisian in Germany and the Netherlands, Basque and Catalan in Spain and France, Breton in France, Sorbian in Germany, Romansch in Switzerland or Welsh (Jones 1998), still the 'healthiest' among the Celtic languages, and Gaelic in the UK (for a complete list giving numbers of speakers see Fill 1993:22). Even national languages like Irish are in danger (cf. Hindley 1990).

Obviously, both governments and minority speakers have to cope with the challenges of multilingualism (cf. Trudgill 2000:122f.) and the status of minority languages varies considerably in different states (for the situation of Romany cf. Trudgill 2000:127). In this context, Trudgill (2000:123-126) also describes the current Welsh bilingual policy as a model approach in contrast to former times (see footnote 10).

White (1991:51) remarks that practically all members of linguistic minorities in Western Europe are at least bilingual, hence the existence of these language communities depends on a continuing state of diglossia (see above 1.3).

Whenever an ethnic minority group defines itself through a distinct language, the language issue plays a strong symbolic role for the minority movement to attempt to achieve (semi-)independence (e.g. the Basques in Spain). Governments may then react tolerantly, intolerantly or indifferently, nevertheless the European Union has established a number of control bodies and linguistic protection measures that are regarded with envy by revival organizations outside Europe (Crystal 2004:48, see below chapter 3).

The next section will consider the influence of the powerful *lingua franca* English, which has frequently been held responsible for the phenomenon of language globalization.

1.5.7 The role of English in the context of globalization

The modern history of the spread of English is unique in that English has been extraordinarily successful in expanding its functions, the number of its speakers and its prestige not only on the continent of its origin but all over the world. It has official or co-official status in numerous countries all over the world (for a complete list of states see Viereck, V. and Ramisch 2002:241) and serves as the base language for a number of creole and pidgin languages, e.g. Tok Pisin in Papua New Guinea (Fill 1993:24).

In North America and Australia alone, speakers of hundreds of indigenous languages have shifted to English, "the world's most dangerous language" (Bradley and Bradley 2002a:351). Bradley and Bradley (2002:xv) also mention that countries that were originally inhabited by Anglophone settlers, such as the US, Canada and Australia, have until recently not really encouraged native communities to continue speaking their mother tongues.[27]

---

[26] *Regional* is another adjective commonly used to denote minority languages in the European Union. For alternative terminology and a categorization of EU language communities see chapter 3.1.1.

[27] Dalby (2002:218) states that until 1969 the government of New South Wales separated half-white half aboriginal children from their families.

In Europe, the Celtic languages, with the exception of Breton, share the same fate: they have become the victims of the same language, English. One of the factors, which caused the decline of Cornish, was the dominant role of English as the language of commerce. In this connection, Price (2000) raises the question why the British Isles, since the arrival of the Saxons, has nurtured such a monolingual culture.

Phillipson (2003:64f.) lists fifteen structural and ideological factors that are responsible for the growing use of English in Europe. Crystal (2004:11-21) has identified ten domains in which English has become dominant: politics, economics, the press, advertising, broadcasting, motion pictures, popular music, international safety and travel, education and communications. In addition, Viereck, Viereck and Ramisch (2002:245) stress the importance of English in the fields of trade, technology and science and Fill (1993:24) refers to its prevailing role as technical language taught in worldwide ESP courses (English for Specific Purposes) and in the domain of sports.

It is therefore not surprising that borrowing from English is a widespread habit and even · a *Großsprache* like French (see 1.5.2) is "deathly afraid of the worldwide [...] power of English" (Fishman 2001b:457), militantly refusing to accept international, technical English terms as loanwords, e.g. 'computer' in German is *Computer*, in French *ordinateur* or 'walkman' *Walkman* (German), *baladeur* (French). On the other hand, Pinker (1999:183) reports that Japanese companies even use meaningless English names and slogans for the sake of prestige.

As we have seen in subsections 1.5.1, 1.5.2 and 1.5.5, difficulties arise when one has to work out an exact number, in this case of actual English speakers. If you add the number of native speakers of English to those using English as a second or foreign language, the total does not even amount to 10% of the world population (Haarmann 2001:19).

In another survey, Haarmann (2002a, cit. in Wuketits 2003:167) claims 573 million as equivalent to 11.3% of the overall population. Crystal (2004:8f.), however, arrives at a grand total of about 1,400 million (= 400 million first language + 400 million second language + 600 million foreign language speakers) which rougly equals a quarter of the world's population.[28] In comparison, Chinese, spoken by 1.210 million (Haarmann 2002a), threatens all minority languages in China.

Since English is relatively poor in terms of inflectional morphology but rich and flexible when it comes to word-formation, it achieves its purpose of a practical, international language ideally.

Moreover, it is a mother tongue, already known by millions of people as a second or foreign language and a literary language (Fill 1993:25). One could argue that the adoption of a neutral artificial language like Esperanto as a *lingua franca* would not only solve problems of multilingualism in multi-national communities, but also ensure the further use of the mother tongue as Esperanto is neither native to anyone nor a national language. From another point of view, however, this argument would not be

---

[28] Concerning foreign language learners, Crystal (ibid.) stresses the uncertainty of estimates, e.g. it is not known how many Chinese people are learning English. The British Council has estimated a billion learners of English, so the number of 600 million is reached from a deduction of one-third of absolute beginners, another guess.

acceptable because Esperanto, in spite of being easy to study than other languages, would privilege Europeans on whose languages it is mainly based (Trudgill 2000:135).[29]

Whereas Price (2000) explicitly terms English "a killer", Görlach (1995:46) calls "[...] the villain English [...] a tempter and seducer rather than a killer." because as a matter of fact, the knowledge of English promises better job opportunities and an improved lifestyle. It seems as if the economic and communicative advantages that the adaptation to the new language entails outweigh everything else. Bradley and Bradley (2002:xx) claim that "economic rationalism" and cutting budgets everywhere are "linked with widespread elite attitudes in favour of English as the global language".

According to the *Volkswagenstiftung* (quoted in *Salzburger Nachrichten*, 7 September 2004, p.11), globalization, often realized in the form of mass communications, media and information technology, is the main cause for the decline of many languages. Even isolated areas cannot escape from it, for instance when the first TV set in an Indian village of the Brasilian jungle introduces the luxury of the western consumer society to the smallest hut.

However, the Anglo-American tongue should not be blamed alone since it is also in distress due to the growing influence of Spanish. In fact, Spanish and Portuguese have been responsible for the loss of a number of local languages in South America and even US Americans feel threatened by Spanish. But also the power of Arabic, Russian and Mandarin Chinese in Asia should not be underestimated (*Die Zeit*, 28 February 2002). Moreover, whereas creoles may be endangered by decreolization towards English (e.g. Norfolk creole spoken on Norfolk Island, east of Australia, cf. Mühlhäusler 2002b), creoles like Tok Pisin or Kriol of northern Australia threaten a number of indigenous languages themselves (Bradley and Bradley 2002:xvi).

For Fishman (2001a:6), the globalization of economy, communication and media can have a boomerang effect as it is both "unifying" and "divisive", "constructive" and "destructive". In fact, globalization, which need not exclude "particularism", even enhances a "greater recognition of local co-identity" (Fishman 2001b:480).[30]

In Haarmann's view (2001:18-20), globalization is not directly responsible for the fragile state of many smaller languages. He argues that this perspective is one-sided since everyday life is not only restricted to economic and technological goals, to the consumption of mass media or fashion trends and highly specialized topics. Therefore English remains excluded from a number of domains, in particular the private one and smaller languages, whose speakers tend to be bi-or even trilingual, will keep their own functional space. Yet one should not regard these developments as diametrically opposed but complementary processes. Parallel to the international linguistic network, people have also become more conscious of the global multiculturalism and multilingualism in the past few years.

---

[29] Around 75% of Esperanto morphemes are of Romance and 20% of Germanic origin (Viereck, Viereck and Ramisch 2002:237).

[30] In general terms, *globalization* is defined as "the free movement of population and goods" (Fishman 2001b:480).

Leading up to the next chapter (see 2.3), Table 2 sets the two extreme language policy paradigms (probably best simplified by the catchwords 'globalization' vs. 'diversity') against each other in a framework consisting of ten parameters (for a detailed interpretation cf. Phillipson 2003:160-163):

Diffusion of English	**Ecology of Languages**
1. monolingualism and linguistic genocide	1. multilingualism and linguistic diversity
2. promotion of subtractive learning of dominant languages	2. promotion of additive foreign/second language learning
3. linguistic, cultural and media imperialism	3. equality in communication
4. americanization and homogenization of world culture	4. maintenance and exchange of cultures
5. ideological globalization and internationalization	5. ideological localization and exchange
6. capitalism, hierarchization	6. economic democratization
7. rationalization based on science and technology	7. human right perspective, holistic integrative values
8. modernization and economic efficiency; quantitative growth	8. sustainability through promotion of diversity; qualitative growth
9. transnationalization	9. protection of local production and national sovereignties
10. growing polarization and gaps between haves and never-to-haves	10. redistribution of the world's resources

Table 2: The Diffusion of English and Ecology of Languages paradigm (Skutnabb-Kangas 2000:657)

Finally, it seems useful to introduce the distinction between three coherent terms that are relevant to the field at this point: language *practice*, *ideology* and *policy* (after Spolsky and Shoamy 2001:356). The language practice of a community (Hymes 1974 called it ethnography of communication) consists of the rules for using the language and its actual uses. Language ideology is the set of beliefs about the motives and values for those uses and their rules. Language policy is an official endeavour to change language use or ideology of a speech community.

1.6 A typology of conditions for minority languages

Before assessing ways of how to save or revive minority languages in chapter 2, a sociopolitical framework to classify different conditions that *Kleinsprachen* have to cope with will be presented (adopted from Anderson 1990:127ff., for details see Haarmann 2001:23-28):

Type 1:   Conditions which promote the vitality of *Kleinsprachen*

Example: Papua New Guinea has a range of languages with varying numbers of speakers (from 2 million speaking Tok Pisin to languages with just 5 speakers left). Geographical isolation has encouraged the unity of local communities and thus keeps the pressure of assimilation at a minimum.

Type 2:   Ecological conditions which easily bring about the death of *Kleinsprachen*

Example: In Australia, a majority of aboriginal languages are spoken by fewer than 10 speakers and therefore endangered. Huge pressure to assimilate to the dominant languages (above all English, but also creole and immigrant languages like German)[31] has resulted in an ecolinguistic catastrophe for most indigenous languages (Bradley and Bradley 2002a:348).

English has influenced the lexicon of many native languages (e.g. *bugu-*'book', *dawun-*'town' in Dyirbal, English verbs plus native suffixes), also grammatical structures (native stems plus English derivational affixes) have been affected. Only about 20 (out of around 250) aboriginal languages are considered 'healthy' as they are used by all generations and passed on to the children (cf. Haarmann 2001:35).

Type 3:   Different local contact conditions which favour certain *Kleinsprachen* and threaten others

Example: In Brazil, Portuguese is dominating the 236 languages, among them many Indian ones. It depends on the contact behaviour of the tribes to what extent their language assimilates to the majority language (e.g. in some tribes it is forbidden to marry someone from the same group).

Type 4:   *Kleinsprachen* as objects of language planning ranging from promotion to suppression depending on ideological trends

Example: Although Russia is home to 137 languages, Russian has been the official language since 1991. Through autonomy of the new federation, some languages have gained the right to be used in administration. However, a knowledge of Russian is the only key to mobility in professional life (for details cf. Haarmann 2001:39-48).

Type 5:   Political systems which grant *Kleinsprachen* cultural and political rights

Example: The benevolent conditions in Finland, which is home to 11 languages, are a rare exception. In the province of Lapland, Sami (Lapp) was established as optional official language for 2,100 native speakers in 1991. According to Haarmann (2001:50), there is no other country in the world where a language with such a small number of speakers is granted such a special status (notice the status of Welsh as compared to the number of speakers, see 1.5.5 and 1.5.6).

---

[31] Fill (1993:23f.) surprisedly notes that Australia's 58 'community languages' only include immigrant languages but no aboriginal languages. This means that immigrants are able to listen to radio and watch TV programmes in their native languages, a service that is denied to the native people of Australia.

Since the 1970s, Sami has been a regular school subject and medium for the written entrance examination at universities and official buildings, forms and traffic signs are bilingual (Finnish and Sami). At the beginning, the only problem was to find enough staff being able to communicate in the three quite different varieties of Sami but this obstacle was overcome by providing adequate training. Haarmann (2001:228) illustrates the special circumstances by including a job advertisement from a Finnish daily newspaper (October 1999) written in three different versions.

Recently, the sociopolitical conditions for Cornish have improved so that its position would now be based somewhere in-between types 4 and 5 (see below 3.6.1).

2   Reversing Language Shift

A people without its language is a people without its soul.

(Translated from a Gaelic saying, cit. in Edwards 1991:271)

Since the late twentieth century, the preservation of the environment has become an acute topic. Just as species of fauna or flora are threatened, so are increasingly languages. And as more and more people realize that whales or rain forests have to be protected, a growing number of scholars and organizations encourage the revival of dying languages because they have understood that the destruction of a language implies the destruction of something unique shared by a community, something that contributes to cultural pluralism.

2.1   Multilingualism – a cost-benefit issue or a vicious circle?

With each newly learned language you acquire a new soul.

(Slovakian proverb, cit. in. Crystal 2004:61)

Would not communication be easier if there were just a handful of languages? The biblical story of Babel tells us that the "proliferation of languages in the world was a penalty imposed on humanity" (Crystal 2000:27). The legend expresses a widely held view that the existence of only one language would bring worldwide peace and reduce mutual misunderstanding (cf. Mühlhäusler 1994/2001:159f.). It goes without saying that supporters of this idea tend to be members of major monolingual nations. Unfortunately, numerous examples of mainly monolingual countries involved in wars refute this conception.

These thoughts suggest an economically based view and allude to the evolutionist theory of Darwin's 'survival of the fittest', where strong languages survive and weaker ones have to adapt themselves (see above 1.3; see also Mufwene 2001:147).

Phillipson (2003:49) underlines the failure of "ideologies of linguistic superiority" and stresses the fact that "any language has the potential to serve any purpose" as long as the resources allocated to it are sufficient. Although irrational fears often influence arguments in favour of a single world language, the economic argument seems very convincing at first sight. In order to ensure international communication, the diversity of languages requires enormous translation and interpretation costs which are additionally time-consuming.

This argument can immediately be countered by the 'human capital theory' (Crystal 2000:31) which suggests that the individual's knowledge of more than one language certainly contributes to the productivity of society as bi- and multilingualism and accompanying biculturalism endow speakers with economic, "intellectual, emotional and social advantages over monolinguals" (Wurm 2002:16). From a broader perspective, the economy does not only influence language but also vice versa, e.g. tourism can benefit from the cultural heritage of a language. As we have seen above, economic factors are frequently responsible for language shift, so these very same factors could also help to promote a language (Crystal 2000:30f.).

In conclusion, the advantages of a global *lingua franca* cannot be denied but do not necessarily have to affect the "well-being" of smaller languages. In fact, the command of two languages, one's native and an international *lingua franca*, would be "highly desirable" (Crystal 2000:29).[32] As their purposes would not overlap, they are supposed to co-exist in harmony. The main task is to convince governments to adopt a bi- or even multilingual policy, which again raises the question of money.

Finally, a statement made by a British government spokesman in 1988 that "3/4 of the translators for Britain in London, Strasbourg and Brussels are Welsh speakers"[33] should speak for itself (Climo 2002:6).

2.2   Why should we care about language diversity?

> If [...] languages are regarded as mere practical tools of communication, the fundamental way in which languages create and shape the way we see and understand the world is ignored. [...] Language is not simply a reflection of reality, it is a conceptual filter through which we constitute reality and see the world. (Phillipson 2003:108)

The current drive for preservation is not based upon a romantic illusion, but upon the objective fact that each language is a unique repository of the experiences and thoughts of a community and, according to the Sapir-Whorf hypothesis, the loss of linguistic diversity involves losing the range of potential ways of experiencing the world (for examples cf. Mühlhäusler 1994/2001:161f.). But why is it then so difficult to direct the public's attention to the language issue in the same way as the environmental issue? As Climo (2002:5) expresses, "We have lost Etruscan, Toltec, Aztek, Mayan, Tocarian, East Prussian, Norn, Scythian and a great many more – and the world still seems to carry on!"

Unquestionably, the loss of a language does not have the same life-threatening consequences as famine or diseases (Crystal 2000:32). Therefore it is even more important to come up with facts and reasonable arguments and combine them with awareness-raising actions (see below). Bradley and Bradley (2002:xif.) list four reasons why work on endangered languages is worthwhile:

a.   **Linguistic reasons**: Linguistics is a young discipline with a number of enigmas that remain to be revealed through extensive research, such as the field of linguistic universals. For example Ica, a language spoken in the north of Colombia, seems to lack a personal pronoun system, which had long been thought of as a linguistic universal. If rare structures of dying languages are not recorded, then the limits of certain grammatical phenomena will never be known, e.g. in terms of plural formation, some Australian aboriginal languages have four different forms for each noun: singular, dual, trial (denoting three of a kind) and plural, three among them are even characterized by five forms (Gibbs 2002:68;

---

[32] In this ideal situation, Esperanto would be a neutral alternative to English (see above 1.5.7).

[33] The Welsh-speaking population of Wales makes up approximately 1% of the UK population.

for further examples see Hale 1998:193-204). Moreover, linguists who investigate the occurrence of loanwords in unrelated languages can retrace ancient migration movements whose implications are not only relevant to historical linguistics but also to anthroplogy. The more sources of material there are, the more reliable the findings will be (Gibbs 2002:64).

b.   **Ethical reasons**: It is the responsibility of the older generations to enable their offspring to gain access to their traditional language and the knowledge and culture it contains.

c.   **Scientific reasons**: Every community shares special knowledge about its environment that is uniquely described by its mother tongue. If the language dies out, important scientific know-how could be irrevocably lost, e.g. about rare plants that could be crucial for the progress in modern medicine (cf. also Wuketits 2003:182,203).

d.   **Symbolic reasons**: Languages are medium, symbol and source of culture, history and literature, in short an essential part of a community's identity.

Similarly, Crystal (2000:32-67) presents five arguments to answer this chapter's title and underpin it in great detail:

i.   We need diversity

ii.   Languages express identity

iii.   Languages are repositories of history

iv.   Languages contribute to the sum of human knowledge

v.   Languages are interesting in themselves

Fishman (1991, see below 2.6.1) and Mühlhäusler (2002b:171) share the view "that the wish to maintain linguistic diversity" is not "a case of sentimentality or irrational nostalgia" but "rational". Mühlhäusler (ibid.), who is in favour of "taking active steps rather than adopting a free market rationalist or laissez faire approach", comes up with three arguments justifying language revival:

- Scientific argument: This does not correspond to Bradley and Bradley's category c) above, but stresses the fact that multilinguals have access to more information and are therefore capable of achieving better intellectual results.

- Economic argument: This refers to the aforementioned possibility of cultural tourism (see 2.1) for extra income.

- Moral argument: This obviously coincides with Bradley and Bradley's ethical reasons as a "loss of linguistic diversity" deprives "future generations of choices, resources and their spiritual home".

For Climo (2002:4), languages are "living things" as they "[…] develop, thrive, cross-polinate, grow old, rejuvenate and sometimes die". Cross-pollinating means "interchanging ideas or words" as in the case of English whose lexicon would be reduced to about 6,000 words instead of more than a million if there had not been influence from Latin, Greek, Hebrew, Celtic, French, Italian, Spanish, Hindi etc.

In addition, languages "interact, borrow, refine, export ideas and challenge the minds of their speakers, helping to shape a *weltanschauung*". Language does not only consist of grammar and vocabulary, but also of "ideas, attitudes, beliefs, songs, poems, proverbs, history, land and heritage", therefore it is unique (Climo 2002:5). Moreover, a "translated culture" becomes "inauthentic" (Fishman 2001a:3).

Haarmann (2001:76) regards the protection of minority languages as an element of a general growing ecological awareness that seeks to maintain a global ecological balance. The following chapter will introduce a new branch of linguistics that specifically deals with the relation between linguistic and biological diversity.

2.3   Ecolinguistics

> The plight of the world's endangered languages should be at the top of any environmental linguistic agenda. It is time to promote a new ecolinguistics - [...] one which is full of colourful and wide-awake green ideas [...]. It needs to be promoted urgently, furiously, because languages are dying as I write. (Crystal 2000:ix, preface)

From a morphological point of view, adding the clipped version of the neoclassical compound 'ecology' as a prefix to the lexeme 'linguistics' results in a new lexeme which denotes a new field within this discipline. For Gould (1993), *ecology* is responsible for competition and selection processes among species.

Applying the term to socio- and psycholinguistics, Haugen (1972) was the first scholar who connected the concept ecology with language. In the natural world, species of fauna and flora depend on each other and similarly, languages compete or keep their balance both within language communities (states) and in the brain of multilingual individuals. Therefore, research areas in Haugen's ecology of language include language change, languages in contact and conflict, language death and planning and also bilingualism and language acquisition.

For Mufwene (2001:11f.), the term *evolution* covers language change that does not necessarily imply any improvement or purpose (see also Gould 1993:303). Ecology brings about natural selection which is important in language evolution (cf. Mufwene 2001:147,153).

Denison (1982) stresses the parallel between biology and linguistics by comparing threatened animals and plants to moribund languages:

> If the sperm whale is worthy of special protection as a unique and threatened species of biological evolution, then surely so is Gaelic as a unique and threatened specimen of human linguistic evolution and tradition. (Denison 1982:8)

This comparison finds expression in the frequent use of metaphors transferred from biological ecology, such as "death" and "survival" (cf. Fill 1993:1f.), or "healthy", "moribund" and "dying" from the semantic field of medicine. For example, Görlach (1995:46) calls Welsh "the strongest Celtic patient" which has also become "infected with the immune deficiency syndrome" and regards Irish as "dangerously ill" (Görlach

1995:45). The influential sociolinguist Fishman, who compares language decimation with the struggle against "cancer" (2001:xiv) tries to "diagnose" the problems linked with language shift and to "prescribe (...) restorative efforts" (1991:1). What weaker languages need is the development of therapeutical approaches "to tackle (...) the same illness in patient after patient" (Fishman 2001a:1, see below 2.6.1).

Ecolinguistics, which investigates the role of languages in interaction with ecological and environmental issues, consists of several branches that are described in Fill's introduction (1993:7-9). The subfield relevant to the present study following Haugen's idea is called sociolinguistic **language ecology**.[34]

According to Wuketits (2003:19), diversity always presupposes a certain degree of inequality. As ecolinguists prefer small and weak (minority languages) to big and powerful (world languages), a particular aim is the preservation of linguistic and biological diversity. Despite the moral obligation to protect our threatened biological and cultural heritage, the costs of multilingualism and the justification of planning interventions from outside should be taken into consideration (Denison 1982:8f., cit. in Fill 1993:15-17).

Whereas Kurdish has repeatedly and successfully resisted state suppression, the status of Irish Gaelic in Ireland proves that the actual use of a language cannot be "prescribed" by a government (*Die Zeit*, 28 February 2002). Also the example of Welsh in Wales shows that official bilingual policies without "vigorous educational policies and the teeth of effective environmental planning and development" do not necessarily guarantee the effect that has been hoped for. On the other hand, Scotland will not be able to retain its Gaelic-speaking population "without some form of positive discrimination" (MacKinnon 1991:145). Although considered artificial, similar policies (e.g. language regeneration with the help of a specially supported local industry) have saved Irish in the *Gaeltachtaí* (cf. Hindley 1990 and Ó Murchú 1993). However, language planning measures can only be successful if the actual speakers can identify with them (Haarmann 2001:77).

For Climo (2002:4), who compares monolingualism with unicultures, species diversity is a measure of ecological health. Unicultures may bring about ecological degradation, resulting in "disasters" such as the Dutch Elm disease or the loss of the dodo on Mauritius.[35] Also Wuketits (2003:16) warns of the consequences of monocultures: as a result of overbreeding, the banana is threatened by extinction. Only few farsighted economists have already understood that the current biodiversity crisis and the ignorant attitude towards indigenous peoples' knowledge about natural resources will lead to big economic problems and prevent any further evolution (Wuketits 2003:19,183).

Wuketits (2003:173,156f.) points out another connection between the loss of species, peoples and languages. Due to deforestation most species are lost in the tropical rain forests which are home to many peoples whose decline goes hand in hand with the destruction of their habitats.

---

[34] The other subfield, psycholinguistic language ecology, deals with individual bi- and multilingualism and overlaps with its sociolinguistic counterpart in terms of language loss (cf. Fill 1993:12-15).

[35] The whole ecosystem of Mauritius was almost destroyed by the loss of one species as the germination of an essential plant which binds the soil depends on the bird.

As a result of the inevitable "involuntary incorporation of indigenous peoples" into the dominant society, "language death has become part of a human rights struggle" (Hinton 2001a:4, Nettle and Romaine 2000), which will be the topic of the following chapter.

2.4   The right to speak one's native tongue?

With the growing awareness of human rights, the interest in minorities is on the increase too as a discussion of basic human rights also implies the role of the mother tongue in society (cf. Skutnabb-Kangas and Phillipson 1994). The right to use one's mother tongue in administrative and legal affairs, church, school and the media is anchored in a still relevant outline of human rights by Kloss (1969:130) and in various international agreements claiming the protection of minority languages and cultures (for a more current description of conditions and tendencies in Europe, see Blumenwitz 1996 and Pan and Pfeil 2000, parts III and IV).

As a matter of fact, if the human rights are recognized as a whole, then the right to use one's native tongue and to live with one's culture should be automatically accepted. The United Nations and other non-governmental organizations (NGOs) signed the 'Universal Declaration of Linguistic Rights' in Barcelona in 1996, respecting "language rights as a basic component of human rights" (Bradley and Bradley 2002a:349).

The nominal acceptance of minority protection regulations by a state due to an international treaty is normally not the problem (e.g. the 'European Charter for Regional and Minority Languages')[36], but the sore point is whether and how protective measures are put into practice and who assumes responsibility (Haarmann 2001:70f.,76). Depending on the policies of the respective governments, minority language communities are faced with different attitudes, ranging from benevolence (e.g. Ireland) and indifference (e.g. China) to disapproval and hostility (e.g. Australia, Bradley and Bradley 2002a:348).

In analogy to the definitions of the terms 'racism' and 'sexism' as "inequality between groups […] identified on the basis of 'race' and 'gender'", *linguicism* refers to the violation of linguistic human rights (Phillipson 2003:66,145). An increasing number of indigenous groups in developed countries are beginning to insist on their linguistic rights and can be regarded as victims of linguicism if they are not entitled to receive funds in the absence of laws securing a status of their language in e.g. education.

Since the upgrading of local cultures and languages is idealistically motivated, it is independent of global intercommunication (Haarmann 2001:19). Haarmann (2001:7,16-18) criticizes the current practice of degrading minority languages as instruments to condemn the "ghost of globalization" and creating a very gloomy atmosphere. He compares the situation with Job's news on the ecological problems of our environment which have repeatedly turned out to be mass media "scaremongering".

Emotional "commonplaces" about society's ethical commitment to protect minorities are dangerous, a factual approach to this "explosive" topic would be more helpful.

---

[36] The French parliament, however, has frequently rejected the amendment of its constitution in order to allow a ratification of the European Charter for Regional or Minority Languages (see below 3.5.1).

Above all, the crucial point is the community's **attitude** towards its culture and language (Haarmann 2001:77), which will be discussed in the subsequent section.

2.4.1 Attitudes

> Why is it that one minority group assimilates and its language dies, while another maintains its linguistic and cultural identity? (Bradley 2002:1)

> Fostering positive language attitudes is, accordingly, one of the most important initiatives to be achieved in the task of language preservation. […] Languages decline when these positive attitudes are missing. And in so many cases they *are* missing. The climate is against them, often for political reasons. (Crystal 2000:81f.)

In the course of discussing language death and revival, the term *attitude* has already turned up several times. Many experts attach enormous importance to the attitude of a speech community towards its language (e.g Crystal 2000:81, Trudgill 2000:193, Haarmann 2001:77 and Wurm 2002:15), for some it even determines life or death of an endangered language (Jones 1998:360, Bradley 2002:1). In the 1940s, Einar Haugen already remarked that attitudes towards endangered languages tend to become better as soon as their impending death is apparent (Fishman 2001b:464).

Attitudes towards language use and support can vary a lot among members of a speech community. While some speakers appreciate their language as a symbol of separate identity and therefore may treat it as "sacred", others represent a more "profane" way of thinking, regarding the shift to a more dominant language as necessary (Broderick 1999:173). According to Ladefoged (1992:809-811), these two groups would often be equal in terms of size. In many cases, there is also a third group, the monolingual speakers of the dominant language in the area, whose policies and knowledge or ignorance play a crucial role. Speakers of that kind tend to think that "monolingualism is the natural state" (Wurm 2002:16). Such a discrepant situation applies to the revival of Cornish, which will be demonstrated in chapters 7.9 and 9.10.

In this connection, Bradley (2002:1-3) has raised several significant questions regarding the convictions and preferences of both minority and majority groups:

- Is bilingualism generally accepted?

- How do monolingual majority language speakers react to the use of the minority language in their presence?

- How do both minority and majority communities assess the usefulness, significance and beauty of the repective languages? Do parents speak the majority language to their children in order to enable future social and economic integration to take place? In this context, Nelde et al. (1996) have pointed out the factor of usefulness for social advancement in their report ("Parents want the best for their kids"; cf. also Mithun 1998:185).

- Are younger speakers discouraged from using the minority language due to purist attitudes of the older generation (Bradley 2002:6f., Dorian 1994)?

- Does society altogether promote, only just accept or even suppress the use of minority languages?

- How is the minority language lexically enriched, e.g. in terms of modern concepts? Are loanwords from the majority language welcome or are neologisms created from within? To what extent do code switching or mixing occur? Is the "semispeaker version" tolerated (Bradley 2002:7)?

- Is there a standard orthography? To what degree are speakers literate? Are there internal dialect varieties?

Although linguists can contribute to building up self-esteem and changing attitudes and consequently linguistic behaviour to some extent (see below 2.5), the willingness to maintain a mother tongue is up to its speakers. The situation in Ireland (see below 2.6.2.1) is exemplary of how active language use and attitudes may differ widely (Fishman 2001b:464).

2.5   The role of linguistics: demands and limitations

As a top priority, linguists have been busy gathering comparative data in the course of the past two decades and several major surveys have brought new information and figures to light. According to Bradley and Bradley (2002:xix), it is the duty of linguists to document and preserve languages, which also entails involvement with the respective language communities. However, they deplore that more funding tends to be made available for academic than practical research, the latter necessarily implying a slow long-term process (Bradley and Bradley 2002:xx). Although there are a number of archives which store endangered language data digitally, fears of a new tower of Babel exist. The problem is that different projects work with incompatible data formats and terminology which certainly complicates cooperation enormously (Gibbs 2002:68).

It is also a major task to "raise the consciousness" of both minority and majority speech communities, about how "precious and unique the resource of human linguistic diversity really is" (Bradley and Bradley 2002:xx). For Wurm (2002:20f.), linguists should primarily assist minority language speakers, develop learning materials and also older speakers should be integrated as "advisers and instructors".

Preceding chapters have outlined that languages undergo a series of structural and functional changes before they may eventually fall out of use. Thieberger's view (2002:310f.) is based on concepts of ecolinguistics: Which parts of a language must be preserved in order to avoid the term 'language extinction'? If a complex (e.g. noun) system is lost but the language is still spoken as a marker of identity, are endeavours to maintain it really necessary? For Mühlhäusler (2002a:38), the main question that should concern language maintenance is, "How can we preserve or recreate the ecological conditions for linguistic diversity?" Fill (1993:25), another main representative of ecolinguistics, does not believe that linguistics alone is capable of counteracting the ongoing loss of language diversity. Only a radical change of attitudes in terms of "ecological awareness" could be effective.

2.5.1 Criticism

> The task of investigating, documenting and perhaps saving the many endangered languages on this planet (as attempted by such organizations as TERRALINGUA) would be worth the while of more aspiring newcomers to ecolinguistics. (Fill 2001:44)

Despite the aforementioned current boom in linguistics and even fashion to work on endangered languages, "the field has accomplished depressingly little" (Gibbs 2002:67). Mühlhäusler (2002a:34) accuses linguists of having "operated with a concept of language that is ill-suited to the business of reversing the decline of the world's linguistic diversity and indeed may be one of the causes that accelerates it." In addition, he advises them to "rethink their discipline radically" if they want to achieve something (Mühlhäusler 2002a:38). Another critical comment is raised by Thieberger (2002:311) who, as already indicated above (2.5), argues that a few linguists' main motive for saving a language might be a special linguistic feature that is irrelevant to the speakers.

From an ecolinguistic point of view, linguistics is badly neglecting its most imperative task: the documentation and study of little-known *Kleinsprachen* and to strengthen threatened tongues. Instead, further details regarding world languages are being investigated with energy which could be summoned up for preserving the cultural heritage of small indigenous peoples (Fill 1993:25; Fill 1998).

To sum up, although growing enthusiasm within the scientific community can be observed now, "hit and run" fieldwork, by which Bradley and Bradley (2002a:351f.) mean the process of collecting data, publishing papers in academic journals (in a major language), pursuing an academic career and leaving the speakers behind, might not really help endangered language communities. They suggest that the linguist's work should be made more accessible by in-depth cooperation with the language community, resulting in the provision of attractive materials and audio/video tapes and the training of competent community members who can carry on with the job.[37]

On the other hand, money for research grants is very limited and as a staff member of the University of Pennsylvania expresses, "anyone who wants to work on endangered languages has to forgo a more lucrative and secure career." (Gibbs 2002:67). Further implications for the linguistic profession are outlined by Grinevald (1998:153-159).

2.6   Where are we now?

Since Einar Haugen's call for a 'typology of ecological classification' (1971:25) some efforts have been made to compare the status of languages, e.g. Edwards's typological model for minority languages (1992), extended by Grenoble and Whaley (1998a) with a hierarchical organization of factors (see below 2.6.2.4). Yet the problem is that there are no objective criteria as to the assessment of the grade of endangerment. Crystal (2000:92f.) demands a general theoretical framework based on case studies which should supply guidelines for diagnosis and provide common terminology (cf. 1.5.3 above). Krauss's work (1997) on age groups of small language communities has been an important step into this direction.

---

[37] In this connection, Bradley (2002:8f.) mentions the positive example of the Bisu in Thailand.

The following section will present Joshua Fishman's **Graded Intergenerational Disruption Scale** (1991), commonly known under the acronym GIDS, which is at present the most widely approved method to assess the vitality of obsolescent languages.

2.6.1 Fishman's model

Chapter 2 has been named after the title of a study by the American sociolinguist Fishman (1991), which marked an important milestone in the sociology of languages and whose publication established the field of *Reversing Language Shift* (RLS). Joshua A. Fishman is also known as the founder of other subfields of sociolinguistics, e.g. language maintenance and language shift, language and ethnic identity, language and nationalism, language planning and the sociology of bilingual education (Bartens 2001).

The theory postulates an eight-stage model in two phases (GIDS) which charts various levels of targets or obstacles that a dying language must overcome on the way towards the goal of revitalization. Yet each problem must be tackled before the following (Jones 1998:37), a sequence, which, as we will later see, does not always work. The ultimate aim of RLS is to re-establish intergenerational transmission, from which the name of the scale is derived, and to foster the unique role of languages in their own environment.

Table 3 shows the steps in reversing language shift which should be read from the bottom up, starting with reconstruction and aiming towards maximum communal and institutional use. The model adapted to Cornish will be represented in a graphically simplified form in chapter 10.2.6.

---

1. Education, work sphere, mass media and governmental operations at higher and nationwide levels
2. Local/regional mass media and governmental services
3. The local/regional (i.e. non-neighborhood) work sphere, both among Xmen and among Ymen
4b. Public schools for Xish children, offering some instruction via Xish, but substantially under Yish curricular and and staffing control
4a. Schools in lieu of compulsory education and substantially under Xish curricular and staffing control

II. RLS to transcend diglossia, subsequent to its attainment

5. Schools for literacy acquisition, for the old and for the young, and not in lieu of compulsory education
6. **The intergenerational and demographically concentrated home-family-neighborhood: the basis of mother tongue transmission**
7. Cultural interaction in Xish primarily involving the community-based older generation
8. Reconstructing Xish and adult acquisition of X S[tandard] L[anguage]

I. RLS to attain diglossia (for a definition see 1.3)

Table 3: Stages of RLS (after Fishman 1991:395, 2001b:466)

Explanations: Xish ... the obsolescent language   Xmen ...speakers of the obsolescent language
                    Yish ... the dominant language   Ymen ... speakers of the dominant language [38]

---

[38] The convention of using variables (generic terms) as abbreviations has been criticized since they depict languages and humans as lifeless symbols (Fishman 2001b:481).

Gorter (2001) and Hornberger and King (2001) help to clarify some definitions in Table 3 by adding comments based on Fishman's original work (1991):

Ad stage 8: With the help of the remaining (mostly elderly and isolated) speakers of the nearly extinct language, folksongs, proverbs and tales should be put together and on the basis of these, grammars and dictionaries should be reconstructed (Fishman 1991:88, 2001b:468). The aim is to "build up a core of those who have at least some knowledge of it" and to make sure that this knowledge is spread (Fishman 1991:90).

Ad stage 7: Since the use of Xish in cultural activities so far rather involves the committed generation "beyond child-bearing age" (Fishman 1991:89), the goal of stage 7 is to develop a younger group of second language learners who may use Xish regularly. This may be achieved through the establishment of youth groups, associations and ideally, neighbourhoods where seniors could act as guides (Fishman 1991:91, 2001b:468f.).

Ad stage 6: This has been found to be the "*sine qua non*", the pivotal stage most difficult to attain and if it is not "satisfied, all else can amount to little more than biding time" (Fishman 1991:398f.). Unless all other measures are linked to it, the whole process of RLS is likely to fail eventually, as the case of Irish demonstrates (Bartens 2001, see below 2.6.2.1). At this stage, Xish becomes the normal informal language spoken not only within the family but also with playmates, friends and neighbours who live nearby (="demographically concentrated"; Fishman 1991:92f.). This also implies an appropriate linguistic landscape: place names, street and road signs, shop and building names and advertising in Xish.

Ad stage 5: Both children and adults should have access to (private) courses in Xish, organized through e.g. volunteer teachers, local schools or local religious groups, that are neither funded by the state nor part of compulsory education (Fishman 1991:97).

While stages 8 to 5 are supposed to consolidate diglossia and represent the minimum programme of RLS for which the minority language community does not necessarily require the cooperation of dominant authorities (Fishman 1991:400), the second phase of the RLS process, also called "high power" stages (Fishman 2001b:473), depends on "approval of those in power" (Bartens 2001).

Ad stage 4: Stage 4, concerned with the use of Xish in compulsory education systems, is split into a and b depending on whether the minority community or the state have control over the public school system (Bartens 2001).

4a: Here, not the state but the minority community controls both staff and curriculum, aiming to spread Xish into extracurricular activities.

4b: Schools of that type are under state control with the school language differing from the home language. Fishman (2001b:481) warns of the consequences: the school variety might weaken the vernacular and even substitute for it.

Ad stage 3: This implies the use of Xish in the workplace together with the dominant language.

Fishman (1991:105-107) admits that the remaining two stages are reached by few RLS movements.

Ad stage 2: Although the minority language is only introduced in the lower spheres, it involves decision-making processes (e.g. how to distribute public resources) on the part of politicians.

Ad stage 1: In the final phase, Xish is even officially used by institutional bodies to some extent and has functions in all domains. If Xish reaches this "highest level of cultural autonomy" without the safety of political independence it can be regarded as fully restored (Azurmendi et al. 2001:256).

Keeping the order of stages, as suggested by the theory, has often been criticized and relativized by Fishman himself (2001a:16) because what is most important is how the stages are linked (Bartens 2001).

According to Dauenhauer and Dauenhauer (1998:61), RLS "means to alter the current trend toward loss by taking decisive and appropriate action". In Fishman's terms (2001b:452), RLS, the theoretical result of his experience with small endangered language communities, is "concerned with the recovery, recreation and retention of *a complete way of life*".[39]

RLS can be seen as an alternative rather than an opposition to globalization (Fishman 2001b:459), asks for a "compromise of multilingual and multicultural coexistence" and does not utterly refuse the dominating culture and language (Bartens 2001). The activity of 'reversing language shift' combines sociolinguistic know-how, devoted work on the spot and ideally, sources of money (Trudgill 2000:193).

Fishman insists that it is the duty of "lesser-used language elites" to judge the particular circumstances realistically in order to avoid erroneous expectations (Williams 2000:67).

Haarmann (2001:80) notes that Fishman's strategies are mainly intended for states where all citizens are integrated into society and not for isolated ethnic groups, e.g. in Brazil's rain forest. It also has to be mentioned that the scale is qualitative rather than quantitative since it neither considers the actual numbers of the minority or majority speech communities nor the respective proportions (MacKinnon 2000:23).

The next step is to examine the first revival stages with reference to the situation in Cornwall.

2.6.1.1   *The position of Cornish on the GIDS scale*

Although it has been proven that there was an "unbroken lineage of Cornish (...) through to the 20th century" through oral transmission (Lyon 2001:21), the revival is generally considered to start with the publication of Henry Jenner's *Handbook of the Cornish Language* (1904), with its stirring call:

> Why should Cornishmen learn Cornish? There is no money in it, it serves no practical purpose, and the literature is scanty and of no great originality or value. The question is a fair one, the answer is simple. Because they are Cornish. (Berresford Ellis 1998:22)

---

[39] The language communities Fishman chose for his case studies in 1991 include Navajo, New York City Puerto Rican Spanish, Secular and Ultra-Orthodox Yiddish in New York City, French in Quebec, Irish, Frisian, Basque, Catalan, Modern Hebrew, immigrant and aboriginal languages in Australia and Maori.

In the same year, Cornwall as a Celtic nation was accepted to become a member of the Celtic Congress. By 1920, the number of interested people was sufficient to found the 'Old Cornwall Society' to preserve anything Celtic in Cornwall, above all the language. 8 years later, the *Gorsedh*, a college of Bards, along Welsh lines was established in order to promote the language and culture of Cornwall. Since then, the ceremony, attracting a huge audience, has taken place annually (except during the war).[40]

Scene at the Bardic ceremony in September 2000

In 1929, Robert Morton Nance, together with Jenner a key figure in the revival of Cornish, answered the needs of a growing number of people eager to learn Cornish in publishing 'Cornish for All'. After studying the extensive body of Middle Cornish literature in detail, he standardized revived Cornish by introducing a new spelling system called Unified Cornish (Berresford Ellis 1998:23f.). The problem with reconstruction was that syntax, semantics and the lexicon of traditional Cornish were incomplete and since there were no native speakers of Cornish available any more, the gaps had to be filled by analogy with the help of cognates from the related languages Breton and Welsh (for details see George 1993b and 4.3.4).

From that time onwards, dictionaries, text books, poems, plays and short stories were produced increasingly to adapt to the growing demand for Cornish classes (for details cf. Berresford Ellis 1998).

By the beginning of World War II, an active group of young people had learned the language so progress of the revival has already passed stages 8 and 7 (MacKinnon 2000:23). This is where Strubell (2001:268) has placed the language on the scale because planning is still an "unofficial, social group activity".

MacKinnon (2000:23) goes further by trying to justify stage 6: After the war, a new generation who had known Cornish since childhood formed a network creating Cornish language organizations and social events. This view will have to be revised in the course of this book.

---

[40] Bards are admitted to the *Gorsedh* for special achievements in literature, music, history and particularly in the Cornish language.

A kind of official body dealing with education, research, publishing and examinations, the Cornish Language Board (*Kesva an Taves Kernewek),* came into being in 1967. In 1979, it induced an associate membership with 'The Cornish Language Fellowship' (*Kowethas an Yeth* Kernewek), an organization open for anyone interested in the Cornish language (around 260 members in 2005, see Hirner 1997:65-68).

In the same year, another very effective initiative was launched under the name *Dalleth* ('Beginning'). Its major aim was to attract more young people by publishing children's books and tapes, by encouraging children to learn Cornish and promoting social activities and playgroups. However, it was very hard to bring parents and their children from all parts of Cornwall together and as soon as the children entered English-speaking primary schools, the project was doomed to failure (see Berresford Ellis 1998:28). Although at present, a number of children are brought up with Cornish, the scattered distribution of Cornish speakers is still a problem. As "there is in Cornwall no village where Cornish is spoken by most of the people for most of the time" (George 1993b:645), it is not a living community language.

In 2000, an independent and impartial academic study carried out on behalf of the Government Office for the South West (see below 3.6.1), the MacKinnon Report, attested Cornish to be a living language but suffering from a huge lack of funding.

According to MacKinnon (2000:23), the Cornish language movement was then situated at stage 5 of Fishman's scale. 378 adult learners were catered for in 38 evening classes, 297 students were enrolled in the correspondence course *Kernewek dre Lyther* (KDL = 'Cornish through letter')[41] and some schools had initiated lunchtime clubs (MacKinnon 2002:272).

Two years later, due to language activists' pressure based on that report, the British Government finally recognized Cornish as an official minority language (see below 3.6.1). Although it is still a long way to attain balanced diglossia in Cornwall, the recognition has certainly given Cornish access to the 'high power' stages. Considering the amendments made to RLS in 2.6.2.7 as a result of observing some individual cases, the consequences of the implementation of the Charter will be discussed in chapter 4.5.

2.6.2 Reversing Language Shift revisited

A decade later, Fishman's theory of 1991 was critically (self)evaluated by referring to the language communities (see footnote 39) he had chosen to back up his model plus examining additional cases such as Otomí (Mexico), Quechua (in the Andean highlands of Peru, Bolivia and Ecuador), Oko (Nigeria), Andamanese[42] and Ainu (Fishman 2001). Altogether, 18 cases spread over all continents should supply information on whether RLS goals are bound to succeed or fail. Since the individual situations are so complex, few selected ones will only be outlined in the following sections.

---

[41] The course aims to prepare students for the examinations of the Cornish Language Board. Of the more than three hundred students that have enrolled since 1983, many have been successful in one or more of the Board's four-level examinations, with 32 achieving the highest grade and thus being made Bards of the Cornish *Gorsedh.*

[42] This language spoken in the Andaman Islands east of India represents a special case: although in 2001 there were only 35 speakers left, three among them were under the age of five (Bartens 2001).

2.6.2.1 *Irish*

In *Bunreacht na hÉireann* (The Constitution of Ireland 1937), it is stated that "the Irish language as the national language is the first official language". It is then stated that "the English language is recognised as a second official language", but sociolinguistic reality is different. Irish is regarded as "dangerously ill" (Görlach 1995:45) and English is predominantly the language of the State and of its population (cf. actual figures in Ó Murchú 1993, Ó Riagáin 2001 and Ahlqvist 2002). The "symbolic value" of Irish is still significant, e.g. Aer Lingus attendants receive passengers first in Irish, then in English. Yet the "real" life communication, such as safety announcements, happens in English only (Ahlqvist 2002:47).

Ó Riagáin (2001:195) finds it difficult to apply the Fishman model to Irish since the Irish government is obliged by the special constitutional status to have an interest in re-establishing it as a national language. Only after giving in to pressure from Irish language groups, it requested full official status for Irish in the EU in November 2004. In June 2005, it was announced that Irish will become the 21st official language of the European Union, which means that important EU legislation documents will be translated into Irish (Celtic League newsletter, 13 June 2005).

In addition, as part of the Official Languages Act of 2003, which aims to increase both quality and quantity of services provided by public bodies and government departments through Irish, the office of a Language Commissioner was initiated in 2004 to keep an eye on its realization.[43]

Irish, which has also undergone standardization, is predominantly represented in the upper stages of the GIDS, e.g. economic advancement in the *Gaeltacht* areas, "recruitment procedures in the public sector", higher education[44] and the mass media (stage1), but the stages have not been passed gradually (Ó Riagáin 2001:196). On the one hand, new Irish-medium schools are opened (Eurolang newsletter, 20 April 2005), on the other hand, attempts to make Irish optional in schools are frequent, e.g. in April 2005 an Internet poll was initiated asking whether students should be able to opt out of studying Irish (http://www.skool.ie). Comments to this survey reflect the contradictory picture of the prevailing mood in Ireland, e.g.:

> *Consider how many schools would drop Irish altogether or schedule Irish against 'easier' options, just what happened to Latin. (11/04/2005)*

> *I am a leaving certificate student and Irish is a waste of a subject and only serves to take much needed time away from other subjects. (06/04/2005)*

> *Should be our own choice. (06/04/2005)*

> *Students should not be able to opt out of studying Irish. The language is part of our heritage and it is important to preserve this. I do believe, however, that a lot of the "stair na gaeilge" section of the curriculum is extremely boring and that*

---

[43] The first annual report by the Language Commissioner criticizes the lack of Irish language usage in education and administration (Eurolang newsletter, 20 April 2005).

[44] Irish is universally taught in schools and still a requirement for matriculation in the National University of Ireland and at teacher training colleges.

Irish students find it difficult to relate to it. A change in this area would perhaps make the subject more interesting/attractive to students. (05/04/2005)

Everyone should learn Irish if they are Irish born because the Irish is getting less common in Ireland and might eventually disappear. (05/04/2005)

No because then no one will choose to do it, and then it will die out. (05/04/2005)

Will you do a poll to see if students can opt out of English, religion or other subjects? (05/04/2005)

I believe that Gaeilge is one of the hardest subjects [...]. I've been doing it four about 9 years now and I am really ashamed to say I can't speak a word. [...] I think there should be a complete review into the way Irish is taught because I don't think the current way is working. (04/04/2005)

It's our native language, we should have some sort of understanding of it. We should be proud that we have something unique and different. Personally I think it's a lovely language. [...] (04/04/2005)

It is our native tongue. If we don't speak it our traditions will soon fade away. (04/04/2005)

I am a student myself and love Irish and know that given a choice most students would not choose to study Irish so the school would probably not be able to give me a teacher. Most adults who didn't really make a decent attempt of learning Irish when they were young will tell you that they wish they had to. The Irish language is an integral part of being Irish and is right now the only cultural difference between us and the UK/USA etc. Irish is our heritage and if you opt out of learning it you are abandoning your heritage. (04/04/2005)

Irish is never going to be needed in any job or subject in life (apart from teaching it!). (04/04/2005)

No way it is so hard to concentrate on two languages. I keep letting French slip out when I am practising for my Irish orals and really when do you ever use Irish. It's pointless. (04/04/2005)

Ó Riagáin (2001:204,211) provides the factual background to the negative comments: Since 1980 only 10-15% of students per age-class have chosen higher level courses in Irish, a growing number fail exams and even after 13 years of study, the oral ability of a majority of 2nd language learners is only "moderate" and according to Ó Muirthile (1999), only about 500 people have a high standard in written Irish. Also TV and radio services do not help to create bilingual communities; the stability of a language depends on the "social network of users", which is not concentrated enough in Ireland (Ó Riagáin 2001:210f.).

To sum up, RLS efforts in Ireland have not been successful but useful as the process of language shift has been retarded. The main problem is related to stage 6 of the scale: while the number of middle-class people passively using the language (with a focus on reading, listening to/watching Irish language programmes) has risen, original Irish-speaking communities have declined, for instance, married couples with both partners having Irish as their native tongue (Ó Riagáin 2001:197,209).

Hence, intergenerational transmission, the heart of the GIDS, is not properly linked to the higher stages, particularly since language group loyalty and language usefulness cannot be taken for granted. Schools are still chiefly responsible to maintain a competence in Irish, but as we have seen above, this role is being questioned (Ó Riagáin 2001:206).

2.6.2.2   Catalan

Along with Modern Hebrew and French in Quebec, Catalan in Spain counts as revival success story. In 1991, Fishman classified Catalan as having reached the highest GIDS stage, 10 years later, Strubell (2001:260) assesses whether it will continue to hold this position.

Concerning mainstream attitude, the Catalan language movement is still seen as a "fanatical mania" in the rest of Spain (Strubell 2001:261), but the situation is passively accepted. For a majority of young Catalans, who definitely identify themselves as Catalans and not Spaniards, the language is not a symbol of identity though. The use of the language in institutions and at school seems to be "artificially fostered" even and it is characteristic that students have their highest linguistic competence between the ages of 15 and 19 (Strubell 2001:269, 276).

The influence of the media is considerable: it promotes a sense of community, represents a formal model of the minority language and provides jobs (as in Ireland, Scotland and Wales; Strubell 2001:262). Still, Catalan is nowhere the only language used and due to "massive immigration and low birth rates, the only long-term hope (…) is to recruit new speakers among the immigrant groups" (Strubell 2001:269). Official language policies cannot interfere with families' lives and attitudes, in fact, they might even have the opposite effect: although the use of Catalan was forbidden during the Civil War, people could not be forced to speak Spanish in their houses (Strubell 2001:268f.).

To conclude, Strubell (2001:279f.) complements Fishman's theory with a circular model of language status change titled 'Catherine wheel'. Learning and using a language and being positively motivated to continue studying it are combined to a social mechanism with the individual in the role of the consumer at the centre of any social change but external or internal factors may hinder the process. In the circular model, increased consumption of goods and services in the language leads to a greater awareness of the language's value, which enhances the motivation to learn and use it. In turn, additional studying of the language demands more goods and services in the language which necessarily results in more supply. If any of the six steps is blocked, language planners (policy makers) should identify the obstacle and then take specific measures to remove it.

2.6.2.3   Frisian

Frisian, like several other European minority languages, has been recognized as a European autochthonous minority language in the Charter for Regional or Minority Languages of the Council of Europe since 1998 (see below 3.5.1). The West Germanic language consists of three dialects which differ from each other considerably. While two of them are spoken in the north of Germany by around 10,000 people, some

400,000 in the Netherlands speak the third (details in Janich and Greule 2002:73-77). Evidently, the status of and support for the Frisian varieties in Germany cannot be compared to the infrastructure and provisions made in the Netherlands. In this section, only the status of Frisian in the Netherlands is dealt with (for the situation of the other varieties cf. Munske 2001).

Gorter (2001:216) notes that Fishman's GIDS lacks this context as even stage 1 is confined to "nationwide levels". Although new language laws have increased the prestige and awareness of language issues in the Netherlands, politicians still ignore Frisian. Whereas Frisian is strong in the domains of family, work and village life, its use is limited in the more formal spheres of education, media, public administration and law despite the framework of regulations that should have taken effect since the recognition. Frisian can be used in most administrative affairs, but in reality civil servants prefer Dutch. This behaviour can be explained by the fact that all Frisian speakers are bilingual and Frisian is the marked, Dutch the unmarked, the expected language (Gorter 2001:218-223,231).

In his RLS study, Fishman (1991:173) noticed weaknesses of Frisian at levels 6, 5 and 4 which could seriously threaten its future. Gorter (2001:225-231) comments on the application of the Frisian situation to GIDS as follows (stages 8 and 7 can obviously be omitted here):

Ad stage 6: Out of 621,000 inhabitants of the province Friesland, 55% speak Frisian as their mother tongue. Notwithstanding almost three quarters of the overall population claiming "reasonable proficiency", mixed marriages could have the potential to destabilize, which may be compensated by Frisian-speaking families blessed with a large offspring. Moreover, Frisian has "more speakers in absolute numbers than ever before", so the situation seems to be stabilized (Gorter 2001:215f.,225,231).

Ad stage 5: A network of adult courses, also for "special target groups such as legal professionals", is distributed over the province (Gorter 2001:226).

Ad stage 4: In 1989, a group of parents founded Frisian language playgroups for both Frisian- and Dutch-speaking children. Ten years later, 11 all-Frisian playgroups had to compete with 200 other playgroups in Friesland. Most primary schools teach Frisian as a subject (for 45 minutes a week), 20% use it as a medium of instruction. Strangely, the standard a pupil should achieve in Frisian after primary school is the same as for Dutch. In 1993, Frisian became a compulsory subject in the first stage of secondary education, a concession which RLS activists are not content with either (Gorter 2001:227; further details in Gorter, Riemersma and Ytsma 2001:113-116).

Ad stage 3: Whereas 94% of the population understand Frisian, writing in Frisian is still the exception. Although Frisian is frequently spoken on the workfloor, it plays a minor role at management level. Apart from teachers and civil servants (the attitude of the latter group does not always encourage the use of Frisian), the work sphere has not been subject to RLS efforts yet (Gorter 2001:228).

Ad stage 2: The position of the media has definitely improved, e.g. a daily 1-hour-early-evening TV broadcast attracts many viewers. In 1999, a monthly magazine was established, yet on the whole, regional newspaper coverage with less than 5% is quite meagre. In terms of the new media, an all-Frisian search engine is available, but no online-course or dictionary (Gorter 2001:228f.).

Ad stage 1: Although Frisian is a popular topic for academics (in the 1990s four doctoral dissertations were printed in Frisian and eight had a Frisian topic), budget cuts dissolved two of the five chairs in Frisian linguistics outside Friesland (Gorter 2001:230; cf. also Gorter, Riemersma and Ytsma 2001:116f.). Concerning the mass media, a positive trend can be observed as the main public channel of the Netherlands broadcast a popular Frisian soap during the summer of 2005 (Eurolang newsletter, 6 June 2005).

To sum up, despite the attention Frisian got due to recognition (e.g. Frisian place-names), the implementation of new measures is not satisfying. Although the inclusion in the Charter was important in terms of symbolic and legal respect, Frisian ambitions were kept down as also other dialects were recognized by the Dutch government. Gorter (2001:230f.) raises the concern that Frisian might even "dissolve into Dutch" since diglossia with Frisian being used in intimate spheres (L) and Dutch in the higher domains (H) is gradually losing its balance in favour of Dutch. As defined by RLS theory, Frisian has entered the prestigious domains (stages 4-1), yet Dutch also increasingly intrudes on people's private lives.

2.6.2.4 *Quechua*

Although Dorian (1998:4) rates Quechua as being threatened, it is the most widely spoken indigenous language in the Americas with about 10 million speakers. However, Quechua monolingualism is gradually shifting to temporary bilingualism in the following generation, eventually giving way to Spanish monolingualism (for actual figures cf. Hornberger and King 2001:166f.).

In order to improve their economic position, peasants who had lived in virtual isolation from the Spanish-speaking dominant group had to learn Spanish and adapt to strange customs and more urban kinds of work since the monolingual Spanish speakers in general had not been interested in supporting their language. Although the use of Quechua in the elementary education of Indian children has been experimented with, the prevalent attitude of Quechua-speaking parents has been that their children, as long as they go to school at all, should learn Spanish (cf. Pap 1979:203f.). Nowadays, Quechua is still associated with the "rural, uneducated and poor" as opposed to Spanish, the language of "literacy […] education and […] success" (Hornberger and King 2001:166f.).

Hornberger and King (2001:176) question the position of stage 6 in the Fishman model as they think that stages 7 and 8 are inadequate to encourage intergenerational transmission, which may need the support of higher stage efforts. Furthermore, they criticize that the two sub-stages 4a and 4b are not strong enough to "capture the diverse configurations of community and government involvement and education", alluding to the lack of cooperation with authorities and the absence of regular instruction via Quechua even if the schools are run by the indigenous community (Hornberger and King 2001:181).

Stage 3 has not been reached yet as Quechua is normally not used outside traditional community boundaries, even much less by non-natives. The only field where Quechua plays a role is tourist industry, e.g. in agencies, souvenir shops, art galleries and open-air markets (ibid.).

At level 2, Quechua is even less manifest than in local education and work spheres and stage 1 is mainly under Spanish control. After Quechua had become the second official language of Peru in 1975, it was supposed to be used in administrative affairs. Also a national daily Quechua newspaper was set up, but due to a lack of readership and the resistance of the Spanish majority, the project was doomed to fail. Still, Quechua is highly esteemed internationally and subject of many websites. Thanks to the enthusiasm of linguists and anthropologists, Quechua is taught as an academic subject at universities worldwide and although native speakers serve as instructors, it is difficult for indigenous Quechuas to participate in these courses (Hornberger and King 2001:182f.). The paradoxical status of Quechua was referred to by Coronel-Molina (1999:171) who remarked that "it is more likely that Quechua speakers, given the proper technology, could communicate with foreigners from around the globe than with the majority of their own countrymen".

Yet Fishman (1991:106) stated that the international reputation and support could also have a negative effect if stage 2 was reached: intellectual leaders could become braindrainers and leave their communities behind. In this connection, Hornberger and King (2001:184f.) note that GIDS only considers members of the minority language community as RLS activists, leaving out groups like international linguists or institutions like churches.

Grenoble and Whaley (1998a:52) propose the distinction between micro-level (community-internal) and macro-level variables outside the community which can refer to local, regional, national and extra-national levels. To combine the international with the domestic and the global with the national, cooperation between international organizations that are otherwise too big to be sensitive to local circumstances and NGOs whose role is ususally confined to being initiators would be ideal.

Hornberger and King (2001:185f.,189) go on to criticize the sometimes ambiguous and indistinct sequence of the stages, e.g. stages 8 and 1 overlap because the adult acquisition of Quechua (stage 8) tends to take place in higher education institutes (stage 1). Most important of all, stage 6, which seems to hold an outsider position, should be aimed at before, during and after all RLS renewal practices so that multiple stages can work simultaneously.

Also Fettes (1997:311) believes that stage 6, which he calls 'living relationships', should have an "overarching" function, yet it may take up to several generations till "stable transmission as a first language" is achieved. As a compromise, Hornberger and King (2001:185) suggest that the stages should be regarded as a useful "heuristic" method "rather than a step-by-step prescription". In the end, they mention a current promising programme that comprises efforts to promote Quechua at various stages (1, 3, 4, 7 and 8; for details see Hornberger and King 2001:189).

2.6.2.5   *Basque*

Azurmendi et al. (2001:234-236) have tried to "diagnose" the situation of the non-Indo-European Basque language (Euskara), which is spoken in both Spain and France. Whereas the French government does not recognize any language other than French, there is some official support for the Basque language in Spain. As a reaction against Franco's dictatorship (1939-1975), which brutally suppressed Basque culture and language, the notorious terrorist group ETA came into existence. Nowadays, the Spanish Basque country is already one of the most autonomous regions in Europe where Basque and Spanish have equal status as official languages, but plans for a complete separation from Spain are on the way (*Salzburger Nachrichten*, 15 January 2005, p.10).

For Azurmendi et al. (2001:247), sociostructural and sociodemographic factors (density of speakers, social network) are most significant, followed by psycholinguistic factors (degree of competence as compared to Spanish or French) and psychosocial factors (interest, motivation, attitude or identity).

The sound status of Basque in terms of the mass media (stages 7 and 8) can be observed by means of the number of publications (over 1,000 books a year). There is also a daily newspaper, Radio and TV audiences have grown as well and obviously, the more readers/listeners/viewers are attracted, the less financial backing is needed. All these initiatives promote the crucial use of the minority language in different social environments and provide a link to stage 6 (Azurmendi et al. 2001:251).

The interdependence between the home-neighbourhood community and education is supported by schooling innovations, e.g. Euskara-medium pre-schools starting from the age of two (further details in Cenoz 2001:50-54). Also sport and leisure activities for young people and cultural centres are sponsored by the government (Azurmendi et al. 2001:252). Although Basque is increasingly being used at school and in university courses, one has to take a closer look at the competence level of speakers (note: there are no Basque monolingual speakers). Generally, adults' reading and writing skills tend to be better than their oral ones, therefore they do not really benefit from the closeness to the language environment. Hence, achievements at stage 5 do not necessarily ensure intergenerational transmission (Azurmendi et al. 2001:243f.,253f.).

The authors conclude that the biggest strides due to education in the 1990s are of quantitative rather than qualitative nature. The circumstances are illustrated by a recent protest of temporary teachers over the requirement to learn Basque (Eurolang newsletter, 13 April 2005). The process of recovery is not exclusively "linear, but rather spiral, and (…) overlapping", which implies that the aims related to the different stages of RLS theory have to be "pursued simultaneously" (Azurmendi et al. 2001:256f.), an amendment that has also been mady by Hornberger and King (2001, see above 2.6.2.4).

2.6.2.6   *Hebrew*

> The revival of Cornish is the only true parallel to the Hebrew case.
>
> (Chaim Rabin, Professor of Hebrew at the Hebrew
> University of Jerusalem, quoted in Berresford Ellis 1998:29)

Hebrew, often cited as unique and unprecedented example of language reinvigoration, had always been taught as a literary and sacred language at school. For this reason, Spolsky (1991, 1996) prefers the term 'revitalisation' to 'revival' but also Fishman's use of the term 'revernacularisation', which expresses the transformation of classical Hebrew into an everyday "vernacular", is appropriate (Spolsky and Shohamy 2001:350f.).

The revitalisation process, which religious preservers of literacy had long objected to, started at the end of the 19th century and did not strictly follow the GIDS model.

Obviously, stage 8 was not necessary and step 5 (literacy at school and in the community) preceded 7 and 6. The real breakthrough of spoken Hebrew was due to the establishment of Hebrew-only nursery schools (Haarmann 2001:79). Although it is difficult to adapt this case to GIDS, the identification of common objectives is useful (Spolsky and Shoamy 2001:352-354).

In a new approach, Spolsky and Shoamy (2001:357) also raise the issue of victims of successful RLS activities: for example, Hebrew ousted Arabic, Yiddish and more than thirty other languages which would require RLS efforts themselves. They suggest that an "ideological acceptance of pluralism" would allow a "policy that treats RLS not as a struggle for existence but as the fine-tuning of complementary functional and social use of languages" (Spolsky and Shoamy 2001:361). The price of successful revitalisation entailed the loss of plurilingualism and only English, which is more prestigious, could be a threat to Hebrew spoken in Israel by around 5 million people (details in Haarmann 2001:80). This once more shows that RLS efforts do not only focus on the language per se (which is the main interest of linguists) but are often economically and politically motivated. For the language user, the linguistic aspect is just one of many "complex social and cultural and economic choices" (Spolsky and Shoamy 2001:357), illustrated by the following extract:

> A Navajo student of mine once put the problem quite starkly: if I have to choose, she said, between living in a hogan a mile from the nearest water where my son will grow up speaking Navajo or moving to a house in the city with indoor plumbing where he will speak English with the neighbors, I'll pick English and a bathroom! (Spolsky 1989:451)

2.6.2.7   *Conclusions*

> In most cases, the best that RLS can hope for, as a starting point for its never ending road into the future, is to disengage from dependence upon and supervision by the Yish authorities. (Fishman 2001b:475)

As the preceding chapters have demonstrated, some adjustments and modifications were put forward by the contributors who, on the whole, did not yet observe any striking improvements due to RLS efforts (cf. Fishman 2001b:478-480; Bartens 2001). The "scenario" is "ambiguous" due to "discrepancies between attitudes and performance" (Fishman 2001b:479f.) as Fishman (2001a:12) also notices a "new spirit" thanks to the increasing acceptance of international conventions and the promotion of 'lesser-used' languages by the EU (see chapters 3.1 and 3.2) which both cannot replace developments in the minority language communities though. The "real secret weapon" of RLS is *Gemeinschaft*, "the intimate community" (Fishman 2001b:458f.).

Cooperation is only successful if functions are kept separate and at the same time shared. In addition, the meagre resources must not be wasted (Fishman 2001a:13), therefore a priority is to set up facilities for young people so that they can also communicate in Xish after and outside school (e.g. clubs, sport teams) otherwise schools might be reduced to 2nd language institutions (Fishman 2001a:15). In fact, stage 4 has been criticized most and some Third World groups (e.g. the Hopi or Quechua) consciously rely on stage 5 education in order to avoid Yish education authorities (see

Fishman 2001b:470-472). RLS related schools must be equipped with "special methods and materials" because of the limited use Xish has outside school:

> These schools cannot afford to teach imaginary Xish conversations at airports, hotel check-ins, luxury-car salesoffices and other social mobility related and Yish dominated interactions. (Fishman 2001b:473)

Furthermore, Fishman amends that the obligatory sequence of functional stages which are only supposed to serve "diagnostic location" ("where to start and what to aim at when") is not necessary (Fishman 2001b:465). What is more important is "strategic support" and the linkage of stages and of goals and efforts, both "anticipatory to and subsequent to any crucial target function" (Fishman 2001a:16). Different language communities have different problems, aims, resources and strategies. What they should all concentrate on is the consolidation of strong functions that the dominant language lacks. Contrary to the GIDS stages, human life and society are not linear, which may also imply leaving out a particular stage (e.g. 5 or 4a; Fishman 2001b:476). Although stage 6 is commonly considered the "crux-stage", other stages may be targeted first depending on the circumstances (e.g. religious or learned languages will require different efforts than decaying vernaculars; cf. Fishman 2001b:467). Unfortunately, modern intrusions on traditional family functions such as divorce, intermarriage or frequent moving during childhood may weaken the power of stage 6 (Fishman 2001b:470).

In the last chapter of his book, Fishman (2001b:452-456) identifies "five ideological challenges to RLS" from the position of the majority language group, which will be briefly summarized here:

a.   **Monetary values, ethnocultural values and cultural democracy**: RLS efforts are more and more being conceived as a fundamental right for indigenous peoples and immigrants by democratic states and international organizations (see below chapter 3). Yet opponents frequently assert that successful language policies are always linked to the demands of the labour market which is naturally dominated by the majority language. Therefore, parents must be "reassured that they will not be handicapping their own children by socialising them and educating them in Xish" (Fishman 2001b:453; see Grin 1999). Fishman (ibid.) counters that Xish children are bilingual anyway and thus not "cut off from the economic rewards" which Yish offers at all.

b.   **The 'normality' of minority language death**: Most Ymen see language shift only as a natural result of an uneven minority-majority relationship and "RLSers [...] [as] trouble-makers, [and] disturbers of civility" (Fishman 2001b:454). For Fishman, the term 'natural' is only used as an excuse for the "power play" (ibid.).

c.   **The dominant language is peaceful; RLS is inherently conflictual**: This argument is flatly refused by Fishman as the absence of a language policy, still a reality in many democracies, is actually a deliberate "anti-minority-languages policy" of ignorance. Moreover, GIDS stages 8-5 are not confrontational as all their endeavours to gather support and recognition are aimed at both the Yian and the Xian "camp". Compulsory education in Xish, the goal of stage 4, depends on the conditions of Yian auhorities and the remaining high power stages cannot be called conflictual either because RLS efforts are based on democratic methods such as "compromise, [...] coalition building" and negotiating (Fishman 2001b:454f.).[45]

d. **Your nationalism is worse than mine**: Only if their expression of identity is oppressed, ethnocultural movements have to find a way to make aware of their situation (Fishman 2001b:455).

e. **One language per country is enough (particularly if it is my language in my country)**: Going back to 19th century imperialism, territoriality can be improperly put forward as an argument for a majority language policy. Translated into figures, 4,000 to 6,000 languages are shared by only about 200 states. Countering this statement, Fishman (2001b:456) comes up with the following comparison:

> To expect Xians to give up Xish merely because they are living in Yland, is tantamount to expecting Yians to give up Yish just because they are living in a world increasingly dominated by Anglophone technological-economic-military power.

Therefore, RLS activities aim to make both Xians and Yians more aware and informed about what is lost (Fishman 2001b:463).

Although an empirically-grounded answer to the basic question of the book 'Can threatened languages be saved?' cannot be given yet (2001b:478), Fishman concludes vaguely but somewhat optimistically, pleading for international cooperation and peaceful coexistence:

> Yes, more [languages] can be saved than has been the case in the past, but only by following careful strategies that focus on priorities and on strong linkages to them, and only if the true complexity of local human identity, linguistic competence and global interdependence are fully recognised. More languages are threatened than we think, and they are not necessarily only the smaller, more disadvantaged ones either. The languages of the world will either all help one another survive or they will succumb separately to the global dangers that must assuredly await us all (English included) in the century ahead. (Fishman 2001b:481)

The following chapter discusses the consequences of the increasing digitalization of the world, in particular of the new medium Internet, for minority languages (based on Crystal 2001, 2004).

2.7   The role of the Internet

Although new technology now enables people all over the world to gather enormous knowledge in most fields, the distribution of resources is not even in terms of geography (developing countries), work (brainworkers vs. labourers) and generation. In order to organize knowledge sensibly, human beings are still dependent on the oldest technology, language (Haarmann 2001:66-68).

Crystal (2004:88) guesses that at least a quarter of the world's languages are present on the Web, not only as academic subjects but actually as media. In 1998 it was estimated

---

[45] Negative exceptions resorting to force can never be excluded though.

that English dominated the Net with around 80%, four years later, the Web contained less than 50% in English and this tendency is continuing (Crystal 2004:87).

Search engines already provide references about almost any endangered language (Buszard-Welcher 2001:331), however, international language organizations' resources and website references are still mostly in English for practical reasons (Bradley and Bradley 2002a:351). This fact expresses the equivocal effect media in general and electronic media in particular have on minority languages: for one thing declining languages are supposed to be represented in them, for another majority languages make substantial use of them to influence and in the worst case manipulate weaker languages (Williams 1991a:37).

For Crystal (2004:89), who regards the Internet as a "lifeline" and "ideal medium" for endangered languages, advantages outweigh possible risks. Before the public acquisition of the Internet in the 1990s, members of a minority language community were only able to call widespread attention to their case at great expense, e.g. through rarely published articles in newspapers. Radio and television programmes were even more difficult if not impossible to get involved in the issue. Nowadays, with the help of e-mails and websites, messages can be sent out to a potentially global audience which can also be accessed for a longer period than newspaper and radio or TV contributions. In addition, chatrooms are beneficial to isolated speakers because they can now participate in a virtual speech community.

Recently (May 2005), a Bushman language spoken by only seven people in South Africa was reported to have been saved from extinction. Specialists recorded the formerly widely used language by means of multimedia and transferred it into a computer language programme.

However, Crystal (2004:89f.) admits that "developing a significant cyber-presence" is not so easy either as he identifies inherent hurdles that could automatically exclude a number of indigenous languages:

a.   The necessary infrastructure is not yet satisfying in several parts of the world and according to Gibbs (2002:66), "last speakers are typically old, poor and computer illiterate. Few have e-mail addresses."

b.   Making use of the Web implies that the languages are fully documented; from chapter 1.5.4 above we know that this is not the case for about 2,000 languages.

c.   Some languages contain particular letters that can be encoded and decoded only with difficulty.

Moreover, a kind of "critical mass" of content in the minority language is needed to make browsing worthwhile and enjoyable which up to now only a few hundred languages have managed. Language experts foresee a growing supply and demand for multilingual websites (e.g. Thomas 2000:2) and the topic itself has already become a field of research.

For instance, a conference paper at the 'International Conference on Minority Languages' in Trieste (see below 2.8) deals with bilingual websites that have been legally required to include minority languages (Deere and Cunliffe 2005).

Also *The Green Book of Language Revitalization in Practice* (Hinton and Hale 2001, see below 2.8.2) devotes part VII, consisting of 10 contributions, to media and technology, e.g. Buszard-Welcher (2001) has investigated a sample of endangered-language websites.

Last but not least, the Linguapax Institute, an NGO founded in 2001, among many other functions and objectives, aims to "contribute to the presence of multilingualism in cyberspace" (http://www.linguapax.org; for further online-supported projects see below 2.8 and 3.).

What the growing influence of the Internet implies for the process of RLS and Cornish in particular will be outlined in the following passage.

2.7.1 Consequences for RLS

> Without an *actual* ethnolinguistic community home, the greater prestige of a thousand computer specialists constituting a *virtual* interactive community, or a dozen Nobel prize laureates posting their works on the internet, will not augur nearly as well for the future of Xish as a thousand intergenerationally related ordinary 'rank and file' daily speakers living in proximity to one-another. (Fishman 2001b:465)

In terms of RLS objectives, modern technologies can be very useful as far as communication among Xian teenagers, parents, teachers and activists is concerned (Fishman 2001b:458,482). Especially teachers should be linked in order to benefit from each other's ideas and materials (Fishman 2001a:15f.). E-mails, computer programmes, search engines and chatrooms can certainly facilitate RLS efforts at all stages, but they can never "substitute for face-to-face interaction with *real family embedded in real community*" (Fishman 2001b:458).

2.7.1.1   Cornish on the computer

The fact that there are Cornish words for 'computer' (*jynn-amontya* = 'engine-to count') and 'Internet' *Kesroesweyth* (literally 'co-network', *roes* = 'net', *kes* ='inter' *gweyth* = 'work') confirms that the adaptation of Cornish to modern concepts has been successful (see Hirner 1997:117).

For the sake of communication among Cornish speakers/learners, the Internet also plays an important role. Cornish speakers/learners benefit from 80% broadband coverage, the highest percentage of any rural area in Britain (*First Great Western* magazine, issue 3, spring 2005, p.14), which certainly helps to reduce distances.

Since 1997, the Cornish language correspondence course KDL (see 2.6.1.1) has been available online and thus makes learning Cornish easier and more accessible. The First Grade Course, consisting of 25 lessons and a number of past examination papers, costs £10, includes an accompanying audio cassette and is cheaper than the traditional postal method. Answers to the lessons which can be submitted via email will be marked and then emailed back (the first lesson can be tried out free of charge: http://www.kdlcornish.freeserve.co.uk). Students who have passed the First Grade, can continue their studies with the Second and Third Grade courses which are also offered online.

In addition, a number of interactive learning CD-Roms have been produced to assist learners (see below). The CD on the left was successfully trialled on pupils at Hayle Community College (see 6.2.1) in order to "get the newest language of Europe to the people" (http://www.languageresourceonline.com/languages/learn_cornish.htm). So far, the company has produced interactive learning material for about 100 languages, including minority languages such as Welsh, Manx, Scottish and Irish Gaelic.

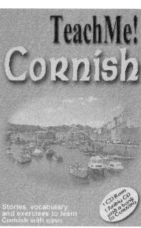

Recent Cornish software supporting learners

Moreover, 'The Cornish Language Fellowship' (cf. 2.6.1.1) plans to release a Cornish CD and magazine for nursery and primary school children which should help them to express their identity and understand Cornish place names. The organization has also created a website called *Warlinenn* ('Online') which offers information on the Cornish language and the latest revival developments, supports learners and serves as a forum for members (http://www.cornish-language.org/). Other organizations, such as *Agan Tavas* ('Our Tongue') provide resource sites containing news, publications, classes and a member forum (http://www.agantavas.org.uk/). There is also a website which regularly presents regional and international news in Cornish (http://www.geocities.com/cornishnews/) and one can even listen to news read in Cornish (http://www.bbc.co.uk/cornwall/connected/stories/cornish_news.shtml).

Electronic newsletters are also a significant instrument to distribute and receive information on endangered languages. For example, the Celtic League newsletter provides current information on developments and events concerning the Celtic languages.[46] Further minority language initiatives that are represented through the Internet or projects based on modern technology will be described below in sections 2.8.1, 2.8.2 and chapter 3.

To sum up, the presence of Cornish on the World Wide Web is significant and seems to be on the increase all the time. If you search for "Cornish language", the engine 'Google' comes up with more than one million entries. This network can only advance RLS efforts in Cornwall.

---

[46] The Celtic League is an inter-Celtic organization that campaigns for the social, political and cultural rights of the six Celtic nations Wales, Scotland, Ireland, Isle of Man, Cornwall and Brittany (http://www.manxman.co.im/cleague/).

The chapter on RLS will be completed by introducing concrete revitalization initiatives worldwide.

2.8 What can be done concretely? Realistic perspectives or a Sisyphean task?

The protection of linguistic diversity has never received more attention through international promotion than during the past decade. In developing countries, the support for endangered languages is obviously less important than education or health (Bradley and Bradley 2002a:348), but generally speaking, fund-raising is the most difficult issue in most cases (cf. Crystal 2004:62f.). Since initiatives seem to be exploding at the moment, only a limited selection of recent ones can be presented or referred to here (some organizations were already mentioned in chapter 1.5.1, further contact addresses can be looked up in Crystal's appendix (2000:167-169)).

2.8.1 Projects and organizations worldwide

- The UNESCO sees work on endangered languages as a priority and has therefore initiated various international conferences on the issue. Moreover, it supports numerous projects and publications, among them the Linguapax Institute which has worked on a 'World Languages Report' (Bradley and Bradley 2002a:349). The most prominent UNESCO project of that kind is an electronic databank, the *Red Book on Endangered Languages*. Under the Endangered Languages Programme, an expert team has recently started an online 'Register of Good Practices in Language Preservation' in order to collect reports of community-based initiatives and disseminate knowledge, expertise and experience (for details cf. http://www.unesco.org/culture/endangeredlanguages/goodpractices).

- The UK-based 'Foundation for Endangered Languages' is involved in numerous activities, exerts political pressure for linguistic rights and monitors linguistic policies (for further aims see http://www.ogmios.org). In its annual conferences, participation by members of "real" minority communities is encouraged (see below 2.8.3).

- A new British philantropy, the 'Lisbet Rausing Charitable Fund', has donated 30 million dollars to a huge documentation project (around 100 languages). The money will be mainly spent on fieldwork but also on specific training of linguists (see Gibbs 2002:67).

- In Germany, the 'Gesellschaft für bedrohte Sprachen' and the 'Volkswagen Foundation' (see *Volkswagenstiftung* 1.5.1) promote projects both practical and academic. The latter has commissioned field linguists to document some 15 endangered languages in all parts of the world and is also funding a resource centre in Cologne and a multimedia archive at the Max Planck Institute for Psycholinguistics in the Netherlands (Bradley and Bradley 2002a:348f., Gibbs 2002:67).

- Linguists from the Max Planck Institute for Evolutionary Anthropology in Leipzig, in the course of their work on language universals and typology, became interested in the moribund language of the Krenak tribe in the Brasilian rain forest. The offspring of a chieftain and his mother in law are trying to transmit fragments of their native tongue with the help of old documents to the family (source: the Austrian weekly scientific TV programme 'Modern Times', broadcast on 14 January 2005).

- In the USA, to name just a few, the 'Society for the Study of Indigenous Languages of the Americas' and 'The Endangered Languages and Their Preservation Committee of the Linguistic Society of America' cooperated in assembling the 'Endangered Language Database' (http://www.indigenous-language.org/endangered). Further American organizations include the pressure group 'Terralingua: Partnerships for Linguistic and Biological Diversity', 'The Endangered Language Fund' based at Yale University and the most comprehensive present-day survey, the *Ethnologue,* which is a product of the Dallas Summer Institute of Linguistics (see above 1.5.1).[47]

- The 'Ford Foundation' has funded Leanne Hinton's master-apprentice approach that was developed specifically to revitalize some 50 native American languages in California. Fluent speakers get paid if they teach younger relatives (who also receive money) in their native tongue (cf. Gibbs 2002:67).

- The 'Long Now Foundation' in San Francisco supervises the Rosetta Project (http://www.rosettaproject.org) which got its name from a disk which, like the original stone, stores parallel texts and also descriptions of 1,000 languages in microprint (for details see Gibbs 2002:66). Moreover, the research team (with the help of voluntary linguists and native speakers) aims to produce a database of words for up to 5,000 languages for the benefit of future generations of waning languages.

- Also in Japan endangered languages are treated as a priority research area, e.g. the Ministry of Education gave a grant to a project on 'Endangered Languages of the Pacific Rim' (Bradley and Bradley 2002a:350). The 'International Clearing House for Endangered Languages' at the University of Tokyo also contributed to the 'Endangered Language Database' (see above, for the development of clearinghouses see Hinton 2001a:11).

2.8.2 Publications

New books on the topic, both theoretical and practical, are mushrooming up, e.g. Hinton, Vera and Steele's guidebook *How to keep your language alive* (2002), Janse and Tol's (2003) and Tsunoda's (2005) overviews, or Grenoble and Whaley's (2006) reference guide.

---

[47] To illustrate the difficulty of fund-raising, Gibbs (2002:67) reports of the 'Endangered Language Fund' and the 'Foundation for Endangered Languages' which were only able to collect 80,000 and 8,000 dollars respectively within a period of five to seven years. More encouragingly, the 'Volkswagen Foundation' had more than 2 million dollars at its disposal.

- Already a classic in the field, *The Green Book of Language Revitalization in Practice* by Hinton and Hale (2001) is an answer to UNESCO's *Red Book on Endangered Languages*. The editors of the *Green Book*, Leanne Hinton and Ken Hale, who devote it to "the brave people who work against all odds to help their endangered heritage languages survive", hope that the it "will be of use to everyone who wants it to be no longer necessary for their language to be listed in the Red Book" (Hinton and Hale 2001:xi). It is a collection of detailed accounts about concrete revitalization projects in all parts of the world and thus can be used as a manual.

- A *World Atlas of Language Structures* illustrating the geographical distribution of 2,560 languages was recently developed by researchers from the Max Planck Institute for Evolutionary Anthropology in Leipzig. This collection of data opens up new perspectives as its analysis surprisingly revealed considerable structural similarites between unrelated languages in particular geographical areas. The "monumental work" also makes comparative linguistics accessible in an attractive way, e.g. an appended CD-ROM enables the users, including linguistic laymen, to verify hypotheses and create their own maps (*Salzburger Nachrichten*, 2 August 2005, p.19).

2.8.3 Conferences

Especially with the announcement of international conferences, e-mails and Internet have proved to be extremely helpful. Limitations on the scope of this study only allow for mention of the following (see also 3.4):

- The biennial International Conference on Minority Languages (ICML), typically hosted by minority language regions, is already regarded as an institution. For example, the 9th conference took place in Kiruna (in the Swedish province of Lapland with Sami as the minority language) in June 2003, the most recent one in Trieste (in an Italian province with a Slovenian minority) in July 2005 was entitled 'Minority Languages in post-2004 Europe: Problems and Challenges'.

- The 'Foundation for Endangered Languages' (see above 2.8.1) held its Ninth Conference in South Africa from 18-20 November 2005 with the title: 'Creating Outsiders: Endangered Languages, Migration and Marginalization' (source: Mercator newsletter, April 2005).

Although some initiatives from Europe were already included at this point, chapter 3 will concentrate on European institutions that are specifically linked with and relevant to the advancement of Cornish.

3 Cornish as a Lesser-Used Language in a European Context

EU Promotes Cornish

Following a remarkable revival in the Cornish language, the EU is now considering allowing the language to be used at the EU headquarters in Brussels. If Cornish is to be used at Brussels, then the EU would have to employ a Cornish translator.

(extract from *Cornish World* magazine, issue 38, summer 2004, p.9)

In terms of the protection of linguistic rights, Europe, represented through the European Union (henceforward EU) and various control bodies, is regarded as a model from outside (see above 1.5.6).[48]

This chapter is supposed to concentrate on initiatives and documents that have significantly contributed to the official recognition of Cornish, omitting many preceding resolutions supporting linguistic minorities.

At the beginning, it seems worth mentioning that Cornwall (and the nearby Isles of Scilly) has been chosen by the administrative body of the EU, the European Commission (EC), as an Objective One Priority area because of its low economy rate (65% of the UK with its gross domestic product per head less than 75% of the European average). The aim of the programme, which started in 2000 and will run until the end of 2006, is to invest in projects (with a grant of over £300 million) that should regenerate the economy and enhance environmental and cultural opportunities.

One important project was the establishment of Cornwall's first university campus near Penryn and Falmouth, which was completed in 2004 (see photo below). Tremough Campus, which now hosts more than 1,600 students, is shared by the University of Exeter in Cornwall and University College Falmouth as part of the 'Combined Universities in Cornwall' initiative. Also the Institute of Cornish Studies, an academic centre which coordinates and carries out all sorts of research relating to Cornish matters including the language, has moved there.

---

[48] Rare criticism of the EU in that respect concerns the assimilation of the Sami (Wuketits 2003:137). Also Kronenthal (2003) reports of failing EU measures based on data gathered from the Galician community in Spain.

Picture taken at Cornwall's first university campus (March 2005)[49]

In the following section, general principles and definitions with regard to different linguistic situations in different EU member states will be laid out.

3.1 Unity in diversity

> Of course, as lingua franca, English has a role to play and this should not be opposed, but knowing English is not cure-all. Replacing English as lingua franca by another language, as some people would like, would be very expensive. And that is not what citizens want. We should rather invest positively in promoting linguistic diversity and language learning.
>
> (EU commissioner for information, society and media Viviane Reding, EBLUL contact bulletin, May 2003, p.5)

The enlargement of the EU in 2004 did not only imply membership of ten new states but also a considerable growth in the number of languages and language communities as illustrated in Table 4:

15 member states	25 member states (2004)
11 official languages	21 official languages[50]
42 regional or minority languages	54 regional or minority languages
73 language communities	156 language communities
40 million regional or minority language speakers	45-46 million regional or minority language speakers
(Pan and Pfeil 2003)	(Bojan Brezigar 2003)[51]

Table 4: Languages in the EU before and after 2004.

---

[49] All the photos, if not stated otherwise, were taken during the stay in March 2005.

[50] As mentioned in section 2.6.2.1, Irish gained official status in 2005.

[51] As quoted in the speech of the President of the European Bureau for Lesser Used Languages at the 9th ICML (see 2.8.3) in Kiruna, entitled "The regional or minority languages in the EU reform process".

Whereas all states that wanted to become a member of the EU had to conform to linguistic human rights (e.g. Latvia, see Ozolins 1999), countries discriminating against their own minorities (e.g. Romania) had not been accepted yet (Fishman 2001a:12, Fishman 2001b:452).[52]

The fact that approximately 10% of all EU citizens (n = 455,000,000) speak a language other than the official language of the state in which they live explains the EU's principle of respect for minorities and linguistic diversity:[53]

> [...] all European languages are equal in value and dignity from the cultural point of view and form an integral part of European culture. (Resolution by the Council of the EU 2002)

3.1.1 The problem of definition

Europe's non-official languages differ enormously in size, constitutional recognition, socioeconomic status, cohesion and level of decline (Williams 1991a:12). That is why defining them has turned out to be somewhat problematic, which the following examples are meant to demonstrate:

The term 'trans-frontier' has been coined to refer to a language that is spoken by a minority in one state but by a majority of another, e.g. Slovenian in Austria or Polish in the Czech Republic (Mercator newsletter February 2005).

Catalan has the status of a minority language in Spain and France but is spoken by more people than Danish, an official EU language (5.2 vs. around 8.5 million speakers, Janich and Greule 2002:32,121).

'Non-territorial' minority languages have been traditionally used in a state but are different from the language(s) spoken by the rest of state's population and cannot be identified with a particular area thereof, e.g. Romani and Yiddish (as defined in part I of the European Charter for Regional or Minority Languages 1992, see 3.5.1).

Other general expressions in use are 'neglected', 'small', 'menaced' or 'minoritized' (see EBLUL contact bulletin, September 2002, p.5). The lack of a precise umbrella term has led the EU to adopt **'lesser-used'** as the least antagonizing, allowing for a sub-classification into five categories (see Extra and Gorter 2001a:10f.).

For the four Celtic languages Welsh, Scottish Gaelic, Breton and Cornish the category of **'unique regional minority languages'** applies as they are spoken in one part of only one EU member state.[54]

According to the European Charter for Regional or Minority Languages definition (article 1, see 3.5.1), **'regional or minority languages'** are "traditionally used within a

---

[52] In the meantime, an important step forward was Romania's ratification of the European Charter for Regional or Minority Languages (see 3.5.1, Dumitrescu 2003).

[53] According to Article 22 of the Charter of Fundamental Rights of December 2000, the EU is bound to respect that. Article 21 forbids discrimination on the basis of language.

[54] Manx is exluded because the Isle of Man is a semi-autonomous crown dependency with its own government and as such not member of the EU. Irish, before it gained official status within the EU, was defined as a 'working' language.

given territory of a State who form a group numerically smaller than the rest of the State's population; and different from the official language(s) of that State."

What the inclusion of Cornish into this definition means in practice will be taken up later. In the following sections, important EU support structures, foremost the 'European Bureau for Lesser Used Languages', will be presented.

3.2 The European Bureau for Lesser Used Languages (EBLUL)

> The European Union's 'Bureau of Lesser Used Languages' and various of its treaties, charters and conventions have established the significance of such languages for the unity and progress of Europe [...]. Certainly this is an ideological precedent that RLSers can and should broadcast, both within Europe and elsewhere as well. (Fishman 2001b:458)

Established in 1982 on the initiative of the European Parliament and mainly financed by the EC, the EBLUL is an independent NGO. It closely cooperates with the EC and the Council of Europe in terms of funding and language legislation (see below 3.5).

Its general aim is to represent, preserve and promote the regional and/or minority languages of the EU, and its activities are manifold (publishing, organizing conferences and exchanges etc., cf. http://www.eblul.org). The association is based on a network of Member State Committees in most EU member states which represent the interests of their communities.

For example, the UK Committee successfully applied for a grant to publish a Cornish dictionary and a grammar. In 1995, a Cornish sub-committee was set up which in turn represents various organizations of the Cornish language movement.

Also most of the new member states of the EU are well-represented. A conference on 'Lesser-Used Languages in Estonia and Europe' was organized by the Estonian Bureau for Lesser Used Languages on 30 September and 1 October 2005 aiming to provide information for language communities in the Baltic Sea area about EU related initiatives (such as Mercator, see below 3.3) as well as about the situation of these communities themselves.

Among the many projects the EBLUL is involved in, the running of a news agency has become vital for the spread of information.

3.2.1 Eurolang

Eurolang, the online European news agency for minority languages, was founded in 2000 to cover events and issues related to the lesser-used languages on a daily basis (cf. http://www.eurolang.net). Reports from the various regions of EU member states are provided by a (growing) number of journalists who speak lesser-used languages themselves.

It is possible for everybody to subscribe to a weekly newsletter which concretely informs the readership of current positive and negative developments dependent on the benevolent or hostile attitude of the respective governments. As the following news item shows, decisions made by EU institutions that are relevant for regional and/or minority language communities, are also covered:

> **BREAKTHROUGH IN EU STATUS FOR 'OFFICIAL 'LESSER-USED LANGUAGES (Brussel / Bruxelles 6/14/2005 by Davyth Hicks)**
>
> Following the Spanish proposal of December 2004, the European Council of Foreign Ministers decided yesterday in Luxembourg to allow the usage of all official lesser-used languages in European institutions. [...] It means that they can be used at Council meetings, by the Commission, that legislation will be translated into the lesser-used language, and that speakers can write using their own language to EU institutions.

3.2.2 Cornish Language News Website

The Cornish Branch of the EBLUL has its own website which is partly funded by Cornwall County Council (http://www.cornish-language-news.org). It provides news about Cornwall, Cornish culture and the language in English and three versions of Cornish (see below 4.3.3).

The EBLUL also cooperates with Mercator, a European service network for research, documentation and information on lesser-used languages, which provides it with back-up material.

3.3 The Mercator network

The Mercator Project (http://www.mercator-central.org), launched by the EC in 1987, consists of three core centres that are thematically specialized:[55]

- Mercator **Legislation** at the CIEMEN foundation in Barcelona is concerned with language legislation, linguistic rights and the use of lesser-used languages in Public administration (http://www.ciemen.org/mercator/index-gb.htm).

- Mercator **Education** at the Fryske Akademy in Ljouwert deals with minority language education (www.mercator-education.org).

- Mercator **Media** at the University of Wales, Aberystwyth focuses on the relationship between lesser-used languages and the mass media, including the new technologies (http://www.aber.ac.uk/~merwww).

Apart from the attractive, multilingual websites operated by each of the centres which announce and describe a multitude of publications, ongoing events, projects and symposia, a monthly common newsletter with updated information has been available since January 2005.

In the following section some other new projects and recent or future events will be introduced.

---

[55] The centres are situated in parts of the EU member states where lesser-used languages are spoken (Catalonia/Spain, Friesland/The Netherlands, Wales/UK).

3.4 Other projects and meetings

- The ADUM project, established in 2004 and partially funded by the EC, helps European minority language organizations and communities to effectively access EU programmes in order to get funding for language promoting projects (http://www.adum.info).

- Besides, a new Internet platform EuroLinguistiX was founded in July 2004 which provides an academic journal, an open discussion forum and a useful collection of information materials (internet links, bibliography of studies) on European language culture including language politics (http://www.eurolinguistix.com).

- 'The European Association of Daily Newspapers in Minority and Regional Languages' (MIDAS) gathered in Bautzen, Germany at its 5th annual general assembly. While the association has articulated its support for the needs of the local Sorbian-speaking minority (cf. Kimura 2002), MIDAS member newspapers are planning to publish a joint e-paper on the Internet (Eurolang newsletter, 3 June 2005).

- The 'First European Conference on Higher Education in the Languages of National Minorities' took place in Romania and online with participants from all over Europe in June 2005. Possibilities of developing higher education in national minority languages based on principles of the EU and the Bologna Process were discussed and a 'Charter of Higher Education' in European minority languages was agreed on (Eurolang newsletter, 8 June 2005).

- *Urdd Gobaith Cymru,* Wales' largest youth movement*,* plans to conduct a European Youth Seminar in 2006 focussing on minority languages, culture and traditions.

In the next section, the oldest pan-European political organization (founded in 1949), the 'Council of Europe', will be introduced with regard to its prominent commitment to national and linguistic minorities.

3.5   The Council of Europe

The Council of Europe (CoE), an international organization with 46 democratic member states, all of them EU members, has its headquarters in Strasbourg (http://www.coe.int). Although distinct from the EU, the CoE is based on the same values, which has led to close cooperation between the two. For example, at their initiative, 2001 was designated as the 'European Year of Languages'.

Two legal instruments which were designed and issued by the CoE have been (and hopefully will be) of major consequence to the status of the Cornish language and identity.

3.5.1 The European Charter for Regional or Minority Languages (ECRML)

In 1992, after some 10 years of preparatory work, the CoE launched the Charter to be signed by its member states. After ratification by five member states, the Charter became effective in 1998. Once put into force by a state, it is a legally binding document.

It applies to languages as defined in 3.1.1, excluding local dialects of official or majority languages immigrant languages. Although Irish Gaelic is a minority language, it cannot be included because Irish is the first official language of the Republic of Ireland. On the other hand, Irish in Northern Ireland has been ratified by the UK. Whereas 19 member states have signed and ratified the ECRML so far, 13 states, among them France, only signed but have not ratified the document yet.

The Charter, which supplies a multitude of measures that state parties can take to safeguard and promote their regional or minority languages (RM), consists of 5 parts.

Parts I and V contain general provisions including the definition of 'regional or minority languages' (see above 3.1.1).

In Part II, Article 7.1, which automatically applies to any qualifying language, nine general principles and objectives are stated, e.g.:[56]

a.   recognition of the RM as an expression of cultural wealth;

b.   respect for the geographical are of each RM in order to ensure that existing or new administrative divisions do not constitute an obstacle to the promotion of the RM in question;

d.   the facilitation and/or encouragement of the use of RM, in speech and writing, in public and private life;

f.   the provision of appropriate forms and means for the teaching and study of RM at all appropriate stages;

g.   the provision of facilities enabling non-speakers of a RM living in the area where it is used to learn it if they so desire;

h.   the promotion of study and research on RM at universities or equivalent institutions;

If a state considers a RM worth of a higher level of protection, then it can be included in Part III, which lists a wide range of specific commitments in the fields of education, public administration, judicature, the media, cultural activities and economic and social life. The signatory must bind itself to at least 35 (out of about 100) appropriate (sub-) paragraphs.[57]

---

[56] Since Article 7 of Part II applies to Cornish, the given passages will be literally quoted. The full text in English can be retrieved at http://conventions.coe.int/treaty/en/Treaties/Word/148.doc.
[57] This practice has been criticized as "à la carte" system as it gives states too much room for implementation (Pan and Pfeil 2000:203).

To demonstrate the difference between Parts II and III, let us choose the field of education. Whereas in Part II only three paragraphs, f), g) and h), relate to it, Article 8 of Part III consists of 9 paragraphs and more than 20 sub-paragraphs. For example, sub-paragraph a)i of Part III demands pre-school education or paragraph h) of Part III teacher training, both of which are not concretely mentioned in Part II.

Part IV, which concerns monitoring, specifies periodical reports (the first after one year, then every three years) on the implementation of the ECRML which the respective governments have to present to the Secretary General of the CoE and which will then be evaluated by an expert committee followed by recommendations of the CoE Committee of Ministers. This report system has been considered a too weak control mechanism (Pan and Pfeil 2000:203).

Another shortcoming of the Charter is the almost exclusive reference to minority languages but not to their speakers. The second legal instrument which was adopted under the auspices of the CoE addresses minority rights in general and also includes the linguistic dimension.

3.5.2 The Framework Convention for the Protection of National Minorities (FCNM)

The Framework Convention for the Protection of National Minorities was signed in Strasbourg in 1995 and came into force three years later. So far, 37 states have signed and ratified it and 5 states have only signed it.

The document represents the first legally binding instrument to protect minorities from violations of their rights. In fact, "a climate of tolerance and dialogue" between a state's majority population and its national minorities (NM), as stated in the preamble, should be created. In particular, the Convention aims to put forward the equality of NM by defining principles that have to be complied with in order to ensure preservation of their cultures and identities. Those principles, inter alia, involve freedom of expression, thought and conscience, as well as access to the media.

Article 10 of the Convention specifically refers to the "right of every person belonging to a NM to use his or her minority language freely" (§1,63), extending it to the contact with administrative authorities (§2,64).

The obligation in Article 11, §2,69, "concerns an individual's right to display 'in his or her minority language signs, inscriptions and other information of a private nature visible to the public'." The possibility of having public place and street names (without official recognition) in the minority language is mentioned in §3,70.

Article 13 concedes NM the right "to set up and manage their own private educational and training establishments" (§1,72). However, this does not necessarily involve "any financial obligation" on the part of the states (§2,73).

Although Article 14 goes further to state "the right of every person belonging to a NM to learn his or her minority language" (§1,74), it does not insist on financial support either. The teaching of the minority language must imply "sufficient demand" from NM and depends on "available resources" (§2,75). Knowledge of the official language is taken for granted as it guarantees "social cohesion and integration" (§3,78).

The full text can be accessed at http://www.coe.int/T/E/human_rights/minorities.

As the decision to determine who counts as a minority and which language is worth being protected under which part of the ECRML is still left to the states, the attitude of the UK towards its minority languages, above all Cornish, will be commented on next.

3.6 The British government's minority policy

In the past, Cornish campaigners frequently deplored the fact that the Cornish were treated better by Brussels and Strasbourg than by Westminster. In recent years, the attitude of the British, unlike the French state, towards its Celtic minorities has become more benign though (Celtic League newsletter, 27 August 2005). Due to the process of devolution under Prime Minister Tony Blair, Scotland and Wales were given more autonomy and at the beginning of the new millennium, an important step was taken to promote Britain's lesser-used languages.

3.6.1 Ratification of the ECRML

On the motion by the Cornish Member of Parliament Andrew George, the Government commissioned an independent, academic study on the status of the Cornish language in 2000, which should guide it in its decision whether Cornish should be added to a number of languages that were designated for inclusion in the Charter (MacKinnon 2000, see above 2.6.1.1).

By that time, the British Government had already signed the ECRML which was put into force in 2001. Whereas Irish Gaelic and Ulster Scots (in Northern Ireland), Welsh, Scottish Gaelic and Scots were officially recognized, Cornish was excluded. What Cornish speakers found most outrageous was that Ulster Scots, apart from vocabulary grammatically almost identical to English and therefore just a dialect of English, was included. Moreover, the fact that Ulster Scots is spoken by the Unionists of Northern Ireland who want to stick with the UK made this decision look like a rather politically motivated one. As a consequence, the status of Scots and Ulster Scots as autochthonous languages in their own right were hotly debated among language activist groups. Also the EBLUL adopted a resolution in which it urged the UK Government to consider a Cornish inclusion. Finally, in November 2002, after a seven-year-campaign and also owing to MacKinnon's report, Cornish, like Scots and Ulster Scots, was added under Part II of the Charter.[58]

Welsh, Scottish and Irish Gaelic have been granted the highest level of protection under Part III with 52 binding paragraphs for Welsh, 39 for Scottish Gaelic and almost a minimum of 36 for Irish Gaelic in Northern Ireland. In Wales, however, the implementation of the Charter is not very likely to have a profound effect because most of the provisions already exist (McLeod 2003).

On the other hand, for Cornish, which had up to then suffered from a lack of regular financial support and had mainly been dependent on private initiatives, the

---

[58] The Isle of Man Government has also designated Manx under Part II of the Charter.

breakthrough was received with enthusiasm and hope for a boost. Still, the priority for all RM that have been entered under Part II is working towards elevation to level III protection.

As a first step, Cornwall County Council, entrusted with the implementation, prepared a 'Cornish Language Strategy', integrating representatives of Cornish language organizations and the Government Office for the South West. After a long process of consultation, the document was published in January 2005 (see below 4.5).

Despite the rather dilatory policy at the beginning, some gradual improvement for the UK's lesser-used languages has been observed since the ratification of the Charter. The CoE expert committee's reaction to a preliminary report in 2002 and a visit to the UK at the beginning of the following year approved of the work done so far.

Now that Cornish has been recognized as a European RM, what about the Cornish people?

3.6.2 Are the Cornish a national minority?

> It is intrinsic in the nature of the Union that we have multiple allegiances; we can comfortably be Scottish and British or Cornish and British or Geordie and British or Pakistani and British.
>
> (Tony Blair, *The Times*, February 2000, quoted by Payton 2004a:296)

In 1998, a number of Commonwealth immigrant communities, the Roma, the Irish Travellers and the autochthonous people of Scotland, Northern Ireland and Wales have been identified as ethnic groups under the terms of the FCNM and thus require special protection (Pan and Pfeil 2002:155). Although the Prime Minister's words above seem to express benevolence and acknowledgement of the distinctive status of the Cornish and in the 2001 Census, people living in Cornwall could state 'Cornish' as their ethnic identity for the first time, the UK Home Office has so far refused to extend the benefits of recognition under the FCNM to the Cornish (Payton 2004a:296).

A number of public figures have contributed to the publication of the 'Cornish National Minority Report' (1999), which concludes that the Cornish have clearly a "distinct historic identity" from the English and that there are "constitutional, linguistic and cultural 'differences'" (http://www.geecee.co.uk/CNMR/summary.htm). Also the Civil Rights groups 'Cornwall 2000', 'CharterWatch' and the national party of Cornwall, *Mebyon Kernow* ('Sons of Cornwall'), have been campaigning to overturn that resistance (see Lee 2003; their current campaign can be accessed at: http://www.mebyonkernow.org/Public/Stories/160-1.shtml).

Paradoxically, the issue has also been raised by the Cornish language organization *Agan Tavas* at a discussion forum of a website that promotes learning English (http://www.antimoon.com/forum/ posts/6801.htm). They accuse the UK Government of ignoring Cornish culture, pointing out that according to Article 7.1.c of the ECRML, "resolute action to promote" Cornish is necessary. The fact that the Cornish do not qualify as a NM under UK criteria seems therefore highly contradictory.

Within Cornwall, such lobbying has already been successful as pupils can now be registered as 'Cornish' at school (*Cornish World* magazine, issue 40, winter 2004, p.10). The topic will be taken up again in chapter 4.1.1.

3.6.3 Concluding remarks

Despite the negative picture presented with regard to Cornish and the FCNM, on an overall scale measuring the level of minority protection in Europe, Great Britain was ranked 6th out of 36 states together with Germany, Austria, Slovenia and Lithuania.[59]

The other side of the coin is that around 200 different mother tongues are represented in British schools so that it is far from realistic to meet all demands. A priority of the UK Government is the full integration of all immigrants into British society, which presupposes fluency in English. Therefore, the main responsibility for the maintenance of native languages lies with the language community themselves (Pan and Pfeil 2002:158f.).

Still, although Celtic minority languages are only spoken by a low percentage of the UK population (estimates range from 1.2% (Pan and Pfeil 2000:81) up to 5% (McLeod 2005)), bilingual schools in Scotland and Wales have received considerable financial support. This has resulted in an increasing number of pupils being educated in Gaelic and Welsh (cf. Robertson 2001, Pan and Pfeil 2002:158f.). For Cornish, which has so far mainly been taught on a voluntary basis, this would be the next step.

---

[59] In this context, Belgium, Denmark and Finland have turned out to be exemplary (see Pan and Pfeil 2002:11).

4   Revived Cornish at its Centenary – The End of the Struggle?

> Cornish has literally been resuscitated in this century, several generations after the last speaker of the language died. (Strubell 2001:268)

This chapter has been named after the paper presented at the 9th ICML in Kiruna, Sweden (June 2003) and a subsequent article that was translated into Estonian (Hirner 2004).

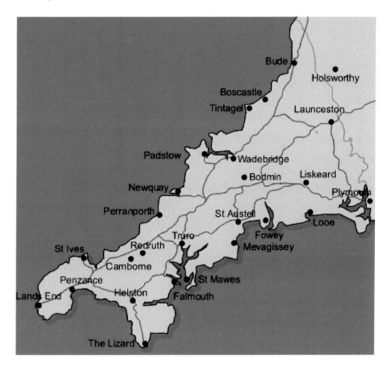

Map 3: Places in Cornwall

In the following chapters, places in Cornwall are frequently mentioned. This map serves as a reference point. Source: http://www.chycor.co.uk/camping/maps/campmap1.htm

4.1   Why is Cornwall different?

On Sunday, 28 July 2002, *The Observer*, an English Sunday quality paper, presented the following headline:

ONE HOT HOGGAN – AND A CRASH COURSE IN CORNISH, PLEASE

Visitors to Cornwall this summer should not ask for a pasty – they should order a *hoggan* instead. Swimmers should head for the *treth* rather than the beach. And they shouldn't say Cornwall at all; they should call it *Kernow*. [...] [60]

Cornwall is not only well-known in Germany and Austria due to Rosamunde Pilcher's novels and (some people call them kitschy) films set in picturesque landscape but it is

---

[60] A pasty is a Cornish speciality with meat and vegetables baked in a pie. *Hoggan* is a dialect variation of *hogenn*.

also popular as an attractive holiday resort for English people. Although a considerable number of tourists may still not be aware of the fact that the Cornish language is not a dialect of English but a separate Celtic language, they cannot escape the "strange, mellifluous place names that give it a flavour quite different from English counties. Many must wonder where they all come from" (Holmes 2000:3).

A popular old mnemonic saying by Richard Carew ('Survey of Cornwall', 1602) makes aware of typically Cornish prefixes: "By *Tre*, *Pol* and *Pen* you shall know the Cornishmen." *Tre-* ('farm, village, town, home'), *pol(l)-* ('pool') and p*en(n)-* ('head, end, top') often occur in combination with (place) names: e.g. in the common surname *Trevenna* ('homestead on hill'), the town of *Penzance* ('holy head'), *Pentreath* (as in Dolly *Pentreath,* 'end of the beach') or the village *Polperro*.[61] The above mentioned *Tremough* Campus near *Penryn* (from *penn rynn* 'end of a slope') is named after a nearby farm (*tre mogh* = 'pig farm')

In fact, the visibility of Cornish words is striking for someone interested in the language (like the author of this book), but even people who were born in Cornwall take them for granted, often not knowing what they actually mean.

Photo taken in Torpoint (August 2002)

Cornwall is separated from its only neighbour Devon by the river Tamar. If you cross the river Plymouth and arrive at Torpoint, you are welcomed by a bilingual 'Cornwall-*Kernow*' sign.

According to the Cornwall County Council, which uses the slogan *Onen hag Oll* ('One and All') as its logo, the existence of Cornish as an essential symbol of Cornishness and regional distinctiveness was an important factor in Cornwall being eligible for Objective One status.

However, Cornwall, together with adjacent Devon and several other counties as shown on map 2 below, is part of the larger South West Region, represented by the Government Office for the South West (GOSW).

---

[61] Due to historical changes in pronunciation and anglicized spellings, place name components occur in various spellings (for details cf. Holmes 2000:5 and 2003 and Weatherhill 2005).

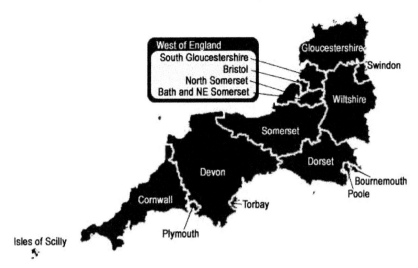

Map 2: South West Region (source:
http://www.gosw.gov.uk/gosw/OurRegion/geographicareas/?a=42496)

Without their own language, the Cornish might be regarded as very similar to the people from scenic Devon or picturesque Dorset. From a constitutional perspective, however, it is not a county but a Duchy, therefore the Queen's son and his wife hold the title of Duke and Duchess of Cornwall. In his foreword to the Millennium book 'Cornwall for ever! *Kernow bys vyken!*' (Payton 2000a:5), an attractive volume celebrating Cornish life and culture, which was given to every schoolchild in Cornwall in 2000, Prince Charles writes:

> I am enormously proud and privileged to be the Duke of Cornwall and I have always believed that Cornwall and the people who live here are very special. [...] The uniqueness of Cornwall lies also in its history. [...] You will all come to carry an important responsibility for preserving the Cornish way of looking at life, the Cornish language and dialect, the Cornish culture and identity [...]

The distinctive local culture and identity also becomes obvious in the local bookshops and libraries which have their own 'Cornish Studies' section. The two bookshops *Gwynn ha Du* ('white and black', derived from the Cornish flag) in Liskeard and 'Just Cornish' in St. Just near St. Ives specialize in Cornish products (the latter also sells Cornish goods on the Internet: http://www.justcornish.com; see Appendix 14.9). In Truro's public library, for example, the visitor can find about 20 books on/in the Cornish language. *Kresenn Kernow* ('The Cornwall Centre') in Redruth is the home of the 'Cornish Studies Library' whose impressive collection exclusively covers Cornish subjects ranging from mining, family history to the Cornish language. The archive contains 269 local and national newspaper articles on the Cornish language which were collected between 1990 to 2002 and make a chronological reconstruction of events possible.

In addition, the existence of an 'Institute of Cornish Studies' which offers Master's and doctoral degrees in 'Cornish Studies' adds to this uniqueness.

The following impressions, which were gathered in St. Ives and Truro in March 2005, should underpin the above observations which suggest a different Cornish identity:

Penwith, from *Pennwydh* ('extremity, end'), is one of Cornwall's six districts, situated in the most westerly part of mainland Britain.

The council's motto *'Kensa Ha Dewetha'* means 'First and Last'.

Porthmeor ('big cove') beach is a famous surf beach in St. Ives (see 9.2).

Cornish landscape

Kernow stickers with the Cornish flag are frequently seen to be displayed on cars.

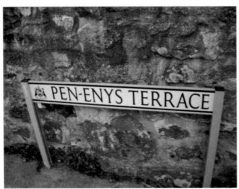

'End of the island' or 'isolated place' *(pen =* 'end', *enys* = 'island')

'White settlement'*(tre* = 'village', (g)*wyn(n)* = 'white')

Cornwall section in a bookshop in Truro, Cornwall's administrative and business centre

Cornish language and local interest books in another bookshop in Truro

4.1.1 A separate identity

Parallel to the revival of the Cornish language and after a long period of assimilation, a felt historical identity has developed. On a small scale, this is for example mirrored in a local primary school survey in St. Just, where 95% of the pupils considered themselves to be Cornish rather than English. On a larger scale, a third of all schoolchildren have been reported to feel Cornish rather than English (*Spotlight* magazine, September 2003, p.21). In Truro hospital, you can even register as 'White Cornish' or 'Black Cornish'.

To this point, we have learned that the Cornish, despite noticeable differences to the English, are not protected under the FCNM yet. The following extract from the summary of the Cornish NM Report 1999 expresses the feelings of those hoping to be recognized as a separate people (source: http://www.geecee.co.uk/CNMR/summary. htm).

- [...] the Cornish are a self-aware and distinct ethnic group and some members of the group see themselves as part of a distinct nation. This has given rise to a cultural and political 'Celtic Renaissance' in Cornwall that indicates its similarities with Wales, Scotland, Ireland, Mann and Brittany and distances it from the majority English culture of the UK state.

- Outsiders also often regard the Cornish as 'different' and a number of (sometimes racist) preconceptions and stereotypes are reproduced about the Cornish.

- This has produced a sense of frustration and powerlessness in Cornish communities.

Moreover, Cornwall's historical constitutional status as a "sovereign Duchy extraterritorial to England", as nationalists insist on, entitles to its independence from England. From 1200 until the 18th century, Cornwall had its own judicial system re-presented by the 'Stannary Parliament' (Latin *stannum* = 'tin') which was closely related to tin mining and never officially abolished (for details of the complex historical development cf. http://en.wikipedia.org/wiki/Constitutional_status_of_Cornwall). Therefore, being subsumed under a south-west identity is not favoured by many Cornish people. In fact, between March 2000 and December 2001 more than 10% of the Cornish population (over 50,000 people) signed a petition calling for a Cornish Assembly on the model of Wales (for a discussion of prospects for devolution in Cornwall see Sandford 2003).

In the next section, we will take a closer look at Cornwall's population which has undergone several changes over the past 50 years.

4.2   Cornwall's population structure

Fishing, mining and farming, the last strongholds of the Cornish language in the 17th and 18th century, used to dominate traditional Cornish industry, but improved communication and transport links have changed Cornwall's economy dramatically. Cornwall's reputation of a relatively deprived economic area has been replaced by one of a rejuvenated business place offering accessible funding (Objective One) and reasonable living costs combined with stunning scenery. Many of the younger generation who formerly had to leave Cornwall in order to study at university or pursue more prosperous careers in the big cities have come back to benefit from a healthier lifestyle. But especially towns like St. Ives (home of the famous Tate Gallery opened in 1993), Truro and Falmouth with a booming arts and culture scene are also attractive for entrepreneurs "flooding in" from all parts of the UK (*Cornwall Today* magazine, January 2005, p. 42f.).[62] This has led to a huge rise in house prices against the background of lower than average wages and a lack of affordable accommodation.

---

[62] Between 2002 and 2003 alone, 142,000 British people moved to the South West region (*First Great Western* magazine, issue 3, spring 2005, p.14).

Obviously, the population movement has affected the structure of Cornwall's population. Whereas in the 1950s, 70-80% of the population had been born in Cornwall, now only 30-50% are estimated to be of Cornish origin.

Despite the positive economic development, it seems as if some initiatives have turned out to be counterproductive with regard to the position of the Cornish language. If the Cornish were recognized as a minority in the FCNM, English people coming to Cornwall would have to show more respect for Cornish culture in general and necessarily more interest for the language in particular, according to language activists.

Paradoxically, the Cornish, being a minority in their homeland, have been accused of being passively racist themselves.[63] Nobody seems alarmed when asylum seekers to Britain should be required to learn English, but when anyone dares to suggest that English people moving to Wales, Scotland or Cornwall should be required to learn Welsh, Gaelic or Cornish, they are quickly labelled as xenophobic or racist. Still, some people fear that the recognition of Cornish could give way to domestic nationalism. In 2002, three members of the Stannary Parliament stole English Heritage signs from local landmarks because of the word 'English', but this incident has remained exceptional.

After giving some background information on the society potential speakers/learners of Cornish are living in, the revived language itself will be brought to the focus of attention again.

4.3 Revived Cornish and its different versions

Although the case of Cornish is generally looked upon as a remarkable success story only comparable with Hebrew (cf. 2.6.2.6), some critics in the past have objected to its somewhat artificial quality:

> So Cornish is not Cornish; 'revived' is not 'real' Cornish. It could perhaps be compared to a painting so heavily restored as no longer to qualify as an authentic work by the artist who originally painted it, or to a piece of music found in fragmentary form and arranged some centuries later by another composer. To envisage the nature and scale of the task facing those who seek to restore it as a living language, one need only think that it is rather as if one were to attempt in our present century to create a form of spoken English on the basis of the 15th century York mystery plays and very little else. (Price 1984:144).

Quite contrarily, others consider the revival of Cornish even more authentic than Hebrew. Fact is that "Cornish is a complex language, capable of expressing every style from the simplest everyday statement to the most involved and abstract political idea" (Brown ²1993, introduction).

---

[63] This is also based on the fact that while only one person in 85 in the South West is black or Asian, the national average is one in 12 (*Cornish World* magazine, issue 40, winter 2004, p.7).

4.3.1 A glimpse at Cornish morphosyntax and morphonology

Like the other Celtic languages, Revived Cornish is more inflected than English, e.g. verbs and prepositions in combination with personal pronouns are conjugable.

The preposition *'dhe'* ('to') combines with 'me', 'you' and so on as follows:

dhymm	'to me'	*dhyn*	'to us'
dhis	'to you'	*dhywgh*	'to you'
dhodho	'to him'	*dhedha*	'to them'
dhedhi	'to her'		

There are not many guiding rules for the complexity of plural forms: various plural endings (e.g. *–ow, -yow, -ys, -s, –ell, -edh, -yn, -yer...*) and the gender of nouns (masculine or feminine) usually have to be learned by heart (cf. Page 1993a:5,30). For example, the plural of *blydhen* (fem., 'year') involves internal change plus suffixation: *blydhynyow*.

Also word order is different and countless morphonological rules and exceptions have to be remembered. The several types of mutations are named after the kind of phonetic change which takes place (cf. Page 1993a:44-46): [64]

- Soft mutation (lenition): P>B, B>V, M>V, T>D, D>DH, CH>J, K>G, G>W or lost. Some causes: the definite article *an* mutates feminine singular nouns and masculine plurals of persons: *mamm* ('mother') – *an vamm*; numeral *unn* ('one') mutates a fem.sgl. noun: *unn venyn* (*benyn* 'woman').

- Aspirate (breathed) mutation: P>F, T>TH, K>H. Caused by e.g. numerals *tri* (masc.) and *teyr* (fem.): *tri hi* (*ki* 'dog'), *teyr hath* (*kath* 'cat').

- Hard mutation: B>P, D>T, G>K.

- Mixed mutation: B>F, D>T, G>H, M>F. Triggered by e.g. interrogative adverbs like *ple* ('where').

The following literal translation of a short passage in *Kernewek Kemmyn* (see below 4.3.3) should give an idea of how Cornish morphosyntax and morphonological rules work in practice.

---

[64] For an outline of the most salient linguistic characteristics of Revived Cornish based on *Kernewek Kemmyn* see Hirner (1997:41-52).

4.3.1.1   *Literal translation of a Cornish text*

The article was published in the magazine *An Gannas* in September 2001.[65]

Kernewek tramor ('Cornish overseas/abroad')

*1   Ute Hirner benyn yowynk   diworth Ostri neb a **dheuth dhe'n Bennseythun** Gernewek*

Ute Hirner   a woman young   from Austria   who   came   to the Weekend Cornish Language

2   warlyna yn Aberfal ow hwithra dasserghyans an yeth a ros areth

last year in Falmouth researching   revival   the language *gave* a talk

3   yn kever studh an yethow keltek dhe 17 studhyer yn Pennskol Graz, Ostri.

about   situation the languages Celtic to 17 students   in/at University Graz, Austria.

4   Tri studhyer a dhewisas oberi yn kever Kernewek ha pareusi paper war agan yeth

Three students chose   to work about   Cornish and prepare a paper on our language

5   a wrons.

they do.

Explanations:

- Ad line 1: In Cornish, adjectives normally follow the noun.

  Dos ('to come') is irregular and *deuth* is the 3rd person sgl. preterite and the verbal particle *a* mutates *d* to *dh*. Cornish verbs are mostly preceded by verbal particles. The particle *a*, for example, is used to link the verb to the subject or object when they precede the verb and softly mutates the verb (see Hirner 1997:49f., Page 1993a, 1993b).

  Dhe'n is the contracted form of *dhe + an*. The preposition *dhe* also causes soft mutation, therefore P>B. The fem. word *pennseythun* in turn mutates *Kernewek*.

- Ad line 2: The present participle '-ing' is formed by placing the verbal particle *ow* in front of the infinitive of the verb.

  The possessive is expressed by putting the thing possessed before the possessor, therefore 'revival of the language' or 'the language's revival'.

  Ros is the preterite form of *ri* = 'to give'.

  The "talk" was actually the Proseminar "The sociolinguistic situation of the Celtic languages in Britain" held in summer term 2001.

- Ad line 3: Possessive construction, therefore 'situation of the Celtic languages'.

- Ad line 4: *Dhewisas* is the mutated preterite (particle *a*) of the infinitive *dewis*.

- Ad line 5: *Wrons* is the mutated 3rd person pl. of the verb *gul* ('to do'), *gwrons* = 'they do'. The function and application of *gul* is very complex (see Page 1993a:38f.), but in this sentence it is actually superfluous.

---

[65] This most successful monthly Cornish language magazine *The Ambassador*, which was initiated by the *Kemmyn* related 'Cornish Language Fellowship' in 1976, has a circulation of more than 300 copies with a few subscribers living outside Cornwall, even in Canada.

4.3.2 Phonology and orthography

With regard to pronunciation, the *Kemmyn* graphemes <eu> (as in French *peur*), <u> (as in French *tu* when *stressed*) and <gh> (as in German *Dach*) could present some problems for English speakers. Due to the absence of native speakers as a control authority, the phonology and orthography of Revived Cornish has sparked off an unforeseen development.

In the 1970s, when the emphasis changed from written to spoken Cornish and more speakers gained proficiency, the question of pronunciation became more important. As a consequence, criticism of Nance's Revived Cornish, in particular of its inconsistency in spelling and pronunciation, began to emerge (examples in Thomas 1992:347, see 2.6.1.1). Much has been written about the fragmentation of the revival movement which followed heated controversy (to name just a few: George 1995, George and Dunbar 1997, MacKinnon 2000:11-15, Payton 2002b:142-162).

4.3.3 Duelling "Cornishes" and their differences

To cut a long story short, four different spelling systems have evolved (listed in chronological order of their "creation"), whose proponents founded their own institutions to promote their varieties:

- **Unified Cornish**, founded on Middle Cornish, is the continuation of Nance's variety.

- **(Kernewek) Kemmyn** ('Common Cornish'), proposed by Dr. Ken George (1986) and adopted by the Cornish Language Board, is based on a systematic computer analysis of medieval texts and more phonemic than Unified Cornish. In terms of numbers (80% of Cornish speakers/learners) and productivity (publications), *Kemmyn* dominates.

- **Late or Modern Cornish** is the variety derived from the last traditionally spoken form based on the corpus of the last texts available (17th and 18th century). Its orthography is naturally most anglicized and there are also some differences in vocabulary and grammar (Gendall 1991).

- **Unified Cornish Revised (UCR)** can be, in simple terms, regarded as a compromise between Unified and Late Cornish (cf. Williams 1995).

Especially the transition from Middle to Late Cornish also saw dramatic changes in morphosyntax, e.g. the breakdown of the system of mutations, increased use of the English plural ending '-s', a breakdown of pronominal prepositions, loss of verbal endings, increased use of periphrastic forms or restricted use of the subjunctive mood. Therefore, those advocating Late Cornish often have to put up with remarks concerning its "poor" constructions and lexicon. Proponents of Late Cornish, on the other hand, argue that their version is more authentic and just as legitimately a language distinct from English as, say, modern Welsh which also borrows from English. The differences are the same as those between Shakespeare's and Dickens's English. In addition, the simplified grammar would facilitate learning and thus become more popular.

In order to illustrate to what extent the forms are mutually intelligible, some examples will be given:

Sometimes, *Kemmyn* and Unified use the same spelling as in *Myttin da* (literally 'morning good') which would be *Metten da* in Late Cornish. *Mis-meurth* ('March') in *Kemmyn* corresponds to *Mys merth* in Unified Cornish (see 1.2.1.1). Referring to the pictures in 4.1, Unified *Kensa ha Dewetha*, *Pen-Enys* and *Trewyn* would be *Kynsa ha Diwettha, Pennynys* and *Trewynn* in *Kemmyn*. Although the spelling deviates, pronunciation is not strikingly different (e.g. *'Kernewek', 'Kernowek', 'Kernuak'* and *'Curnoack'*) and both can be overcome with practice (MacKinnon 2000:15).

Kernuak Es ('Cornish easy'), a beginner's course, is based on UCR and uses the simplified grammar found in the Cornish after 1500 (Climo-Thompson 2001). Still, the learner has to struggle with the rules for mutations. Also the conjugation of the verb 'to be' (*bos*), though a bit more simplified in Late Cornish, has to be studied in all versions:

Lowen of vy	*Lowen ov vy*	'Happy am I' = 'I am happy'
Lowen os ta	*Lowen os ta*	'You are happy'
Lowen yw ef	*Lowen yw ev*	'He is happy'
Lowen yw hy	*Lowen yw hi*	'She is happy'
UCR version	*Kemmyn* version	
(Climo-Thompson 2001:19)	(Sandercock 2004:4)	

In addition to Sandercock's (2004) beginner's course *Cornish This Way* in *Kemmyn*, there is also the informal Unified comic course book *Cornish is Fun* (Chubb 2003). In short, all varieties produce their own learning materials, which one the one hand stimulates productivity, on the other hand is a waste of precious energy and also confuses learners ("Which variety is the best/easiest?", personal comments). Most speakers feel the need for a single standard form, however, as in most other languages (including English and Welsh) which have dialects, the differences do not prevent them from communicating with each other.

The reader him-/herself can compare both differences and similarities by reading the first part of a letter written by one of the last speakers in the 1770s (Late Cornish) and the same extract re-written in *Kemmyn:*

Bluth vee try egance a pemp.	*Ow bloedh vy yw tri-ugens ha pymp.*
Theara vee dean bodgack an puscas.	*Yth ov vy den boghosek an puskes.*
Me rig deskey Cornoack termen	*My a wrug dyski Kernewek termyn*
me vee mawe.	*pan en vy maw.*
Me vee de more gen seara vee	*My eth dhe'n mor gans ow sira vy*
a pemp dean mouy en cock.	*ha pymp den moy y'n kok.*

English:

My age is sixty-five. I am a poor fisherman. I learned Cornish when I was a boy. I went to sea with my father and five other men in a boat.

In addition, a passage from the 'Strategy for the Cornish Language' (which has been published in English and all four Cornish versions) will be appended in all four varieties (see 14.1). The extract also gives a summary of the current status of the language including its media presence.

The next section deals with the level of lexemes, in particular with word-formation in Cornish.

4.3.4 Filling lexical gaps and the realization of modern concepts

The Cornish lexicon consists of 50% Celtic, 40% English and French (*chambour, -yow* masc. = 'bedroom')[66] and 10% Latin words (e.g. *fenester, -tri* f., *eglos, -yow* f.) but in average texts, 85% of the words are of Celtic origin (George 1993c). Consequently, the common English speaker but also any other European knowing Germanic or Romance languages finds it difficult to rely on cognates.

When reconstructing Cornish, two kinds of lexical gaps had to be filled:

- Common words which must have existed in the language but do not happen to have been recorded, e.g. Breton *razh* and Welsh *rhath* indicate that the Cornish word for 'rat' must have been *rath.*

- Words for concepts which did not exist in the 18th century.

One of the greatest challenges has been to make the language fit as vehicle of modern concepts. Whereas *Kemmyn* and Unified Cornish mostly combine a Celtic root and existing words in a descriptive way or refer to Welsh or Breton cognates, Late Cornish tends to borrow from English (*jynn-ebrenn* 'machine'+'sky' vs. *ayrplen*). Still, a Late Cornish speaker is very likely to understand the *Kemmyn* or Unified form as well.

The work of expanding the lexicon has been continued by the Vocabulary and Grammar Committee of the Cornish Language Board (source: dictionary supplements *On the Roads, Kitchen Things and Home and Office*):

The principle adopted was (in order of preference):

a.   an existing Cornish word, with extension of semantic range, e.g.
      maglenn 'gear system', originally 'mesh, snare'
      lost 'queue', originally 'tail'

b.   a new word constructed from familiar Cornish elements, e.g.
      glan gales 'hard shoulder' = *glan* 'border' + *kales* 'hard'

c.   a new word based on Breton or Welsh, e.g.
      oyl-men 'petroleum', Breton *eoul-maen*
      rosva 'promenade (road)', Welsh *rhodfa*

---

[66] Depending on the historical stage, data vary, e.g. 70% Celtic, 20% English and French and 10% Latin.

d.   a new word based on other European languages, without giving English any special priority
tuyow oll, 'through traffic', French 'toutes directions'

e.   direct borrowing, e.g.
patrol 'patrol', French patrouille
radyo 'radio' from international vocabulary
taksi 'taxi'
attes 'at ease'
tennis, ostel 'hotel'
aspyryn, byrger, chekkenn 'cheque'

A semantic problem the compilers of the supplements had to tackle in the absence of traditional speakers was to allocate the following words, all referring to containers of some kind, to present-day kitchen equipment: *bason* ('large basin'), *bolla* ('bowl', 'small basin'), *chek(k)* ('cauldron', 'open kettle', 'large boiling pan'), *lester* ('vessel'), *padel(l)* ('pan'), *seth* ('crock', 'large jar').

When translated, they do not denote the same object as the original one and this is where the Sapir-Whorf hypothesis applies. Language revivalists like to claim that a specific idea can only be expressed perfectly in that specific language (cf. Fishman 2001a:3f.). Likewise, distinctions encoded in one language are not realized in any other (linguistic relativity). Sapir-Whorf's linguistic determinism, however, does not allow for the fact that people manipulate language to convey their perceptions. So if there is a gap for a modern concept, this does not imply that speakers are not able to perceive it (cf. Yule 1996:246-248).

As already mentioned in 2.7.1.1, the creation of neologisms to cover all domains of modern life does not pose any problems. Still, the proportion of coinings and borrowings in Revived Cornish is quite small (e.g. 2.3% in the magazine *An Gannas*). The following examples are supposed to illustrate that word-formation in Cornish is quite natural and logical:

margh-tan	'fire horse'	locomotive
margh-horn	'iron horse'	bicycle
gwaya-myr	'moving show'	cinema
jynn-golghi	'engine-to wash'	washing machine
jynn-skrifa	'engine-to write'	typewriter
pellgowser	'far+speak'	telephone
pellwolok	'far+see'	television
rewer	*rew* = 'ice'	freezer
gwiasva	*gwias* = 'web, texture'	website
	-va = place-name ending	
gwydhea	*gweles* = 'to see'	video
kartenn-gresys	'card' + *kresys* = 'credit'	credit card
carten lendya	Late Cornish	credit card

Some people might argue that if a word is well established internationally (e.g. 'video'), it seems unnecessary to desperately make it look Cornish (e.g. *gwydhea*) or tortuously translate it when many English words are Greek-Latin hybrids anyway (e.g. 'television'). Others consider it essential for a language to be successfully revived that even the most technically complex materials should be translated and more of a genuinely Celtic lexicon should be preserved.

So there may be a few who would prefer *komputa* or *komputenn*, the anglicized form with a Cornish suffix, to *jynn-amontya* ('engine-to count'). On the other hand, a survey of Welsh-speaking pupils found that the Welsh word for 'computer' *cyfrifiadur* ('to compute' = *cyfrifo*) was preferred to "Welshified" *compiwter,* but nobody translated 'Internet' into mutated *rhyngrwyd* ('inter' = *rhyng*, 'net' = *rhwyd*; see Hirner 1997:102).

To sum up, there are various ways of how to create new words in Cornish. Since change and innovation keep a language alive and fluid, keeping a balance between borrowing and combining existing Celtic roots would be ideal. As an important step, speakers of all four versions of Cornish should seize the opportunity and first agree on common neologisms which lack the historical "burden".

4.3.5 On the way to consensus?

Recently, a more tolerant climate among the groups, who have had to cooperate on various occasions, has been observed. The Cornish sub-committee of the EBLUL consists of members of all branches and also the Strategy advisory group included representatives from various organizations.

Most people involved are aware that a successful implementation of the Strategy first requires standardization of Cornish orthography, which was also one of the main themes in the first 'Cornish Language Strategy Conference' entitled "Towards a Cornish Future – Language Planning & Cornish". It took place at Tremough Campus, University College Falmouth, on 17 September 2005. Other topics included public signage, media, commercial use of Cornish and education and experts from outside (Wales, Scotland and the Isle of Man) gave advice derived from experience with their own language communities as well. A Cornish language conference, organized by the Cornwall County Council, is now intended to be held annually.

Especially finding a compromise on place names won't be easy due to the westward retreat of Cornish. In East Cornwall, where the language died much earlier, the spelling of place names naturally derives from an earlier period than in the West, where Late Cornish spellings prevail (MacKinnon 2000:14).

A single written form is also considered absolutely necessary if Cornish is supposed to enter the regular school system.

4.4 Cornish in education

To date (November 2005), Cornish has predominantly been taught by volunteers as an extracurricular activity in lunchtime or after-school clubs and is currently absent from pre-school education. The majority of learners are adults who study the language in evening classes in- and outside Cornwall (see below 4.4.2). Table 5 shows the most recent Cornish education figures available which were provided by MacKinnon (2000) and Mercator-Education (2001):

Type	Total of students	Number of schools	Cornish students
Primary school	39,000	12	approx. 120
Secondary school	32,000	4	approx. 70
Evening class		36 classes	approx. 365

Table 5: Cornish education figures (2000/01)

4.4.1 Pre-school, primary and secondary education

Since circumstances are constantly changing due to headteachers' attitude, teachers' commitment and language skills and pupils' interest, the school figures above are not up-to date any more (cf. Huebner 2001:36). In general, primary schools are keen on teaching local interest and might include Cornish words in assemblies, prayers and songs. Some even use bilingual welcome signs (see picture in 9.4).

Lately, schools in the UK have been able to specialize in certain subjects, which makes it possible to receive extra funding, e.g. for language education. Two specialist language colleges, Hayle Community School near St. Ives and Penrice School and Community College at St. Austell, offer Cornish as part of their curriculum with year 7 (11-12-year olds). In Hayle Community School, around 150 secondary school pupils followed a one-term "taster" course in the school year 2005/06.[67] Therefore, the number of students given in Table 5 must be revised. However, no provisions are made to enable pupils to continue studying Cornish and the teacher is not a fluent Cornish speaker (see below 6.2.1).

Teaching a regular subject implies a special qualification for teachers but a lack of funding and resources for teacher training have so far made it impossible to establish a network of renumerated peripatetic teachers. An annual Teachers Day held by the Cornish Language Board has been the only course so far.

As long as Cornish is not a proper subject, pupils are not likely to take it seriously (personal comments of parents). In that respect, the development has even been backward since Cornish used to be offered as a GCSE subject (General Certificate of Secondary Education) in cooperation with the Welsh Joint Examinations Committee. Then a new cost-saving rule was introduced by the government which required at least

---

[67] No data could be obtained from the other secondary school probably due to a lack of interest on the part of the contact person.

800 entrants a year in order to arrange a GCSE exam. In 1996, the last seven students passed this demanding exam.

Conditions as described above have made the chairman of the 'Cornish Language Strategy Steering Group' state that "education is the biggest nut to crack" (*Cornwall Today* magazine, December 2004, p.60). First and foremost, pre-school children should regularly come into contact with Cornish in nursery schools or playgroups as in Wales and the Isle of Man. The problem of distance as outlined in 2.6.1.1 has already hindered efforts to institutionalize a playgroup in the early 1980s. Meeting once in a month turned out to be too sporadic to be effective so that after three years the project stopped.

4.4.2 Adult education

At present, adult education, in the form of evening classes which are offered in three varieties of Revived Cornish, plays the most important role in terms of enlarging the circle of speakers. The figures in Table 5 above, which vary from year to year, refer to a network of classes throughout Cornwall being made up of 16 classes in *Kernewek Kemmyn,* 9 in Unified and 11 in Late/Modern Cornish. They take place in Further Education Colleges (which hold classes ranging from modern languages to arts and sports) but also more informally at private houses, village halls or pubs. Cornwall County Council provides a list of current classes with teacher contact numbers on its homepage (http://www.cornwall.gov.uk/index.cfm?articleid=6119).

In the autumn term 2004, Truro College, for example, offered a 10-week Beginner's Course in Cornish for 30 pounds. The continuation class which was supposed to start in January 2005 (Tuesday from 7-9 p.m., 15 weeks for 45 pounds with accreditation available) was cancelled because enrolment rates were too low. Outside Cornwall, there is a highly recommended *Kemmyn* class at the City Literary Institute in London Holborn[68], a Unified one in Bristol and Cornish is even learnt in evening classes in Australia and the USA. The opportunity to learn Cornish by post or e-mail (KDL) has also attracted a considerable number of learners living outside Cornwall (see 2.6.1.1 and 2.7.1.1).

By way of illustration, the following extract from the Penwith Adult and Community Education College guidebook 2004/05 (p.15) shows a Cornish course description:

---

[68] In fact, the London class has "produced" a number of fluent speakers who very actively contribute to the promotion of Cornish, e.g. the language teacher and secretary of 'The Cornish Language Fellowship' or a Cornish poet, actor and language teacher, both Bards of the Cornish *Gorsedh.*

> ## Cornish for Beginners
>
> **John Parker**
>
> The emphasis of the course is on spoken Cornish and fluency in conversation. The version of Cornish taught is known as Kemmyn, and the course text for beginners is "Holyewgh an Lergh" ("Follow the Path"), but anyone who has begun learning a different version of Cornish in the past is welcome to come along and sample Kemmyn. The course will lead to the grade 1 examination of the Cornish Language Board and in subsequent years to the examinations for grades 2 and 4. There will be opportunities to take part in various Cornish language events throughout the year and to meet Cornish speakers from elsewhere in Cornwall. Kernewek a'gas dynnergh!
>
> **Penzance – Penwith College**
> **A1014   20 September (20 weeks)**
> **Monday 7.00pm to 9.00pm**
> **FF £99.00   60+ £59.00   RF £59.00**

Most classes in *Kemmyn* and Unified follow the syllabus of the Cornish Language Board examinations which consist of a written and an oral part and usually take place between May and June. The exam results are published in *An Gannas* or can be accessed at the *Kowethas* ('Cornish Language Fellowship') website (since 2004). The number of successful candidates amounts to around 60 per year (e.g. 62 in 1998, 58 in 2001, 57 in 2004) and unsurprisingly decreases with the exam's degree of difficulty. Surprisingly on the other hand, in 1995, only two students from outside Cornwall, *Loundres* ('London') and *Ostrali* ('Australia'), passed the Fourth Grade exam. The latest available results are from 2004, 26 candidates passed the First Grade, 14 the Second, 8 the Third and even 9 students the demanding Fourth Grade.

Apart from the classes, opportunities to practice Cornish orally are not very frequent. In the next section, a useful way of combining social integration and language learning will be described.

4.4.2.1   *Social events supporting language learning*

Apart from the classes, learners get a chance for conversation by meeting in pubs across Cornwall (*Yeth an Werin* = 'informal gathering at which Cornish is spoken', George 1998:53f.)[69] or by attending Fun Days (*Dydhyow Lowender, dydh* = 'day', *-yow* = a common plural suffix) where all activities are organized in *Kernewek*.

Most effectively, immersion in Cornish takes place during language days or weekends which are organized by organizations related to Unified, *Kemmyn* and Late Cornish.

---

[69] 'Language of the People'; the actual noun *gwerin* is feminine and the definite article *an* triggers soft mutation, therefore *werin*.

Especially the *Pennseythun* ('weekend') hosted by the *Kowethas* has been catering for complete beginners through to advanced speakers with a range of classes and activities to suit all levels. In the past, it had even lasted for a whole week, but due to time constraints on the part of organizers, teachers and participants who all have to make their living besides promoting, teaching and learning Cornish, it has been reduced to a long weekend.

The Language Weekend 2005 took place in a caravan park just outside of St. Austell from 11 to 13 March. Experience has shown that staying in caravans encourages contacts among learners who can hear people around them talk fluently in natural situations. Also the early spring season has proved ideal for this event as due to the absence of tourists at that time of the year, the holiday park can exclusively used by Cornish speakers. Central meeting point was a clubhouse where the language classes during the day and entertainment (Cornish music and dancing, singing and poem reading in Cornish) in the evening took place. On Saturday afternoon, a trip around the nearby 'Lost Gardens of Heligan' was organized with explanations in Cornish and bilingual information brochures.

On Saturday and Sunday morning, learners were split into four groups according to their competence and taught by fluent *Kemmyn* speakers from 9.00-12.30. The top group consisted of 20 fluent speakers and the beginner's group was so big that it had to be split again. Altogether, some 70 people, took part in the lessons, among them a significant number of small children (who formed an extra group and were "playfully" introduced to Cornish, e.g. with colours and numbers) and teenagers who had accompanied their parents. In one case, a mother and a friend accompanied a teenager who wanted to learn Cornish (see below 7.1). A few learners who have Cornish roots or study Cornish in London or via KDL also came from outside Cornwall (Wales, Somerset, London, Birmingham). One girl's name (from Somerset) was *Kerensa*, the Cornish word for 'love'. It was also striking that three learners from the Late Cornish movement took part and a renowned researcher and fluent speaker of Late Cornish gave a talk to the most advanced group. Language activities varied from role plays to vocabulary games and the relaxed atmosphere combined with intensive studying certainly contributed to building up more confidence.

In a very positive feedback session, only one negative aspect was mentioned: costs. Apart from accommodation and food and drinks, participants also had to pay 20 pounds which included lessons, materials, evening entertainment and the excursion. This fee seemed to have prevented a few low-income families or unemployed learners from participating. What is more, teachers, especially one student who travelled to Cornwall from London where he teaches Cornish at the City Lit, did not get any refunding. It was agreed that in the future, the charge should be graduated according to income and that some sort of reward for teachers should be considered. Learners also suggested that in addition to the *Pennseythun*, Fun Days should occur quarterly.

Summing up, the Weekend was a success and an encouraging trend could be observed with regard to participants. Compared to the *Pennseythun* 2000 (31 August – 3 September in Falmouth), which I also attended, the number of children and teenagers starting with Cornish has risen considerably. Another positive sign was that *Kemmyn* learners mixed with Late Cornish learners.

The following pictures should capture the experiences as described above:

Accommodation at Duporth Holiday Village

Meeting other speakers in the clubhouse

Studying language materials

The first phrases

Beginner's class

Playgroup

Cornish Language Weekends are not only confined to Cornwall. In August 2005, the 2nd annual Cornish Weekend was held in Berkeley Springs, West Virginia. The American representative of KDL, also a Bard of the *Gorsedh* and PhD in Celtic Languages from Harvard University and two KDL students with Cornish ancestors prepared various activities for practising Cornish. The event seemed to have been so successful that a 3rd American-Cornish Weekend is already planned for August 2006.

Since 1973, the World's Largest Cornish Festival, *Kernewek Lowender,* has been held every two years in three former mining towns in South Australia. From 9-16 May 2005, around 72,000 participants could experience the Cornish heritage. Among the many events related to Cornish history and traditions, an Australian Bard, who also teaches Cornish at the Adult Learning Centre in Adelaide, introduced the Cornish language to beginners. In addition to this 3-hour-session, there was a conversation class for students of Cornish.

Despite all the enthusiasm for the Cornish language and culture shared by people in- and outside Cornwall, there is still one question left. Why does only a fraction of a potential of 50,000 people who signed the petition for a Cornish Assembly speak or bother to learn Cornish? There seem to be a number of factors which prevent them from completing their Cornish identity.

4.4.2.2   *Motivation of learners*

It is estimated that since 1979, roughly 10,000 people have attempted to learn Cornish but only few of those who join a beginner's class may become fluent. Enormous effort is required to study such a complex language, which seems to have been mastered only by some 300 people so far. Given the fact that daily use of the language is not guaranteed, weekly lessons are just not enough. Moreover, the private costs for travelling to and attending Cornish language classes or events should not be underestimated, all the more so since there is no demand for learning Cornish in the context of business life (yet).

But even if classes were free or at least subsidized, the majority of learners who succeed in acquiring some basic principles and phrases would drop out when facing the load of advanced grammatical structures and the mass of new vocabulary. According to Kennedy (2002:286f.), a lack of attractive self-study materials and natural support outside the classroom contribute to the failing of the "ordinary" learner. The result is the production of numerous semi-speakers who certainly serve to increase general support for the revival movement, but also make aware of the limitations of an "imaginary" Cornish-speaking community, which does not live within a "linguistically defined geographic area" (Kennedy 2002:288). As already indicated in 2.7.1.1, this shortcoming is increasingly compensated by communication via the virtual space.

Undeniably, the spelling conflict has been confusing potential learners as well (Payton 2004a:282). In addition to orthographical standardization, existing grammatical forms should be rationalized (Jones 1998:342).

In order to tackle the issues raised above and to enhance the prospects for learners, great hopes are being placed in the concrete implementation of the European Charter, which will be discussed in the following chapter.

4.5   The Strategy for the Cornish Language

The year 2005 will be remembered as another milestone in the history of Cornish. After a one-year period of broad consultation which included a study visit to the Isle of Man and also served as a platform to express the needs of Cornish speakers, the first official "umbrella" document was published by Cornwall County Council (CCC).[70] It clearly has a "long-term vision" of Cornish as a "widely-spoken community language" (p.1). To reach this goal, six domains of priority have been identified which are supposed to be targeted step by step over the next 25 years (p.9).

Cover picture of the document
(source: Cornwall County Council homepage,
http://www.cornwall.gov.uk/cornish/cornishstrategy/default.htm)

4.5.1 Education

Increasing provisions for learning Cornish from pre-school to university and adult education is one of the top priorities (vision 1, p.10f.). In the long run, everybody who wishes to learn Cornish should have the right of access both through schooling and adult education. Special emphasis should be put on the involvement of young children and their families and the needs of semi-speakers.

Vision 2 (p.12) is concerned with raising standards in teaching to attract more learners. This includes the establishment of a network of peripatetic teachers and the training of school teachers who should have the opportunity to obtain a recognized qualification in Cornish.

4.5.2 The visibility of Cornish in public life

For the language to have a much wider public presence, bilingual signs on and in public buildings should be displayed more prolifically as well as bilingual letterheads, websites and promotional materials (vision 3, p.13f.). A long-term aim is to have all

---

[70] Bilingual hard copies of the document (in the four different versions of Cornish) are displayed in all public libraries in Cornwall.

official documents translated into Cornish as this has already become common practice in Wales. Moreover, Cornish should enjoy greater media coverage and be used more prominently in festivals and other public events.

4.5.3 The role of Cornish in Cornwall's economy

Since 1997, the language has been reported to be slowly gaining ground in commerce and advertising. For instance *'Kernow* Mill', a Cornish branch of a popular clothing store chain, has had members of staff greeting coach parties in Cornish and English or holiday guides have had a Cornish message printed on the envelopes which they have been sent out with.

Vision 4 (p.15) is based on the potential appeal of the language as a marketing tool for local products and as serving the tourism industry by drawing visitors. The economic value of "Cornishness" should be encouraged, e.g. by assisting businesses in terms of Cornish branding.

4.5.4 Enhancement of Cornish as a RM language

Vision 5 (p.16) seeks to encourage cultural exchange and cooperation with other language communities as well as public bodies. If the need arises, stronger legislation will be called for.

4.5.5 Supporting infrastructure

In order to realize visions 1-5, a common single written form of Cornish must be agreed on by the different language groups. Joint Cornish language centres where resources can be shared and projects initiated should be established. Language groups should also be assisted in applying for and making use of funding (vision 6, p.17f.).

4.5.6 Immediate aims

Of course, not everybody has been happy with the outcome of the process of consultation. For some who consider the document as too weak Cornish should be treated the same as Welsh and additionally be protected under a domestic Cornish Language Act. The Cornish Branch of the Celtic League for example would have liked to see the compulsory teaching of Cornish in schools, but things being forced upon people often quite have the reverse effect and the possibility of introducing further measures has been left open anyway (4.5.4).

The most immediate aim is to employ a full-time Language Development Officer on the model of Manx (see below 4.6) who can exclusively devote his/her time and expertise to fund-raising and establishing contacts with relevant private and public organizations and individuals (e.g. MPs). In the past, several councils in Cornwall have refused to use Cornish on public signs with the excuse that a standard orthography does not exist yet.

For the language to be used for official purposes, standardization has to be on the agenda first (see 4.3.5).

Yet, the best strategies can only become reality if sufficient funding is guaranteed. Although adherence to the Charter obliges the British Government to promote the language in every way possible, "it isn't required to pledge any hard cash" (*Cornwall Today* magazine, December 2004, p.60). Further, local councils or courts are not committed to use Cornish or pay for its advancement.

In an interview conducted on 17 March 2005, a member of the Steering Group who was enthusiastically involved in the whole process summarized main problems and future aims.

4.5.7 Interview with a Strategy Steering Group member

In her function as the Arts Officer of CCC, the Cornish language has been one component of her wide field of activities. A fluent Cornish speaker and traditional dancer herself, Cornish culture has also been part of her private life.

For her, one of the most difficult challenges are Cornwall's demography (see above 4.2) and the related failing of play groups. She has experienced this backward development with her own daughter. In addition, discussions about the language, which is seen by many as a political issue, even produce racist connotations. Further, reaching agreement among all parties concerned on a common standard for schools won't be very easy, the more so since one form has been dominating.

On the more positive side, a growing number of young people seem to take an interest in Cornish (e.g. at the Cornish Language Weekend). Also businesses are slowly beginning to use Cornish, e.g. a surfing company selling clothes with bilingual labels, thus helping to create a modern image. A lot of structure is already there (e.g. Hayle school project) serving as a base to carry on.

Priorities for the near future are to identify costs and nurture the demand. A professional Language Officer and support staff (part- or full-time, hopefully by autumn) should raise the profile and ensure consolidation. A network of peripatetic teachers should be established but Cornish teaching should not be forced on schools. The local education authority as part of the CCC is supportive as long as there is no extra stress on teachers and no interference with the curriculum. In a pilot scheme, advisory groups for schools will be formed.

In preparing the Strategy, Manx, the closest correlate to Cornish, served as an inspiration. For the Arts Officer, drawing lessons from the successful approach in the Isle of Man is very helpful but it will take some time to feel such an impact in Cornwall.

4.6 Manx

The Isle of Man, located in the north Irish Sea 77 miles northwest of Liverpool, is neither part of the UK nor a full EU member. With its 572 square kilometres it is smaller than Cornwall (3,563 km²) and obviously has fewer inhabitants, according to the latest Census figures 76,315.

Unlike Cornish, Manx, a form of Gaelic, survived into the era of recording devices and was actually revived before it died. Only 17 years after its death, questions regarding the language (who reads, writes and/or speaks it in correlation to age, occupation and place of residence) were asked in the 1991 Census. 1,465 people claimed being able to speak, write or read Manx (details in Broderick 1999:182-186). A decade later, the number had risen to 1,689 as a result of a variety of supportive measures undertaken by the Manx authorities. [71]

Since the introduction of Manx as an optional school subject with the appointment of a Manx Language Officer and two peripatetic full-time teachers in 1992, around 1,000 pupils from the age of eight onwards have been taking part in a weekly lesson each year (details in Stowell 2000). In addition, students now have the opportunity to obtain Manx language qualifications equivalent to the GCSE and A-level and 25 pupils are even reported to attend a Manx Medium School. The Manx Department of Education has also established a favourable framework for families who want to educate their children through Manx from an early age. Although the Isle of Man Government has recognized Manx under Part II of the ECRML, it already fulfils certain Part III requirements in terms of education and the judiciary system (bilingual laws).

In its Government Plan for 2003-2006, the Isle of Man Government intends to continue fostering the Manx identity that is strongly linked to the language and to extend promotion of the language in education and the media. The detailed Manx Language Development Programme by the Manx National Heritage and the Manx Heritage Foundation can be accessed at http://www.gaelg.iofm.net/INFO/program.html. The island's autonomy and its own Parliament are obviously trumps which accelerate the progress of revival.

Apart from the high visibility of the language (e.g. on official buildings, streets), the Cornish delegation was particularly impressed by the positive attitude and enthusiasm Manx people showed for the language in general. A further advantage is the existence of only one form of Manx whose pronunciation is very similar to that of the last speakers.

---

[71] However, only around 50 fluent speakers were identified (Ó hIfearnáin 2005).

5 Interim Summary and Hypotheses

With the recognition of Cornish as a minority language both within Europe and the UK, a unique opportunity has been created for the language to consolidate its position. There is probably a greater sense of confidence amongst Cornish speakers now and more awareness of the language, certainly locally, but because Cornish has only been included under Part II of the Charter (rather than Part III like Irish or Welsh), any extra funding will continue only being voluntary, not statutory. However, there is now an obligation on the part of various bodies to treat the language with more respect and to promote it in various ways. Also, it is illegal to discriminate against a Cornish speaker for speaking the language now.

The following hypotheses, divided into positive expectations and further challenges which may inevitably overlap, can be proposed:

5.1 Positive consequences of the recognition

The strengthening of profile and status that Cornish has enjoyed during the past couple of years is supposed to create a more beneficial climate for Cornish speakers. The Strategy addresses many needs and wishes speakers have expressed in the past (e.g. education at all levels, increased visibility, economic benefits) and its implementation, even though a slow process, is likely to raise the position of Cornish on Fishman's GIDS, approaching the 'high power' stages.

Especially in the field of education, already existent school projects allow for some guarded optimism. Although teaching Cornish as a subject for a limited amount of time will not produce fluent children, it can at least bring about an important change in their minds to appreciate the language (Hinton 2001a:7).

Without doubt, institutional support is a great step forward to reversing language shift, but is it enough to fully restore a formerly extinct vernacular? For Dauenhauer and Dauenhauer (1998:97), who associate a vernacular with "spontaneity and intimacy" and RLS with "planning", this involves a contradiction because it is questionable whether spontaneity and intimacy can be organized at all. In addition, natural and inherent barriers to a successful implementation of the Strategy are still present at most stages.

5.2 Obstacles to overcome

The sociolinguistic status of Cornish as a deliberately learnt, second language is indeed somewhat peculiar and the situation by some even considered artificial. As in the case of Hebrew, its applicability to Fishman's model has to be modified. As long as using the language is linked to organized events and communication takes place in a virtual rather than a real community, intergenerational mother tongue transmission (stage 6) will remain the exception. In addition, the weak demographic basis of the language can only be counterbalanced by the establishment of nursery schools which were observed to involve the whole family in the parallel cases of Hebrew and Manx.

5.2.1 Demography

Only 30-50% of Cornwall's present population were born in Cornwall, which is undoubtedly supposed to have consequences on the general attitude towards the Cornish language. The network of Cornish speakers who normally do not live geographically close together will become looser the more "outsiders" there are. In order to have significant effect on Cornish life, a critical mass of over 1% of the population, equivalent to more than 4,500 people, would have to speak it effectively (George 1993b:653).

5.2.2 Attitudes

Attitudes towards the revival of Cornish will be diverse and depend on whether people were born in Cornwall and have Cornish ancestors or just moved to Cornwall later in their lives. Cornish speakers, no matter if born in or outside Cornwall, will have a different view of the situation and consider the language an essential part of Cornish identity.

For the majority of the non-Cornish-speaking population, Cornishness will not necessarily imply speaking the Cornish language and some might even feel threatened by it. Preserving a dead language may also be regarded as an interference with a natural development (Mithun 1998:185) and revitalization efforts as a waste of time and money. If the language is not seen as a unifying force in the community, the motivation for keeping it alive will be very low, resulting in apathy and unawareness of recent achievements. Also passive acceptance is not enough to bring about an attitudinal change and to attract potential learners. People, above all parents, must be convinced that speaking the language is an enrichment of life.

5.2.3 Education and motivation

Learners must be effectively assisted and motivated in the process of studying a complex language which is so different to their native tongue. More funding can directly improve teaching materials and teacher training, but creating an adequate number of opportunities to speak and practise Cornish outside class will require the support of Cornish radio and national TV stations as well. If learners have easy and regular access to Cornish via the mass media, the burden of time and distance will be reduced to some extent.

As long as there are no Cornish programmes on TV and it is not taught as a proper subject at school, the language will not be taken seriously enough. An official status will increase prestige and might open up economic opportunities and benefits ultimately. Trained and renumerated personnel will be more committed to teaching and convey enthusiasm to their students.

5.2.4 Fragmentation – the spelling debate

Both learners and teachers will find it easier to refer to only one form of the language. Also funds will be invested more effectively in publications, advertising and bilingual signs and learning resources will be shared if there is one common standard. A harmonious and uniform appearance is a must for the revival movement to succeed in the long run.

5.2.5 Intergenerational transmission

According to Fishman (2001b:472), it is not so difficult to start and financially support schools where the minority language is taught but it is hard to create new "fluent and active" speakers of the endangered language. The greatest challenge for effective speakers however is to maintain the level of fluency "until they find an equally committed life-partner and start nuclear families of their own" (ibid.). Only in the home-family-neighbourhood context will the language be successfully transmitted to the next generation. In the case of Cornish, which lay dormant for more than 100 years, this stage is necessarily preceded by the higher stages of schooling. Since the extent to which it is possible to live in Cornish is crucial, the use of the language in different social environments must be guaranteed first.

6   The Investigation

The present empirical survey is an attempt to provide further data illuminating both the current status of Cornish and language attitudes of three different groups of subjects:

1.   Cornish speakers (including learners): n = 100

2.   Pupils who have been instructed in Cornish as part of the curriculum: n = 64

3.   A sample from the non-Cornish-speaking population: n = 101

As Jones (1998:3) has already pointed out, it is very difficult to carry out research in Cornwall since speakers and the few centres of learning are scattered around the whole county. In this case, the advantages of the use of questionnaires are evident as they are quite easy to distribute and collect. The circulation of three different questionnaires took place between February (via e-mail) and March 2005 (on the spot). The data were analyzed statistically using the programme SPSS for Windows.

6.1   Cornish speakers/learners

The nature of this first sample is similar to the one which was investigated in the course of earlier field research (group size n = 85, see Hirner 1997) and, due to the limited number of speakers available, a number of respondents are represented in both surveys. Therefore, in order to point out changes (e.g. in attitude, status of the language), improvements or setbacks that have occurred during that period, the obvious thing to do is to draw a comparison between the results whenever possible (unless questions and categories differ widely) and appropriate. This comparison will be marked with numbers/percentages given in brackets, e.g. (1997: n = 85).

6.1.1 Subjects

The sample is made up of 100 informants[72] (54 male, 46 female) who are either in the process of learning Cornish, learned the language in the past or consider themselves fluent.

---

[72] In this special case, frequency and percentage are equal.

- **Age**

Figure 4 shows the distribution of age:

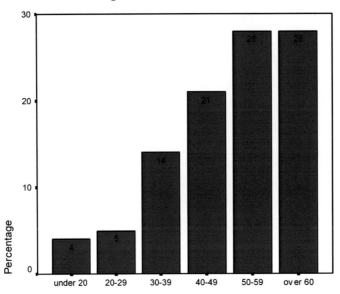

Figure 4: Cornish speakers and their age

Conclusion: The dominant age groups are the 50-59 and over 60-year-olds with each of them having the same representation. Whereas the number of under 20-year-old has doubled (1997: n = 2), there are now fewer 20-29-year olds (1997: n = 12). The 50-59- and over 60-year-olds have remained the dominant age groups.

- **Occupation:**

Figure 5 shows the subjects' occupation:

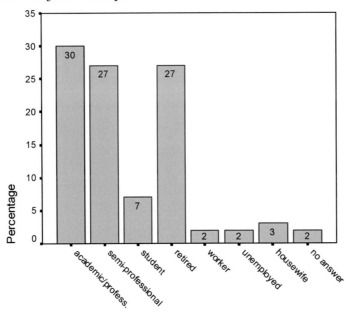

Figure 5: Occupation of speakers

Conclusion: Generally speaking, although Cornish speakers can be found among all social classes, the number of higher educated people stands out. Also noteworthy seems to be the second position of pensioners. Both categories include a considerable number of teachers (altogether 18%), a phenomenon which was also observed in the former sample (cf. Hirner 1997:79).

- **Origin:**

Only 45% were born in Cornwall. A majority of the remaining 55% are from all over Great Britain (without Wales 37%, 10% of them from London), 6% from Wales, 3 USA, 2 Germany, 2 Australia, 1 Ireland, 1 Spain (Basque country), 1 France (Brittany), 1 Hong Kong, 1 Kenya.

- **Residence:**

It seems striking that only 66% of the sample are living in Cornwall, the remaining 34% are dispersed over the United Kingdom (23%, 4 Wales, 4 London, 2 Plymouth which is close to the border of Devon and Cornwall), 4 Australia, 3 USA, 1 Netherlands, 1 France,1 Austria, 1 Germany.

- **Roots:**

24% of the sample have Cornish ancestors but were not born in Cornwall. 4 others were excluded whose explanations for affiliation to the Cornish community were as follows:

Welsh roots, war existence in Cornwall, mother's foster family, Cornish husband

Conclusion: A chi-square analysis was conducted to find out whether residence was dependent on being Cornish. The three degrees of Cornishness are defined as:

a.   Of Cornish origin = **Cornish**

b.   Cornish ancestors but not born in Cornwall = **Cornish roots**

c.   Neither born in Cornwall nor any Cornish roots = **not Cornish**.

The analysis revealed some significant results (χ^2 (2, N = 100) = 8.587, p = 0.014):

a.   Cornish:

- 80% of the people who are of Cornish origin are living in Cornwall, 20% outside.

- 54.5% of the subjects who are living in Cornwall, are of Cornish origin.[73]

- In toto, of the 45% who were born in Cornwall, 36% are living in Cornwall, 9% outside.

---

[73] Percentages are rounded off to one decimal point.

b.   Cornish roots:

- 45.8% of the informants with Cornish roots are living in Cornwall, 54.2% outside.

- 16.7% of the subjects who are living in Cornwall, have Cornish roots.

- In toto, of the 24% who have Cornish roots, 11% are living in Cornwall, 13% outside.

c.   not Cornish:

- A majority of 61.3% who are not Cornish are living in Cornwall, 38.7% outside.

- 28.8% of the informants who are living in Cornwall, are not Cornish.

- *In toto*, of the 31% who are not Cornish, 19% are living in Cornwall, 12% outside.

Figure 6 illustrates the dependence of Cornishness and residence:

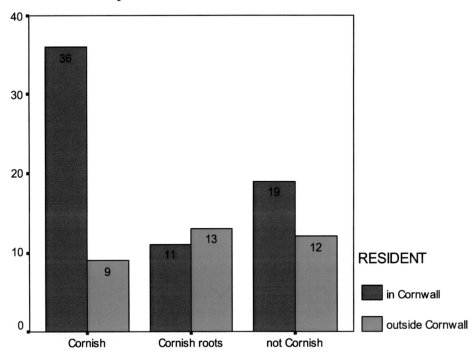

Figure 6: Crosstabulation Cornishness/residence

- **Varieties of Cornish**

Figure 7 shows the distribution of Cornish varieties:

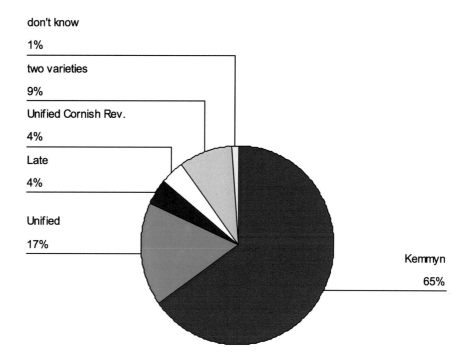

don't know
1%

two varieties
9%

Unified Cornish Rev.
4%

Late
4%

Unified
17%

Kemmyn
65%

Figure 7: Varieties of Cornish

Conclusion: A majority of the sample learn/speak *Kernewek Kemmyn*, followed by 17% Unified speakers. Both Late and Unified Cornish Revised (UCR) are represented by 4 informants. 9 subjects have ticked more than one variety:

- Unified and *Kemmyn*: 7

- Unified and UCR: 1

- Unified, UCR and Late Cornish: 1

The learner who did not know which variety she was studying is a child.

- **Duration, effort and method of learning Cornish:**

Figure 8 shows the varying learning intervals:

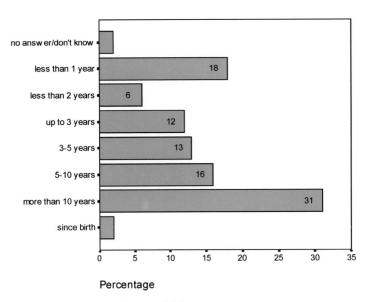

Percentage

Figure 8: How long have you been learning Cornish?

Conclusion: Two bars stand out: whereas 18% have just begun studying the language, 31% have learnt Cornish for more than 10 years, some of them even more than 30 years. As in the 1997 survey, two subjects (aged 20-29 and 40-49) have grown up with the language (1997: both under 20 years old).

The amount of effort put into the study varied accordingly. For example, a Cornish speaker reported having studied almost full time for the first two years. Another respondent mentioned that after 25 years, her studies were irregular and involved active use. The surveyed participants (response rate for this item was 77%) indicated that they studied 3.9 hours a week on average or 2 hours as represented by the median (standard deviation = 4.5). Four respondents stated that they had been studying Cornish more than 15 hours a week, whereas 95% of respondents reported revising Cornish between 1 and 10 hours a week. Only one speaker studies 30 minutes a week. Considering the heavy skew towards a lower number of hours, the median (2.0), which reflects the midpoint of the distribution, probably provides a more accurate representation of the group tendency.

Almost half of the sample (response rate 99%) have attended evening classes (43%), 15% have learnt Cornish via correspondence course, 12% have been autodidacts. 21% have applied two methods, mainly evening class combined with self-study. 4%, obviously beginners, have started with the language at the Cornish Language Weekend 2005. 4% described having used other methods, e.g. having learnt Cornish from the parents at home or via computer course (CD-Rom).

6.1.2 Material

The questionnaire comprises 18 questions (including age, sex, occupation, origin, residence, roots and variety) concerning various aspects of Cornish (e.g. motivation, status and attitude). The questions regarding origin, residence, roots (see 6.1.1) and Cornish language exams (7.4) are based on Kimura (2000/2002), question 7.5 has been adopted from Huebner (2001:47). In addition, respondents were encouraged to add comments. The questions will be presented and dealt with in detail in chapter 7 and the questionnaire will be appended (14.2.1).

6.1.3 Procedure

The questionnaire was already sent to contact addresses via e-mail in February 2005. On the spot, some 70 were distributed at the Cornish Language Weekend in St. Austell (11-13 March 2005, organized by the *Kowethas*, see 4.4.2.1) where most participants either filled in the questionnaire immediately or returned it on the following day. Previous contacts and acquaintances helped a lot. The questionnaire was also made accessible at the *Kowethas* website after the event. In Truro and Redruth, about 30 were handed over to representatives and members of two other groups for further distribution. During my stay, I received 46 completed questionnaires. Between February and July 2005 I obtained 30 responses by mail and 24 via Internet, altogether 100.

6.2 Pupils learning Cornish

Photo taken in front of Hayle school

6.2.1 Subjects

The sample consists of 35 female and 29 male informants who attend Hayle Community School, located on the northern coast of West Cornwall. The comprehensive school for pupils aged 11 to 16 became a language college in 2001 and made history by being the first school to timetable Cornish as part of a one-year language awareness course in Year 7. The 11-12-year-old pupils start with Cornish in the term before Christmas for one lesson a week. Then they have a short Italian course followed by a half-term Japanese module. After Easter they do German. All students learn French (3 lessons per week), so they are more confident in French than any other language. Normally, they would continue with French and add Spanish the following year and the top classes would also do German in Year 9. In 2005/06, there were six classes with an average of 26 pupils in Year 7.

The teacher, who created and teaches the course, is not a Cornish speaker, but a French teacher. Her priority is not competence in the language, but a smattering of a variety of languages which are presented in a variety of ways (computer, native speakers) so that the pupils have an apprenticeship in language learning. They are encouraged to identify their preferred learning style so that they will approach language learning in the future with confidence and enthusiasm.

The Cornish module involves using a CD-Rom (Eurotalk's 'Talk Now', see 2.7.1.1) which the pupils access and work on as a class and individually. It gives them practice in listening and speaking mainly at word level. The CD has also helped to overcome the shortage of Cornish-speaking teachers (*The West Briton*, 30 January 2003). According to the teacher, the CD, a masterpiece of diplomacy using both *Kernewek Kemmyn* and UCR text side by side, brought Cornish into the 21st century. The speakers use *Kemmyn* and Late Cornish.

The second half-term's work involves them researching the vocabulary for a topic of their choice (e.g. the semantic fields of animals or sports) and creating a resource book or powerpoint presentation to teach it to a group of younger children in nearby primary schools the week before Easter. Materials from the Cornish Language Board in *Kemmyn* are used, but any variations from the pupils are accepted. If time allows, a CD-Rom for primary schools may be put together from these materials.

This year there has been no provision made for pupils to carry on with any of these languages (Cornish, Italian, Japanese) further. There was no demand for further opportunities in Cornish studies with local experts when teachers offered this previously, although a number of pupils wanted to carry on using the CD-Rom and did so at lunchtimes. In addition, no staff qualified to teach it to any higher level is available (source: personal communication with the teacher).

- **Age:**

Since Cornish is only taught in Year 7, all girls and boys are between 11 and 12 years old.

- **Parents' occupation:**

The pupils are from a wide range of socio-economic backgrounds. Since no significant differences related to results could be noted, details need not be given.

- **Variety of Cornish:**

All pupils were mainly taught via the CD-Rom which included three varieties (see above) but the focus was on *Kernewek Kemmyn*. Some pupils ticked Late/Modern Cornish because they considered the CD modern. In general, pupils were not aware of different spellings.

- **Duration and intensity of learning Cornish:**

All subjects had 50 minute-lessons once a week over a period of 14 weeks.

- **Ability to speak Cornish:**

Due to the limited exposure to the language, the overall competence was observed to be low. When pupils were asked something in Cornish, they mostly could not respond. Nevertheless, they were asked to assess their competence on a five-point-scale.

Figure 9 illustrates the pupils' estimations:

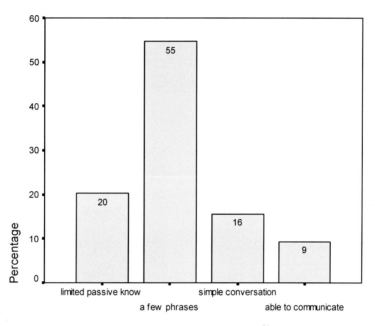

Figure 9: Pupils'self-assessment regarding their level of knowledge[74]

Conclusion: Nobody considered her-/himself to be fluent. A majority chose level 2, knowledge of a few phrases, which corresponds to the observations made in class during my visit.

6.2.2 Material

A questionnaire was designed to find out about students' experiences with the Cornish language, their attitudes, feelings and possible future behaviour. It comprises 20 questions, including those which were dealt with in the section above. The results will be presented in chapter 8 and the questionnaire will be appended (14.2.2).

6.2.3 Procedure

The language teacher distributed the questionnaires in three Year 7 classes. I visited a class of 26 pupils on 10 March 2005 from 11.05-11.55. 23 questionnaires were completed during a lesson in my presence and returned immediately. 41 were sent by post a month later. Altogether, 64 completed questionnaires were obtained for this group.

---

[74] Percentages occurring in the charts are always rounded off to integers.

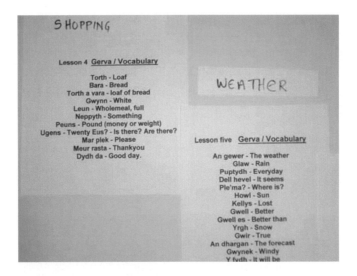

Cornish vocabulary posters in the Year 7 classroom

6.3   The non-Cornish-speaking population

6.3.1 Subjects

The third group includes 101 people who had been living in Cornwall in March 2005, 46 informants are male, 55 female. Their homes are scattered over 28 different places (towns and villages) in Cornwall.

• **Age**

Figure 10 shows the distribution of age:

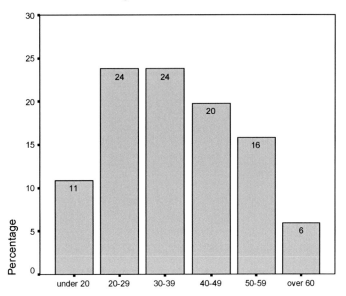

Figure 10: Age of non-Cornish-speaking sample

Conclusion: The dominant age groups are the 20-29- and 30-39-year-olds with each of them having the same representation. For the purposes of this study, it seemed most useful to achieve a relatively even age distribution.

• **Occupation:**

The survey aimed to include a mixture of social classes. 8 primary school teachers from a local school and 26 employees from a construction business form homogenous groups.

Figure 11 shows the subjects' type of occupation:

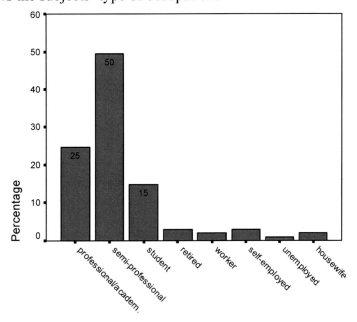

Figure 11: Occupation of non-Cornish-speaking sample

Conclusion: One explanation for the high number of semi-professionals might be the method of distribution (see 6.3.3). Shop and library assistants, clerks and receptionists were easier to access than other occupational groups.

- **Origin and roots:**

Only 44.6% of the sample were born in Cornwall. Of those who are not from Cornwall (55.4%), just 10.7% have Cornish roots (5.9% of the whole sample). Almost half of the sample (49.5%) were neither born in Cornwall nor have Cornish ancestors. A majority of those born outside Cornwall are from all parts of the UK (8 from London), 4 from Germany, 2 from France, 1 from Brazil and 1 from South Africa.

- **Length of stay in Cornwall:**

One question was intended to find out since when people have lived in Cornwall. 10 informants did not answer this question.

Figure 12 shows the subjects' length of stay in Cornwall:

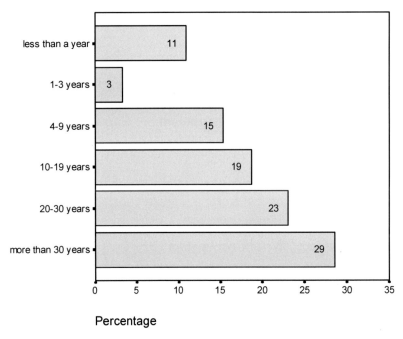

Percentage

Figure 12: Length of stay in Cornwall

Conclusion: Also subjects who were born in Cornwall are included in Figure 12, which explains the high percentages for 20 years and more of residence. For example, whereas 53.3% of the people born in Cornwall have lived there for more than 30 years, only 4.8% of those who are not Cornish (cf. the three degrees of Cornishness in 6.1.1) have stayed there for so long. In addition, the fact that 11% of the sample had only recently moved to Cornwall accounts for some informants' ignorance of the Cornish language (see chapter 9).

6.3.2 Material

The questionnaire comprises 21 questions (including those which describe the subjects in 6.3.1) concerning various aspects of Cornish (e.g. status, attitude and support). Again, the questions regarding origin and roots are based on Kimura's questionnaire (2000) and the formulation of questions 9.2 and 9.15 on Huebner's (cf. Huebner 2001:49-51). Respondents were also encouraged to add comments. The questions will be presented and results discussed in chapter 9. The questionnaire will be attached (14.2.3).

6.3.3 Procedure

Prior to the visit, 5 questionnaires were sent to acquaintances via e-mail. With the help of a friend who works in a construction business in Falmouth, some 40 questionnaires were circulated to the staff, 26 were returned to the contact person and then handed over to me. Most questionnaires were distributed during the research trip in March 2005, 3 of them to friends. 20 questionnaires were left at two primary schools in Hayle, but only one of them returned 8 by mail.[75] The rest was distributed to people working in the following places (see map 3):

- St. Ives: cinema, tearoom, restaurant, friend's neighbours, travel agency, tourist information office, library, taxi company

- Hayle: coffee shop, primary schools

- St. Austell: pub

- Truro: library, bookshops, cafés (also to customers), bank, museum, Cornish County Council reception, chemist's, computer shop, wine shop, art gallery, car rental service, train station (also to passengers waiting for the train)

- Redruth: library

- Penryn/Tremough campus: reception, students, train station, pupils

Most subjects responded immediately or asked me to come back later that day to collect the questionnaires. Altogether, I obtained 101 completed questionnaires.

- **Reactions:**

Although nobody really refused to fill in the questionnaire, a few people became a bit sceptical when they saw the topic. They seemed to be worried about not knowing enough about the Cornish language, let alone speaking it. Others even found the issue a bit ridiculous. One person I addressed turned out to be a Cornish speaker herself, so she was given the 'Cornish speaker' questionnaire.

---

[75] The low interest in one primary school which even has a Cornish motto is somewhat contradictory but could very likely be attributed to time constraints.

7 Results: Cornish Speakers/Learners

7.1 Motives for speaking/learning Cornish

Informants were given eight possible reasons for speaking/learning Cornish and were asked to tick the motives which have inspired them. The formulation of motives has been adopted from Jones's study of Welsh (1998:128ff.). In addition, the Cornish subjects could specify other motives.

Figure 13 shows the overall distribution of motives:

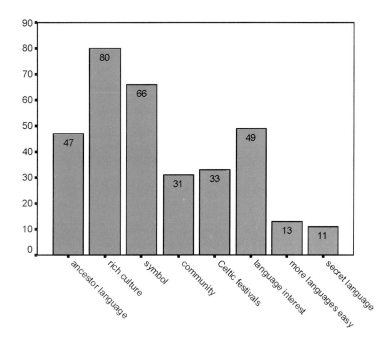

Figure 13: Motivational factors for learning Cornish

Conclusion: The most important reason is Cornwall's rich culture to which the language is a key (80%). The second highly scoring motive is the language's function as the symbol of national identity (66%). Language interest also figured highly among the respondents (49%). These results roughly correspond to the 1997 investigation in which identity and culture were equally ranked highest, followed by linguistic motives (see Hirner 1997:86).

Other motives are summarized and categorized. Most of them are given in the form of *direct quotations* (in italics). If the same motive was stated more than once in a similar way, the number in brackets indicates how often. Relevant information on individual subjects is also given in brackets. The same method will be applied to all questionnaires and groups.

- **Political motives**:
    - *To support the revival movement from outside Cornwall as a Welsh speaker.* (2)

– As a political statement (2)

One informant commented in great detail:

I feel it is important to value and promote languages which have been suppressed for political reasons and to ensure that they are and the history they represent is not erased – to resist 'linguistic imperialism'. The treatment of the Celtic languages of the British Isles is a classic example of this. Very few English people have any knowledge of them even if they have learned other European languages or other languages from outside Europe for academic, professional or personal interest reasons, and (with the exception of Irish in the Irish Republic and Welsh in some parts of Wales) they are not automatically taught and learned as a second language.

- **Cognitive motives:**

  – *Challenge of study of early Cornish manuscripts* (2; 1 PhD student)

  – *Keep brain cells working* (2)

  – *Interest in the concept of language revival*

  – *Research interest*

  – *I wanted to know a Celtic language* (university professor)

- **Personal motives:**

  – *Partner/husband is Cornish and wanted to learn. I am learning to support him.* (2)

  – *Daughter wanted to learn and needed an adult with her at the Cornish Language Weekend.*

  – *Husband is very influential in the Cornish language movement.*

- **Emotional motives** (partly overlapping with identity/community/linguistic motive):

  – *I'm Cornish, what better reason do you need?* (3)

  – *I'm proud of being Cornish.*

  – *I love Cornwall. I wanted to be part of whatever it means to be Cornish. The more I learned the language, the more Cornish I felt. I now have a strong sense of being an 'insider' rather than an 'outsider' as a result of becoming fluent and getting involved in many Cornish activities.*

  – *Special connection to the language, which does not really have to do with my ancestry or national identity.* (from the USA)

  – *It is a beautiful language.*

  – *It's nice not to speak English.*

- **"Celtic" motives:**

– *I am Welsh and Welsh and Cornish are related.* (3)

– *Keep in touch with our other Celtic-speaking nations, e.g. Breton and Welsh.* (2)

– *Use Cornish in Celtic music*

- **Historical motives (partly overlapping with ancestor motive):**

– *Understanding place names, names of farms and villages* (5)

– *Family history (where did our ancestors live)*

7.2 Fluency

The overall fluency rate is distributed as follows:

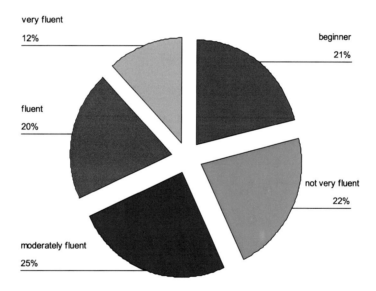

Figure 14: Fluency rate of Cornish speakers

Conclusion: If categories 'beginner' and 'not very fluent' are subsumed under 'beginner', the percentage is 43 (1997: 50%). 'Fluent' and 'very fluent' (32%) correspond to category 'fluent' (1997: 29%). A quarter of the sample consider themselves 'moderately fluent' which is equivalent to 'intermediate' (1997: 21%). Although comparative figures are quite similar, a slight growth in fluent speakers can be observed. The biggest difference seems to lie within the group of beginners: the percentage has fallen by 7%.

7.3   Continuation of studies

When asked whether they were going to continue their studies, a convincing majority of 86% (response rate 97%) answered in the affirmative. 11% did not intend to carry on studying Cornish. Some of the reasons given will be summarized in the following subsection.

7.3.1   Reasons for giving up studies

- *I do not seem to be able to improve.*
- *I can read and write quite well, I just can't speak it.*
- *Lack of time*
- *Grade 4 is too time-consuming and rather boring.* (correspondence course, from Australia)
- *I have achieved my primary aim (fluency, ease in reading).*
- *I am fluent and with little time for studies.*
- *Passed grade 4 (in 4 years).*
- *I am a Bard and now teach Cornish via Internet (KDL; see 2.6.1.1). I also publish in a Cornish magazine to increase vocabulary and fluency.*

Conclusion: Lack of motivation and time and already achieved fluency seem to be the main reasons for giving up studying.

7.4   Cornish language exams

65% of the informants have already taken and passed one or more Cornish Language Board exams and 20% answered that it might be possible that they will take one in the future. 15% definitely excluded that option, stating reasons such as:

- *I did not learn to prove myself to others.*
- *No exam in Late Cornish /UCR available at present.* (2)

7.5   Progress in the language vs. main difficulties

Respondents were asked to assess their progress in Cornish (response rate 75%).

49% wrote that they were pleased with it, 13% felt that it was okay, but another 13% were dissatisfied with their advancement. Most subjects, including those who are happy with their language development and fluent, are nevertheless faced with difficulties. The problems are summarized, categorized and complemented by spontaneous comments as follows:

- **Lack of opportunity to speak** (34):
  - *I'm frustrated at not having anyone to speak Cornish with in my area. (from the Netherlands, USA, but also people living in Cornwall mentioned this)*
  - *Too few people to converse with regularly.*
  - *Difficult to find a group to speak.*
  - *Difficult to practise and keep skills alive.*
  - *Difficult to understand others, I need more practice. (3)*
  - *Difficult to maintain fluency.*
  - *Limited experience with other speakers has halted further advancement.*
  - *It is hard to find social contacts to practise it sometimes.*
  - *It's frustrating that the opportunities for regular exposure to Cornish are so limited (e.g. radio).*
  - *Difficult to find a use for it.*

- **Lack of time (10):**
  - *Pressure of work*

- **Distance (5):**
  - *I am away at university.*
  - *Finding a class locally to carry on studying. The advanced class in Truro was cancelled due to low interest. (2)*

- **Motivation** (17):
  - *Lack of discipline*
  - *It's always a struggle.*
  - *Getting others to make use of what they know.*
  - *Commitment to learning*
  - *Too slow (2)*
  - *Irregular practice (3)*
  - *Getting used to it.*
  - *My spoken language is very poor.*
  - *Memory (2)*
  - *Started too late in life.*
  - *Laziness and lack of persistence*
  - *Need to spend more time working at it.*
  - *Lack of confidence*

- **Grammar** (10):
  - *Mutations* (3)
  - *Pronouns; word order; conjugation; verbs; personal verb endings*[76]

- **Pronunciation** (3)
  - *I am used to Welsh orthography.*
  - *I always go into French pronunciation.*

- **Different spelling systems** (2)

- **Increasing vocabulary**

- **Lack of supporting resources** (7):
  - *Lack of resources for hearing conversational Cornish.*
  - *Lack of teaching and learning resources, lack of training for teachers* (2)
  - *Lack of good books*
  - *Bad dictionary, bad explanations in lessons (KDL)*
  - *Not having a person readily available to explain problems verbally.*
  - *With more structured support, I could have progressed further.*

- **Lack of core media – radio and TV** (3):
  - *If there was a Cornish language radio station which I could listen to for several hours a day, I would have a much higher level of fluency by now (due to experience of this kind of exposure to learn other languages).*

Conclusion: The limited opportunities to speak Cornish regularly are most problematic. Lack of time and motivation seem to be factors that inhibit adult language learning in general. Although grammar was not explicitly asked for, it was mentioned more often than spelling and vocabulary. This corresponds to the results of the 1997 survey (see Hirner 1997:89-92).

7.6 Use of Cornish outside the classroom

The subjects were asked who they spoke Cornish to mostly. Figure 15 shows the most frequent Cornish interlocutors (response rate 97%):

---

[76] If different subjects made different remarks belonging to the same category, the statements are divided by semicolons.

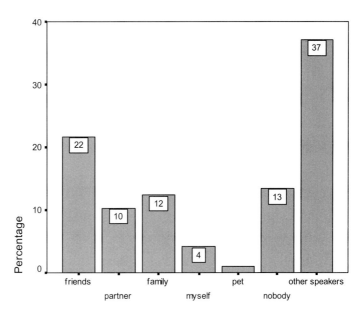

Figure 15: To whom do you speak Cornish?

Conclusion: Friends and other speakers account for 59% of possible interlocutors. 32% reported speaking Cornish with the partner or the family which might also include partners. The other 18% admitted only talking to themselves, the pet or not at all in the course of a typical week.[77]

Additional individual answers which did not fit into the categories above were:

- *Occasionally with customers* (grocer)
- *With some people all the time (on the phone)*
- *With several work colleagues*
- *With my neighbour*

The environments in which Cornish is spoken/used are:

- At home (13%)
- In the pub (13%)
- At cultural and social events (13%)
- At Cornish language meetings (8%)
- On the Internet (6%)
- At work (2%)
- On the phone (2%)[78]
- Nowhere (18%)

---

[77] Obviously, speakers who use the language at home also use it with other speakers.

[78] One respondent noted that phone conversations have now been virtually replaced by e-mail.

- More than one setting (25%):[79]
  - *Internet, phone and holidays* (subject lives outside Cornwall but frequently visits Cornwall)
  - *At the Gorsedd and on the phone*
  - *At home and in the Cornish shop* (3)

- Other settings:
  - *Cornish Language Weekend* (2)[80]
  - *Yeth an Werin once a month* (3)
  - *Sometimes in the street*
  - *In chapel*
  - *Increasingly in a professional context* (project manager)

Conclusion: Cornish is being used in an increasing number of contexts and is also very hesitantly beginning to gain a foothold in professional life. However, the fact that 18% of the sample still do not actually have the opportunity to speak the language to anyone seems quite discouraging (1997: 20%).

7.7 Passing on Cornish to the children

55% of the sample have children (1997: 56%), but only 40% of this group speak Cornish to them (1997: 65%). The most frequent reason was that the children are already adults and most of them have moved away (10). 5 subjects claim that their children are not interested to learn, 4 have mentioned that they speak Cornish to the grandchildren when they visit. One respondent wrote that she used to speak Cornish to them when they were young, but not any more now as all their schooling is in English. Two learners think that they are not fluent enough themselves to pass Cornish on to their offspring. A respondent from Wales reports that his/her children find it confusing when learning Welsh. In another case, the child should not be put off Cornish as with French. One person's children even think that he/she is eccentric because of speaking Cornish. A more optimistic answer was given by a subject who has 8- and 25-year-old children (*"Perhaps, I should."*). A Basque-speaking Spaniard who lives in France in a German-speaking region would definitely speak Cornish to his children if they lived in Cornwall. Three subjects who do not have children (yet) asserted that they would also speak Cornish to their children if they had any.

Conclusion: Although the most frequent factors responsible for not speaking Cornish are external, the development must be considered backward as compared to 1997.

---

[79] Cornish speakers who use the language at home are very likely to use it in many other settings as well.

[80] The Cornish Language Weekend is actually a mixture of language classes and social/cultural events, so this answer was hard to classify.

7.8 Status of Cornish after official recognition

The feelings concerning an improvement in status are mixed: 43% think that the position of Cornish has been strengthened considerably after it was recognized under Part II of the European Charter for Regional or Minority Languages in 2002. 42% think that this is not the case and 15% are uncertain.[81] Respondents were encouraged to give reasons for their answers. As will be seen from the examples below, the spontaneous comments were rich and varied:

- **Yes, the status has improved**:
  - *Public profile has been raised very much in recent years and the charter is one of the reasons as it has raised the status amongst the general public.* (4)
  - *For the first time ever, we now have people in central government who are very favourable to us and to the language.*
  - *More pressure can be applied to the British Government by the Cornish.*
  - *Yes, but not sure if improved visibility for the language resulted from recognition or if recognition resulted from more people using the language and promoting it.*
  - *Cornish speakers have worked hard to promote the language and teach others.*
  - *Thanks to all the Cornishmen who want to preserve our culture.*
  - *Funding is now available and Cornish is being taught.*
  - *It will be part of the curriculum.*
  - *Getting more publicity/ more in the papers.*
  - *It has been given more respect and attention in the press and on TV.*
  - *Possibility of increased financial support and signage.*
  - *More signs in Cornish. In the last census (2001), one could call oneself "Cornish" for the first time.*
  - *There has been a moderate level of funding and publications benefit from this appearing "classier" than before.*
  - *Cornish, more considered as a modern Celtic language and less as a mere "construct", is used more on the Internet.*
  - *It is no longer looked upon as an activity of a few "cranks"; people regard it as less eccentric.* (2)
  - *Cornish is not "quaint" but it is to be taken seriously now.*
  - *More people are attending classes. This Pennseythun has been better attended, new faces around.* (2)
  - *People know about it and want to learn; it is becoming more well-known.* (2)

---

[81] Especially people who live outside Great Britain were not able to answer this and the following question.

- *It has created a greater awareness amongst our English friends.*
- *There is now a much greater awareness of the existence of Cornish and that it is now quite widely spoken.* (2)

- **Uncertain position:**
  - *Status has improved as far as debating goes, but no great change in the actual situation.* (2)
  - *Moderately rather than considerably improved.* (2)
  - *Improving slowly; much more could have been done.* (2)
  - *Now harder to ignore and dismiss but money is needed to back up.*
  - *More awareness of the language now but work is still being done by volunteers.*
  - *Could potentially improve but progress is very slow and I mistrust the government to do all they should to make improvements.*
  - *Publicity was good, but hardly any change in the treatment of the language. Some squeaks of encouragement from officialdom but no direct support.*
  - *May have improved technically and legally, but there is no evidence of this in my daily life.*
  - *Too early to tell as yet, but it will be dramatically in the near future.*
  - *Much will depend on progress in the implementation of the strategy for the Cornish language developed by the Cornish County Council. The recognition will hopefully provide leverage for the implementation of the proposals in the strategy.*
  - *Yes, but not enough, more funding is needed.*
  - *Before I came to Cornwall in 2002* (from Yorkshire) *I was not aware that there was still a Cornish language.*

- **No, the status has not improved:**
  - *Lack of government interest and commitment.* (2)
  - *Lack of government backing (support and money) for resources.* (3)
  - *UK government only grudgingly recognized Cornish and does the minimum it has to under the charter.*
  - *Government was doing as little as necessary to avoid a politic row. Don't want to acknowledge the separate identity of the Cornish, which would lead to increased calls for devolution for Cornwall. Therefore not a penny of government money has come to those who are trying to improve the standing of Cornish although other Celtic languages receive funding.*
  - *Not as much as it should have done, due to the English refusal to consider Cornwall as a country.*

- *Government and local councils are slow to introduce measures, e.g. in schools or signs in Cornish.*
- *Nothing changed: no classes shooting up, no extra signs in Cornish, no lessons in schools.*
- *Government only wants to fill up administrative papers to show they have done some work, but really, they don't believe in Cornish or Cornwall.*
- *Lot of talk, no action yet. (2)*
- *The UK political establishment, dominated by the English, are all anti-minority cultures and will only give as much as they are forced to.*
- *No specific timetable for implementing language support strategy. (3)*
- *We do not have the organization to give it the impetus it requires.*
- *No official body has taken responsibility for its development and funding.*
- *Language is already recognized internationally. British government have used the woolly language of Part II of the charter to do nothing.*
- *Will not improve considerably until it is properly funded: no money has yet been forthcoming. (3)*
- *Low interest of 2nd term classes at Truro College led to cancellation. If status is to improve, colleges must be prepared to either promote the classes or run them with fewer people.*
- *Symbolic status rather than practical.*
- *Not yet, only time will tell. (2)*
- *Still very small group of Cornish speakers.*
- *General resistance from the public, laziness of English speakers, Cornish speakers are regarded as eccentric.*
- *The media in Cornwall have served Cornish badly. Press releases are often sent but not published and some presenters treat the language as a bit of a joke.*

Conclusion: A very different perception among Cornish speakers is noticeable. Whereas one faction has expected a great deal more from the recognition and mainly blames the government for a stagnation of the development, the other group has realized that the position of Cornish has improved at many levels but it will naturally take some time until a real impact can be felt.

7.9   General attitude towards promoting Cornish

The subjects were also asked to rate the general attitude among the Cornish population with regard to promoting the language on a 3-point scale ('very favourable' – 'neither favourable nor disfavourable' – 'unfavourable'). 21% think that the atmosphere is very favourable, a majority of 56% have a neutral opinion and 10% regard the general attitude as clearly unfavourable. 13% believe they cannot assess the situation sufficiently. Again, comments to explain the estimations are abounding:

- **Positive general attitude:**

  - *Resurgence of national pride leading to interest in all things Cornish over the past few years.*

  - *More interest is being shown.*

  - *Improving now – previously obstructive.*

  - *Increasing awareness means more people can participate in some form.*

  - *Most "born" Cornish people are now far more enthusiastic for Cornish than 20 years ago.*

  - *10 years ago many inhabitants of Cornwall even didn't know the language Cornish existed. The Cornish consider the almost lost language as part of their heritage.*

  - *People want to know their heritage.*

  - *In the past 10 years, there has been a dramatic "about turn" of people towards the promotion of Cornish.*

  - *Whenever I speak Cornish, people are interested.*

  - *People are interested and have begun to see economic benefits of using the language with their business.*

  - *Higher profile given to the language commercially and a general feeling that it is important to promote Cornish in Cornwall, a region with such a distinct identity of its own and a strong local feeling and consciousness.*

  - *Many work colleagues have approached me for information regarding learning the language and teaching it in schools at a basic level.* (radiographer)

- **Neutral attitude:**

  - *Some people are very enthusiastic and committed to promoting the language. Having different forms of the language splits up the efforts of these people.*

  - *People are anticipating much easier access to the language through properly funded and programmed education.*

  - *Most people are aware of the language, but too few learn any.*

  - *It varies a great deal. There is a lot of positive will but also a lot of indifference. This may be partly a generational phenomenon.*

  - *Still most people have very little contact with the language and therefore little awareness. We still have much to do to promote the language and get them to "share ownership" with us.*

  - *Most people are indifferent.*

- *I have always encountered a favourable attitude from Cornish people, often accompanied by mention of regret at not having attempted to learn the language themselves. Very rarely have I met with amazement and ridicule at my learning Cornish, but only from people who weren't interested in investigating into the possibility of a national Cornish heritage apart from English heritage.*

- *There are not enough Cornish speakers to have any impact yet. It will be a long time (if ever).*

- *Acceptance of the need for the language among Cornish people is a slow process.*

- *People are glad that there is a language, but it is not "cool" to learn it.*

- *Small pockets of resistance and apathy, but a slow acceptance as part of "tourist attraction" value!*

- *Little interest outside language circles except as a device for promotion of tourism.*

- *Whilst many people are supportive just as many are ambivalent or openly hostile to the language.*

- *Hard to know (not been to Cornwall in about 2 years), but impression I have is that many people think it is nice to have the language around, but aren't interested to do anything about it themselves. Most people not involved have some good will but not enough interest to learn it.*

- *Most Cornish people are proud that the language exists even though most of them haven't the motivation to learn it (possibly due to the appalling lack of language teaching in the UK); perhaps fearing that it may be too difficult for them.*

- *Most local people tolerate my enthusiasm. They are proud to be Cornish but do little for the culture.*

- *There is applause for learning but no wish to join in. Some see learning it as a waste of time.*

- *Many people are unaware of the issue and seem ambivalent towards it.*

- *It varies hugely – some feel really threatened because they don't understand it, but others are very much interested, and this is on the increase.*

- *More favourable than before – people used to think that a Cornish speaker challenged their Cornishness, i.e. that they were somehow less Cornish. More people are interested in learning now.*

- *Still viewed as slightly eccentric; activity by many, pointless by others, but more support than before.*

- *Some are favourable (enthusiasts and people from Cornish families who feel themselves distinct from Shire England), and some aren't interested in their local culture and are satisfied with being Little American.*

- *A mix of anti and support – some will not admit it exists.*

- *Apart from work of the volunteer language groups which are relatively tiny, there is no promotion of the language and the attitude of many people is the language is irrelevant, although this has changed in recent years. The Cornish themselves are becoming more aware, but unfortunately Cornwall is full of wealthy retired solicitors from London.*

- *Some people are very supportive and would like to see it taught in schools; others are indifferent, a few openly hostile especially when they hear Cornish being spoken.*

- *The attitude **outside** of Cornwall is very unfavourable to Cornish culture, especially in the media. Massive immigration from England of people with no knowledge about the language and an unfavourable outlook on Cornish things in general. This means that the favourable attitude in Cornwall is under threat. There is a tendency in England to link Cornish culture to plans to create an autonomous state (I have never actually come across anyone who wants this) and also to mock Cornish language and culture.*

- **Negative attitude:**

  - *Most people don't seem to care very much unfortunately, but they have got used to it not mattering and so don't think about it.*

  - *Nobody really recognizes Cornish as a "plus" for Cornwall. There is APATHY among the people in charge (ex. Cornish County Council and district council).*

  - *In general apathetic and to most it's irrelevant. (2)*

  - *Many people are not interested – also confined by the different forms of the language.*

  - *Non-Cornish are quick to ridicule it, possibly because they feel threatened.*

  - *Even Cornish people seem to view learning the language as a pointless exercise. General ignorance of English people that there is a language.*

  - *Most Cornish people seem to regard "others" who come in as being interested in the language and not themselves. There is a defeatist attitude that Cornish was dead and what has been revived is an invented language.*

  - *Majority ethnic attitudes and centuries of English oppression.*

  - *People think learning Cornish is a waste of time as people think it is a dead language.*

  - *The language has little or no influence on the lives of most people in Cornwall.*

  - *General population don't know much about it and are not interested.*

  - *It is still a bit of a novelty rather than a serious everyday part of Cornish life.*

  - *Cornish is wanting to be learned but upcountry people who move into our communities will have nothing to do with it.*

  - *Majority of Cornish people do not appreciate that they are not English, therefore Cornish is seen as something that is not theirs.*

- *Most of the local people I have met regard themselves as "English" and consider Cornish a dead language.*

- *Some people regard Cornish speakers as active historians or linguists – others regard them as cranks.*

- *Most indigenous Cornish are indifferent or even hostile to their own language.*

- *Many incomers are still unaware of Cornish culture.*

- *Lack of opportunities to learn about the language and use it in public life.*

- *Negative publicity for many years owing to fears on the costs to public money which may be incurred.*

- *Lack of official support, disinterest of much of the population, largely due to lack of education about the language's place in Cornish history.*

- *The apathy of the Cornish people caused the decline, and eventual cessation, of Cornish as the language of everyday conversation. They could see no profit in speaking Cornish, when those around them and from whom they received their livelihood, spoke only English. There is a growing awareness, at this time, of "Cornishness" fuelled in part by success on the rugby field over the past 20 years or so, and awareness of the language is part of that, but the vast majority still cannot see the necessity of learning their own language.*

Conclusion: Although a growing number of people living in Cornwall may be passively sympathetic towards the issue, they are not prepared to contribute to the advancement of the Cornish language.

7.10 Concrete measures to promote Cornish

The only open question was intended to find out which concrete measures to further develop Cornish the informants would like to see implemented in the near future. Participants came up with both very concrete and general suggestions which, although sometimes overlapping, can be divided into the following domains:

- **Support and funding in general:**
  - *Official support and mainstream funding* (2)
  - *Government should give substantial financial aid.*
  - *Provide salaries for those who are currently working hard for the language in their spare time.* (6)

- **Education:**
  - **Pre-school level:**
    - *Funding for/establishment of playgroups/nursery schools* (2)

- *Pre-school education is presently the most important (but not the most difficult) issue since it will create further demand for the language in the education system.* (4)

- *Programmes for children*

- *Cornish rhymes and songs for children; more bilingual children's books and videos*

- *Support and encouragement for children to be taught Cornish from birth until they leave school.*

- *As in Wales, get children interested in learning the language and encourage bilingualism from an early age on (e.g. 3).* (4)

- **Primary-school level:**

  - *Every primary school child should have been given a copy of the CD-Rom 'Teach me Cornish' as part of the centenary celebrations of Jenner's 'Handbook of the Cornish Language'. That would have encouraged them to study further in their own free time.*

  - *Teaching of basic Cornish and the history of the language so that all children in Cornwall have a realistic view.* (3)

  - *Introducing more history/culture in school classes would encourage a broader interest in the language.* (2)

  - *Up to 12 years, teaching of Cornish should be obligatory. Then option to take it further to school-leaving age should be given.* (3)

  - *Provision of Cornish at all levels of education for all children who wish to learn it.* (5)

- **Cornish as part of the National Curriculum** (54):

  - *Recognition by the education authority*

  - *Cornish lessons should be included in the curriculum of every school and the language taught within the normal school day.*

  - *Teaching in schools would change things radically as in Wales.*

  - *Creation of Cornish language schools*

- **Teaching and courses** (10):

  - *Governmental support and funding for teachers (both in schools and evening classes) to be trained.*

  - *Employ a body of peripatetic Cornish teachers*

  - *More class opportunities for learners and free adult classes* (4)

  - *Classes should be advertised and promoted well so that people are encouraged to attend.* (2)

  - *Classes in other cities outside Cornwall* (2)

- *Cornish speakers should come to Australia to help with promotion and speaking.*
- *Running immersion courses, e.g. free Easter and summer schools for children and their parents to learn Cornish.* (2)
- *Develop a body of teaching materials*

- **Research:**
  - *Language should be more widely taught at university.*
  - *A survey is needed.*

- **Official recognition:**
  - *Legislation should empower its official use alongside English.*
  - *More authoritative acceptance of the language by the councils.*
  - *Recognition by all public bodies (councils)*
  - *More commitment by education providers and councils*
  - *A government body to implement the charter* (2)
  - *Adherence to the charter*
  - *A timetable of action; firm programme and funding to support the aim of the agreed policy and strategy document.*
  - *Direct action vs. "token" recognition*
  - *Appointment/funding of a Cornish Language(Planning) Officer* (3)
  - *Funding of Language Officer and support staff to develop resources (books, teaching courses) and locate funding. Progress so far has been depending on the goodwill of individuals who have their "day" jobs, too.*
  - *Part III recognition under the charter*

- **Unity in spelling:**
  - *Accepting one Standard Cornish for official use* (5)
  - *Recognition of one variety (e.g. Kernewek Kemmyn) as best orthography for official documents and education.* (3)
  - *We must end the multiplicity of spelling systems as this causes great confusion to potential learners.*
  - *More unity between groups representing different varieties and less political animosity.* (5)

- **Public presence:**
  - *More Cornish signs everywhere* (12)
  - *Use of bilingual sign-boards with a short explanation of the meaning of place names (e.g. Bodmin=Bosvenegh, meaning 'the place of the monks') should be*

expanded as sign-boards are often people's first contact with the language and could spark their interest in knowing more. That is certainly what first drew me to learn Cornish.

- *Road signs, leaflet*
- *Big publicity campaign (2)*
- *Find Cornish used in all walks of life for it to become cool.*
- *Stigma of it being a "2nd class or dead language" removed by more widespread public use.*

- **Development of Cornish language media (14):**
  - *More radio and TV broadcasting and guaranteed broadcasting time (much more language readily available to general Cornish public without them having to go out of their way to get it).*
  - *Local TV news items in Cornish*
  - *Weekly Cornish programme on TV*
  - *Cornish language on the mainstream radio (at least one hour a week).*
  - *Digital/online radio station would be a good stopgap measure even if only a few hours a day. It would also encourage the development of more modern music in the language – sponsorship would be available.*
  - *More Cornish in local papers, e.g. news and beginners' items.*
  - *More money to support publication of high quality books.*
  - *More positive attitude by the media*

- **Social and economic life:**
  - *Work-centred training*
  - *Cornish Language Resource Centre (2)*
  - *Signs for places where the language is spoken (shops, pubs) and badges for speakers.*
  - *Businesses should introduce the language in their adverts; greater commercial uptake*
  - *Develop tourism around the language, e.g. Cornish language trail which would increase a correct awareness in England.*
  - *Language needs normalisation in social and economic spheres.*

- **Critical remarks:**
  - *Get rid of Kemmyn*
  - *Free Cornwall from English rule*

Conclusion: As in the previous study, the most important field to promote is clearly education (cf. Hirner 1997:98). Suggestions made by almost every respondent ranged from pre-school level to adult classes. Many informants also want to see Cornish established in the media regularly and hope for increased public presence through bilingual signs. A problem that a lot of Cornish speakers would like to get solved in the near future is the spelling disunity.

7.11 Challenges to overcome

The final question dealt with more or less difficult obstacles that have to be tackled on the way to reversing language shift. 12 challenges were listed and respondents had to rank them by writing numbers from 1 (most difficult challenge) – 12 (least difficult challenge) next to them. The overall result is presented in the same hierarchy:

1. **Cornish is no proper subject at school.**

2. **Lack of funding and resources for teacher training**

3. **Few opportunities for daily use**

4. **Absence of Cornish on TV**

5. **Lack of pre-school playgroups**

6. **No concentrated area of speakers**

7. **Fragmentation – spelling mistake**

8. **Lack of interactive teaching materials**

9. **Cornish is not useful for social advancement.**

10. **Growing number of second home owners from outside Cornwall**

11. **Private costs to pay classes**

12. **Difficult grammar (e.g. mutations)**

•   **Additional remarks:**

    – *Most difficult challenge is lack of support from governance and local education authority.*

    – *Most difficult issue is within the Cornwall Local Education Authority – key influencing people (officers and councillors) are against the language.*

    – *ad 10): Some of them want to learn it.*

A leading *Cornish* speaker and proponent of *Kernewek Kemmyn* took the trouble to comment on almost every challenge in great detail:[82]

    – *ad 12): Mutations are an integral part of all Celtic languages. We cannot (even though this has occasionally been suggested) remove them from Cornish to make it easier to learn. It is not an easy language (though others, e.g. Welsh*

---

[82] The overall ranking is not necessarily the same as the commentator's ranking.

and Irish are more difficult), but the introduction of Kernewek Kemmyn has made it much easier to learn than it used to be.

– *Ad 11): I do not see this as a serious problem.*

– *Ad 10): This is a problem in Wales, where English-speaking incomers upset the balance of a Welsh-speaking community, but in Cornwall it is only a political problem; it scarcely affects the language at all.*

– *Ad 9): A "translation industry" such as exists in Wales would change that. Meanwhile it is not a serious issue.*

– *Ad 8): Not a serious difficulty; these could be developed, given the resources, within a year, using Manx as a model.*

– *Ad 7): Fragmentation is sometimes used as an excuse by people not to learn Cornish, or not to support it. This makes it appear a difficult challenge. It must be said that of the various groups the numbers of those using Kemmyn are greater than all other groups put together; but those who do not wish to use Kemmyn make a noise which is out of proportion to their number. The "problem" would be solved at a stroke if these people would simply accept that Kemmyn is the best orthography, and the one which should be used in education and official documents. Such acceptance is unlikely to happen.*

– *Ad 6): This is not important in my view. The distribution of Cornish speakers is similar to that of the general population, i.e. a little more concentrated in the west. There have been occasional suggestions that Cornish speakers should all try to live in the same village; this is impractical and indeed undesirable. With modern means of communication, this is not a challenge.*

– *Ad 5): Quite important, in so far as these groups played a key role in the revitalizing of Welsh, but not too difficult a challenge. We have had Cornish pre-school playgroups before. They depend on the enthusiasm of Cornish-speaking mothers to talk Cornish to other children as well as their own.*

– *Ad 4): This is a difficult challenge. Both the BBC and ITV organize their programmes on a regional basis, and unfortunately Cornwall is treated as if it were part of a region of England. There was a long campaign to get the Welsh TV channel S4C; the Breton TV Breizh is a disappointment, being 90%+ in French. There will be great resistance to overcome to obtain even a short programme per week (probably scheduled at 2.30 a.m.).*

– *ad 3): This is not so difficult as it might appear. Certainly it will be a long time before we can go into a bank or post-office and expect to be served in Cornish (as one can in Welsh in Wales). Yet if families learn together, they can use Cornish at home. 90% of everyday conversation is simple, even banal ("Pass the milk, please."). I would encourage workmates to learn Cornish together and use the language at work (I have done this on occasion.). To sum up, on a collective basis this would appear a great obstacle, but on an individual basis it is more easily overcome.*

– *Ad 2): The difficulty here is the initial persuasion needed to convince the authorities to allocate funds; once that is done, all else can follow. The*

Government is morally and legally obliged to support Cornish after signing the Charter. Nevertheless it is not easy to get funds.

- *Ad 1): This is both important and difficult. Cornish should be available to any pupil who wants to learn it. For this to happen requires a great change in attitude on the part of the authorities or a change in political structure, viz. the establishment of a Cornish Assembly.*

Conclusion: Challenges 1 and 2, both having to do with education, clearly correspond to the result of the previous question (7.10). Also the importance of the media, in particular TV, is reflected in the results of both questions. Concerning fragmentation, a change of priority can be observed. Whereas in 1997 the non-united approach was regarded as the biggest threat (cf. Hirner 1997:99f.), it does not seem to cause as much concern now (ranked 7th).

8   Results: Cornish Pupils

In the Cornish language classroom

8.1   Did you like the Cornish lessons?

An overwhelming majority of 78.1% liked the lessons, 3.1% thought they were okay and 18.8% did not like them. The following reasons were given:

- **Yes:**
  - *They have been fun. (6)*
  - *They were fun and explained a lot.*
  - *They were nice and simple.*
  - *They were interesting. (2)*
  - *They are always interesting and fun.*
  - *It was fun on Eurotalk. (3)*
  - *Because we were on the computers.*
  - *I am interested in other languages.*
  - *It was interesting to learn more about Cornwall.*
  - *It was good learning Cornish as we have never learnt it before.*
  - *I liked making a book with Cornish.*
  - *Interesting words and fun words to use.*

- **Okay:**
  - *Sometimes boring and sometimes fun.*

- **No:**
  - *I didn't really like Cornish because I don't get it.*
  - *I didn't really enjoy them and it was boring.*
  - *Boring* (4; all 4 among lowest level of ability; see Figure 9)
  - *I hate school and it was boring.*
  - *There is no way to learn it.*
  - *I cannot remember the words and nobody speaks Cornish any more.*
  - *My partner kept messing around when I was working on my project.*

8.2 What has made learning Cornish hardest? Grammar, vocabulary or the pronunciation?

20.3% did not answer or misunderstood the question. 10.9% regard all three fields as equally difficult because:

- *It was my 3rd language.*
- *It is very different to English.*
- *All of it was weird.*
- *Learning Cornish was hard when we had to do Eurotalk as a class because people kept being annoying and destructive.*

9 pupils (14.1%) have difficulties with grammar[83], one of them especially with sentence patterns. 14 informants (21.9%) consider vocabulary hardest, particularly because it is so hard to remember. Pronunciation has been identified as the most challenging part by 32.8% because:

- *Cornish sounds different to how it is spelt.* (However, Cornish is much more phonemic than English!)
- *It's like a tongue twister.*
- *It's different to English.*
- *Cornish is such a different language to anything else.*
- *They have a strong accent.* (the speakers on the CD-Rom)
- *I am not a Cornishman.*

[83] As grammar was not really taught explicitly because the focus was on vocabulary, this question is not really suitable for comparison (e.g. with pupils from Wales who learn Welsh as a subject). In addition, some pupils had problems to understand what was meant by the term 'grammar'.

8.3 Have you used Cornish outside the classroom? On what occasions? With whom?

A minority of 15.6% have used Cornish outside the classroom, all but one at home in the context of school. Most of them told their mothers what they had learnt in the lessons and 2 even tried to teach their parents some Cornish. One pupil only used Cornish at home to confuse the mother. Only one informant uses Cornish regularly with the great-uncle who seems to have a qualification in Cornish.

8.4 Do you use Cornish in writing?

Apart from the school project (book or powerpoint presentation), nobody has ever written in Cornish yet.

8.5 Do you learn/speak other foreign language? Which one?

As has been described in 6.2.1, all pupils learn French and have been taught some Italian and Japanese as part of the language awareness course. Strangely, 6 pupils answered that they did not learn any other foreign language, 15 did not mention French, only 23 brought up Japanese and no more than 10 Italian. In addition, 3 pupils referred to English as a foreign language. Other languages included Spanish (3), Arabic (Arabic parent), Korean and Greek.

8.6.1 If yes, do you prefer the other language to Cornish?

For the reasons mentioned above (in fact all pupils learn another language), the evaluation of the original question was slightly changed and the sample taken as a whole. More than half of the subjects (59.4%) prefer other languages:

- *Arabic, because I learned it most.*
- *English, because I speak it.*
- *English is easier than the others. (2)*
- *French is easier (to understand). (7)*
- *French, because I have been learning it longer/for ages. (4)*
- *French uses a better way of teaching.*
- *In French you learn grammar.*
- *Japanese, because I enjoy learning about their culture.*
- *Japanese, because we did some practical learning with the native. (2)*
- *Japanese is fun. (3)*
- *Japanese is easy. (!)*
- *Japanese is a really good culture and you do lots of funny things.*

- *In Japanese, we looked at money, food and pictures.*
- *Japanese, because it's different to other languages. (2)*[84]
- *Greek is cool.*
- *Cornish is boring. (2)*
- *Cornish is pointless as no one speaks it.*

Those who prefer Cornish (40.6%) have given the following reasons:

- *French is even harder (and you have tests). (3)*
- *French is very boring. (2)*
- *Cornish is the best! (2)*
- *Cornish is different (to French).*
- *Cornish is a really good language and sounds nice.*
- *Cornish is easier to speak.*
- *We can relate to Cornish in everyday life.*
- *We get to go on the PC.*

8.6.2 If not, would you prefer learning another language to learning Cornish? Which one and why?

Again, the evaluation was adapted to real conditions and could be reformulated leaving out the "if not". Subjects gave the following answers:

- *English is easier. (2)*
- *Japanese* (5, one because of karate)
- *Spanish would be cool. (3)*
- *Spanish, so I could go there.*
- *Spanish because it seems much easier.*
- *Norwegian sounds interesting.*
- *Chinese because I want to write in symbols.*
- *I fancy Chinese because they have colourful festivals.*
- *I need to learn more languages.*

---

[84] The answers may have been influenced by the fact that Japanese was the most recent module.

8.7 Are you proud of knowing Cornish?

A majority of 62.5% are proud of knowing Cornish. This value is even higher than the one attained from a comparable sample in Wales (1997: n = 39; average age 14) where Welsh is taught as a core subject (Hirner 1997:111, 56%). Girls tend to be prouder than their male counterparts. However, the difference between the two groups (54.7% girls, 45.3% boys) did not reach statistical significance (χ^2 (1, N = 64) = 1.215, p = 0.270).

8.8 Did your parents encourage you to learn Cornish?

Only 23.4% of parents have encouraged their children in the learning process. Parents' education did not have any significant influence (χ^2 (4, N = 64) = 7.439, p = 0.114).

8.9 Advantages of speaking Cornish

Only a quarter of respondents are convinced that being able to speak Cornish has advantages:

- *Some people still speak it. (2)*
- *People in Cornwall speak Cornish.*
- *Because I live here in Cornwall. (2)*
- *Because we can understand more in Cornwall. (2)*
- *It makes me more Cornish.*
- *You can communicate with Cornish people.*
- *Just in case I meet anyone who is/speaks Cornish (e.g. the shopkeeper). (3)*
- *I might marry a Cornish maid.*
- *In case you need to use it in finding jobs.*
- *It helps me read or speak some other languages.*

20.3% did not answer the question and a majority of 54.7% do not see any advantages:

- *They don't speak the language any more. (3)*
- *No one I know speaks Cornish. (3)*
- *Nobody speaks it in Hayle. (2)*
- *Not many people speak it. (2)*
- *I live here and have no problem with speaking.*
- *It's not appropriate.*
- *My mum hates me speaking stupidly.*
- *It's boring. (2)*

– *I don't know much Cornish.*

Conclusion: Compared to their Welsh counterparts (1997:95%), who predominantly referred to the role of Welsh in terms of job prospects in Wales,[85] the Cornish pupils (except for one) have not been able to identify such benefits.

8.10 Apart from school, do you know anybody who speaks Cornish?

18.8% have Cornish speakers among their relatives or circle of acquaintances: grandfather, grandmother (2), neighbours, great-uncle, old fisherman, 2 pupils mentioned the same name of a woman.

8.11 How is the Cornish language noticeable in everyday life?

Subjects were given a list of five domains and could also add their own (only two subjects mentioned books). Multiple answers were possible. Figure 16 shows how and where pupils perceive the existence of Cornish:

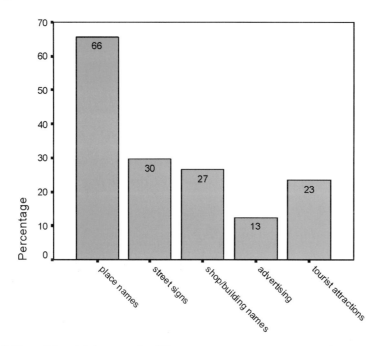

Figure 16: Visibility of Cornish in everyday life

Conclusion: Pupils are mostly aware of Cornish in place names. This might also be due to the bilingual sign 'Hayle' – Cornish *Heyl* (= English 'estuary', Concise Oxford

---

[85] Note that the Welsh informants are older, but the result is mainly due to the different socio-economic status of the two languages.

Dictionary: "a wide tidal mouth of a river") which you see immediately when you enter the town (see also cover of the 'Strategy for the Cornish Language', 4.5).[86]

8.12 Do you think the Cornish language is cool? Why (not)?

43.8% think it is cool, 17.1% have not answered this question and 39.1% do not associate Cornish with coolness. Those who think it is cool have given the following reasons:

- *It is good for Cornish people to learn.*
- *Because I am Cornish.*
- *Because you can have a conversation and no one understands you.* (2)
- *It makes me a proper Cornish person.*
- *It is quite a nice language.*
- *Words are funny.*
- *It makes me different from everyone.*
- *It has a strong accent to it.*
- *I like different languages.*
- *It is different.*

The group who does not find Cornish cool has explained the feeling as follows:

- *It is boring.* (8, 1 of them is proud though)
- *No one knows it.*
- *Not everyone in Cornwall speaks it and it's not appropriate.*
- *Not everyone in Cornwall knows Cornish.*
- *It's hard and there are big words.* (2)
- *Weird names for things.* (would still like to continue with Cornish, see 8.14)
- *You don't really use it in everyday life.*
- *People don't like it.*
- *I don't know much.*

---

[86] People from Hayle are proud of their estuary which serves as a haven and a feeding ground for many types of migratory birds.

8.13 Do you think English is cooler than Cornish? Why (not)?

A majority of 60.9% are of the opinion that English is cooler, 25% think the opposite and 14.1% have left out this question. Although 80.6% of the female respondents consider English cooler than their male counterparts (58.3% of the male participants), the difference between the two groups is not quite statistically significant (χ^2 (1, N = 55) = 3.265, p = 0.071).

Both male and female pupils produced the following statements:

- **English is cooler because …:**
  - *I can speak it more.*
  - *I know how to speak it.*
  - *I can understand it.*
  - *It is easier.* (2)
  - *I live in England and can speak English.*
  - *English people are cool.*

- **English is not cooler because …:**
  - *No one likes it.*
  - *It is used too widely.*
  - *In Cornish nobody knows what you are saying.* (2)
  - *English is not fun.*
  - *It's boring.* (3)
  - *English is so simple and not interesting.*

8.14 Are you going to continue to learn Cornish? Why (not)?

Only 21.9% intend to carry on with Cornish, 62.5% are not going to continue their studies and 15.6% do not seem to have thought about this possibility. A chi-square analysis revealed that 29.2% of boys and 23.3% of girls decided to continue, so there was no significant difference between genders (χ^2 (1, N = 54) = 0.236, p = 0.627). Pupils gave the following reasons to underpin their decisions:

- **Yes:**
  - *It is fun.* (3, 1 of them is not proud of Cornish and doesn't find it cool either)
  - *It's cool.*
  - *It's interesting.*
  - *It's good to learn.* (does not think Cornish is cool)

- **No:**

  - *It is boring.* (3)

  - *It is too hard.* (2)

  - *I don't have the facilities.*

  - *No more lessons.*

  - *I don't want to.* (3, although 1 finds it cool and is proud of Cornish)

  - *No use to anyone.*

  - *I won't really use it.* (although being proud of Cornish)

  - *I want to learn Chinese.*

  - *Not appropriate.*

  - *No point.* (although finds it cool and is proud of Cornish)

  - *No time.*

  - *Too hard and not many people use it anymore.* (proud and cool)

  - *Hard to remember.* (cool)

  - *I want to do something else* (2, 1 is proud and both find Cornish nice/easy)

  - *I can't.*

  - *I don't have someone to teach me.*

Conclusion: One key factor responsible for the result may be the lack of further provisions as reported in 6.2.1. Due to the contradictory attitude of some informants (e.g. not being proud of Cornish but planning to continue studying it and vice versa), a chi-square analysis was carried out in order to verify whether (not) continuing with Cornish was dependent on (not) being proud of knowing the language. The correlation is in fact significant (χ^2 (1, N = 54) = 8.837, p = 0.003), as Table 6 and Figure 17 below demonstrate:

			CONTINUE		Total
			yes	no	
PROUD	yes	Count (=frequency)	**13**	**19**	32
		% within PROUD	40.6%	59.4%	100.0%
		% within CONTINUE	92.9%	47.5%	59.3%
		% of Total	24.1%	35.2%	59.3%
	no	Count	**1**	**21**	22
		% within PROUD	4.5%	95.5%	100.0%
		% within CONTINUE	7.1%	52.5%	40.7%
		% of Total	1.9%	38.9%	40.7%
Total		Count	14	40	54
		% within PROUD	25.9%	74.1%	100.0%
		% within CONTINUE	100.0%	100.0%	100.0%
		% of Total	25.9%	74.1%	100.0%

Table 6: Crosstabulation PROUD/CONTINUE

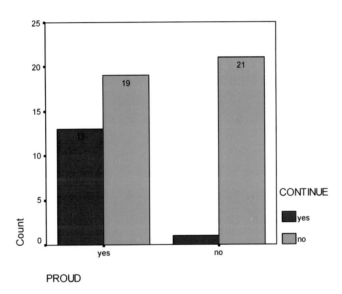

Figure 17: Correlation proud of knowing Cornish/continuing with Cornish

The same technique was used to find out whether there was a correlation between finding Cornish cool and continuing with Cornish. This time, no significant result was obtained (χ^2 (1, N = 52) = 5.450, p = 0.020).

9   Results: The Non-Cornish-Speaking Population

9.1   The Cornish language belongs to the Celtic language group. Do you know of any other Celtic languages? Which ones?

Just about more than half of the sample (54.5%) have heard of one or more other Celtic languages. While answering this question, some respondents were not sure whether knowing also implied being able to understand or speak the languages. The most frequently mentioned language was Welsh (43), followed by Irish or Irish Gaelic (26), Scots/Scottish or Scottish Gaelic (20). 12 informants just wrote Gaelic. Breton was mentioned 26 times (1 called it "*French in Brittany*") and Manx 3 times. No significant correlation between degree of Cornishness (see 6.1.1) and knowledge of other Celtic languages could be detected (χ^2 (2, N = 101) = 0.961, p = 0.618).

9.2   Do you know any Cornish words that are still used in your area? If yes, give examples.

Less than half of the sample (48.5%) have claimed to know Cornish words. However, when it came to giving examples, 11.9% of this group actually referred to dialect and slang words. Several informants gave more than one example. Most frequently, they mentioned names in general (11 place names, 1 personal names without giving examples) and *chy* (10, Unified Cornish (Revised) spelling) or *chi* (1, *Kernewek Kemmyn* spelling) for 'house'.[87]

The photos below, which were all taken in St. Ives, illustrate the frequent public occurrence of this Cornish word, especially for house names:

'bush-house'[88]

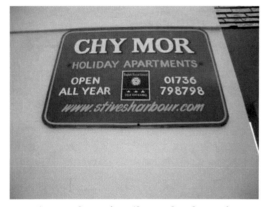

'ocean-house' or 'house by the sea'

---

[87] If not stated otherwise, *Kernewek Kemmyn* will be used as the variety of reference.

[88] The literal translation would be 'house the bush'. The possessive construction 'house of the bush' or more freely 'bush-house' probably denotes a house by a big bush. Since *perth* is feminine and the definite article *an* mutates feminine singular nouns, it should actually say *chy an berth* (see 4.4.2).

'church-house'[89]   'house of/on the hill(side)' or 'on the brow of the hill'

Kernow ('Cornwall') was mentioned 10 times (once written as *Curnow*, a spelling that doesn't exist but would correspond to the Cornish pronunciation), *bys vyken* ('forever') 3 times (twice in combination with *Kernow*),[90] *Kernewek* once and *eglos* ('church') 4 times.

The typically Cornish prefix *Tre-* was mentioned 3 times, *pol(l)-* 4 times and p*en(n)-* 2 times (see above 4.1). Other common Cornish words as found in place names included *carn* (dictionary spelling *karn*, 'rock-pile', 4), *port(h)* ('cove', 2) and *bal* ('mine', 1).

Some respondents produced Late Cornish anglicized spellings, such as b*rea* for *bre* ('hill'), *meor* for *meur* ('great, large, many')[91] or *carrack* for *karrek* ('rock').

The combination *vean* (soft mutated Late Cornish form of *byghan* 'small, little') *Heyl* (see 8.11) seems strange as in Cornish word order, it should be *heyl vyghan* ('small estuary'). Since *heyl* is masculine, the *b* in *byghan* should not mutate.

The same person who mentioned *carrack* also listed *dhu* (soft mutated *du* = 'black') and the orthographically anglicized mixed mutated late form *whidden* for *wynn* (*gwynn* = 'white') showing pre-occlusion of 'nn' to 'dn'.

It is a fact that Cornish survived in hundreds of English dialect words and some of them are still known nowadays (Pool ²1982:29). This may be the reason why a few subjects listed slang and dialect words such as 'dre(c)kl(e)y' ('later', 7), 'oggy' (a slang term for Cornish pasty, 4), 'emmet' ('ant', derogatory: 'tourist, visitor ignoring the Cornish language', 3), 'stank' ('walk' from *stankya* = 'to trample'), 'brare' ('a lot'), 'croust' (actually 'crowst', from *kroust*, 'picnic lunch, snack, meal taken to work'), 'scat' (used now with the meaning 'to demolish or break down', from Cornish *skat* = 'blow', *skwatya* = 'to crush, hit, squash') and a few others that are hard to find a translation for. One subject thought that rude words and curses were of Cornish origin, but did not give any examples.

Conclusion: Whereas 36.6% are aware of Cornish words in their surroundings, the majority mix up the dialectal Cornish variety of English with the Celtic language

---

[89] This holiday estate agency is situated close to the town's church. In former times, the name must have denoted a priest's house or a house owned by the Church.

[90] The phrase *bys vyken* may be familiar due to Philip Payton's Millennium book 'Cornwall for ever! *Kernow bys vyken!*' (2000a), which was given to every Cornish schoolchild in 2000.

[91] For example, the spelling *meor* occurs in *Porthmeor* ('big cove', see photo in chapter 4).

Cornish or do not seem to notice parts of the Cornish lexicon which abound in Cornish (place) names.

People born in Cornwall tend to know more Cornish words (42.2%) than people born outside Cornwall without Cornish roots (26%), but surprisingly less than people who were born outside Cornwall and have Cornish roots (83.3%). However, the overall correlation is just not significant enough (χ^2 (4, N = 101) = 9.212, p = 0.056).

9.3 Do you know anybody who speaks Cornish?

34.7% of the sample have met Cornish speakers. This percentage is considerably higher than the one reached by the pupils of Hayle School (18.8%, see 8.10), which can be obviously explained by the higher age and more social contacts of informants. The following acquaintances have been given:

- Name of a person (5)
- *Many* (3 concrete names)
- 2 names (2)
- *Several individuals and Cornish language groups* (Cornish studies library assistant)
- *School teacher* (3)
- *School governor*
- *Cornish dancing teacher*
- *Our son* (2, people were known to have a Cornish-speaking son)
- *Several of son's friends* (see above)
- *Step father*
- *Step father's sister who is a bard*
- *2 local Cornish bards*
- *Cornish bard*
- *Language group from the Cornish Language Weekend* (2, which took place in the pub they were working)
- *A couple of people in my village*
- *Parents' friends*
- *Friends; a friend*
- *Old next door neighbour*
- *Former work-mate*
- *My boss*
- *Local councillors* (working at Cornwall County Council)

Conclusion: Neither age (χ^2 (5, N = 101) = 4.296, p = 0.508) nor occupation (χ^2 (7, N = 101) = 10.148, p = 0.180) do have a significant influence on knowing Cornish speakers. Although more women tend to know Cornish speakers (40% vs. 28.3% of the male sample), the difference between genders was not significant enough (χ^2 (1, N = 101) = 1.524, p = 0.217).

Also in terms of Cornishness, a certain tendency could be observed: 40% of the people born in Cornwall, 33.3% of the inhabitants with Cornish roots and 30% of those informants who were neither born in Cornwall nor have Cornish ancestors have Cornish acquaintances. Again, the correlation was not significant either (χ^2 (2, N = 101) = 1.051, p = 0.591).

9.4 How is the Cornish language noticeable in everyday life?

Subjects were given a list of five domains and could also add their own category ('other'). Multiple answers were possible. 6 subjects have not noticed any Cornish in their surroundings, which would not have been that surprising if they had just moved to Cornwall. However, half of them were born in Cornwall, aged under 20, 20-29 and 30-39.

Figure 18 shows how and where the existence of Cornish is perceived:

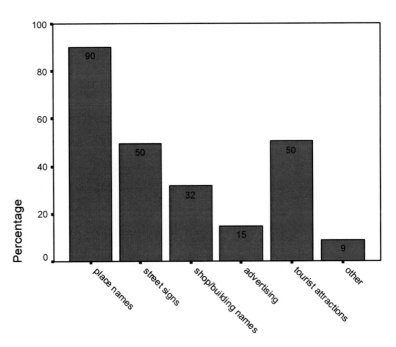

Figure 18: Visibility of Cornish in everyday life

Other places or items where the Cornish language is visible are:

- *Surnames* (2)

- *-The Cornwall County Council website*

- *Some local music features; Cornish songs and tunes*
- *Some artists use Cornish words (place names) as titles for their work.*
- *Schools*
- *Some branches of ASDA have some signage in Cornish.*[92]
- *Some shops*
- *Everything*

Conclusion: An overwhelming majority of 90.1% are aware of Cornish in place names (pupils 66%, see 8.11, Figure 16). Half of the sample have also noticed the use of Cornish on street signs and tourist attractions.

Bilingual school slogan in Hayle

Advertisement poster in Truro

9.5 Have you got the feeling that the media are raising the public awareness of Cornish? If yes, please specify.

37.6% think that newspapers, radio and TV are successful in raising the public appreciation of Cornish. Individual comments helped to grasp the scope of the influence:

- **Newspapers/magazines/books:**
  - *Frequent mentions in local media (e.g. 'The West Briton')*
  - *National papers quite often report on traditional Cornish festivals.*
  - *Letters and articles in local newspapers* (4)
  - *I noticed some words in 'The Cornish Times', mainly in titles.*
  - *'Western Morning News' column, various news articles, Cornish news section* (2)

---

[92] ASDA is a British supermarket chain.

- *More articles about Cornwall in the local press* (2)

- *Plug for classes*

- *Regular articles on Cornish subjects; more coverage of events* (2)

- *Lots of publications (Tor Press especially for Cornish books); monthly magazines 'Cornwall Today' and 'Inside Out'*

- *Article in 'Cornwall Today' about teaching in Hayle Community School*

- **TV and films:**

  - *Local TV features* (3)

  - *Films and TV programmes, but more of Cornwall as a county than the language.*

  - *Talked about on the local news.*

  - *History programmes, Cornish language programmes for Open University, documentaries, news items, e.g. Cornish bard ceremony*

  - *2004 Simpsons Christmas special* (3)[93]

  - *The Cornish separatist movement has even been highlighted by the cartoon 'The Simpsons'!!!*

- **Radio:**

  - *Local radio stations* (3)

  - *Radio Cornwall has a Cornish language programme.* (2)

- **General:**

  - *Sometimes; only a little; not enough*

  - *There has been talk of teaching the Cornish language in local schools.*

  - *Cornish-speaking lessons, local language school*

  - *More local/Cornish names used*

  - *As a tourist attraction (The Tate Gallery in St. Ives)*

  - *Mainly in Cornwall but it is becoming more popular with tourism and Cornwall is recognized now nationally.*

  - *Promotion of Eden Project, surfing, University for Cornwall, tourism*

  - *Cornwall has its own political party.*

Conclusion: Newspapers and magazines seem to be most influential in shaping the public perception of Cornish.

---

[93] Cartoon figure Lisa Simpson shouted '*rydhsys rag Kernow lemmyn*"('freedom for Cornwall now') and held a banner demanding 'UK out of Cornwall'.

9.6 Could it be possible that you start learning Cornish in the future? Why (not)?

Only 17.8% can imagine learning Cornish, another 4% were not sure (e.g. *"I enjoy learning place names (even have a book in my car), but probably wouldn't learn to speak it."* or *"maybe some words and phrases"*). Individual motives to learn the language are:

- *For work* (library assistant at the Cornish Studies Library in Redruth)
- *If we are asked to teach it.* (primary school teaching assistant)
- *I became interested in your language group.* (bar manager at Cornish Language Weekend)
- *I already learnt Cornish 25 years ago and it has been changed now.*
- *Because I would like to learn more about my roots.* (under 20)

The majority of respondents have no intention to study Cornish for the following reasons:

- *Lack of time (at the moment)/time factor/too busy* (14)
- *Not (really) interested* (12)
- *Dead/obsolete language* (2)
- *Dead languages shouldn't be revived "just for the sake of it".*
- *It's not a live spoken language. It is also associated with a narrow and backward looking xenophobia.*
- *It has gone out of fashion.*
- *Cornish is a dying language and it would be no use to me if I learnt it.*
- *Why should I, when no one speaks it?*
- *Too complicated* (2)
- *It is not worth the effort. The language is no longer "alive" and has no literature.*
- *I see little use in it.* (3)
- *No point, no need, not useful in everyday life.* (8)
- *Not enough demand.*
- *It would be of no benefit.*
- *I has only limited use.*
- *Wouldn't be as useful as e.g. Spanish for my travels.*
- *Not a lot of point, i.e. who would I speak it to? French would be more useful.*
- *Too many other things to learn for job opportunities.*

- *Other languages would be more viable.*
- *I wouldn't have anyone to speak to.*
- *I don't know anyone who uses it.*
- *There isn't much of a need to learn it due to other people not speaking it.*
- *Life is too short and other things to do first.*
- *Language is not used over a wide area, so not practical.* (2)
- *Not a priority.*
- *Lack of opportunity to practice in a naturalistic setting.*
- *I am learning French (plan to move there).* (2)
- *Moving to Spain.*
- *I speak already 5 languages, enough!* (from Brazil)
- *I don't feel a connection, but I am learning Italian due to Italian roots.*
- *I do not like the sound of Cornish.*
- *Difficult to find classes in local area.*
- *Too late to start now.* (aged 30-39)
- *Too old.* (2, retired)

Conclusion: Lack of time, interest and immediate benefits seem to prevent the majority from learning the language. The few positive reactions show that Cornish as a formal work qualification (as Welsh in Wales) would give grounds for an effort.

9.7   Have you heard of any Cornish language evening classes that are offered in your area? If yes, where?

Almost half of the sample know about the existence of Cornish language classes in their area (43.6%), 9.9% have heard of classes, but do not know exactly where they take place. A third of respondents, who seemed to be well-informed, listed colleges, schools and pubs scattered all over the county where formal or informal classes are held.

9.8   Motivation for learning Cornish

Five statements as possible reasons for learning Cornish were presented to the subjects who were asked to tick the ones they agree with. These statements are identical with five motives in the corresponding question put to the Cornish speakers (see 7.1, Figure 13). Informants could also specify other motives. 41 informants could not agree with any of the statements, another three just added their own (see below). Figure 19 shows the overall distribution of motives:

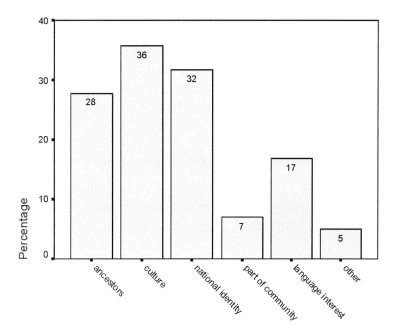

Figure 19: Possible motivational factors for learning Cornish

- **Other motives:**
  - *Understanding place names* (2)
  - *I'd like to sing in Cornish.*
  - *Work* (Cornish Studies library assistant)
  - *Cornwall is different in many ways to other parts of the country and I believe it should strive to maintain that distinction.*

- **Other comments:**
  - *I do not agree with any of these statements* (2)
  - *Not interested, thanks!* (2)
  - *I don't really have a need to learn it.*
  - *I think I can enjoy the undeniably rich culture without the language.*
  - *There is no real reason other than historic to keep Cornish alive.*

Conclusion: In terms of hierarchy, the results are roughly consistent with those obtained for the Cornish-speaking group (cf. 7.1). The most frequent reason is Cornwall's rich culture (35.6% / 80% of Cornish speakers). Also the second highly scoring motive is the language's function as the symbol of national identity (31.7% / 66%).

9.9 Other languages apart from English

This question was intended to find out to what extent informants have a command of other languages. 53.5% speak other languages with varying degrees of fluency. Most frequently mentioned was basic French, often combined with basic Spanish, Italian or German. Obviously, two participants from France and four from Germany claimed native competence. Other languages included Basic Hindi, Urdu, Maltese, Japanese, Portuguese (from Brazil) and Sign Language, Afrikaans (from South Africa) and Dutch, all of them occurring only once or twice. Concerning other Celtic languages, there was one Gaelic speaker.

Since almost the same question was put to Cornish speakers in the 1997 investigation (Hirner 1997:87-89), a comparison of figures seems useful. Whereas only 22.4% of the Cornish sample (n = 85) spoke no other language apart from English and Cornish, the percentage of this sample is more than double (46.5%).

Conclusion: As a consequence of the above percentages, a lower linguistic inclination of the non-Cornish-speaking population can be implied. Although a tendency may be derived from the fact that female respondents have a higher language interest (60% of the female sample speak one or more other languages) than their male counterparts (45.7%), the difference between genders is not significant enough (χ^2 (1, N = 101) = 2.073, p = 0.150).

9.10 How should Cornish be taught in schools in Cornwall?

Surprisingly, only 15% think that Cornish should not be taught in schools at all. 4% would even agree with the compulsory teaching of Cornish and 14% would accept Cornish as a second language on a par with languages such as French or German. A majority of 67% would like to see Cornish taught as an extra/voluntary subject outside the normal timetable.

9.11 General attitude in Cornwall with regard to promoting Cornish

Like the Cornish-speaking group (see 7.9, comparative figures in brackets), the subjects were also asked to rate the general attitude among the Cornish population with regard to promoting the language on a 3-point scale ('very favourable' – 'neither favourable nor disfavourable' – 'unfavourable'). 17.8% think that the atmosphere is very favourable (21% Cornish speakers), a majority of 64.4% have a neutral opinion (56%) and 11.9% regard the general attitude as clearly unfavourable (10%). 5.9% believe they do not know the atmosphere adequately (13%). Again, the varied and often critical comments should give details of respondents' views:

- **Positive general attitude:**
  - *The Cornish language is integral to Cornish identity.*
  - *The Cornish are very nationalist and proud of their culture.*
  - *The Cornish have always done anything to distance themselves from the rest of the UK, this is just another chance.*
  - *Amongst those genuine Cornish left.*
  - *I see it promoted in schools.*
  - *People want to learn.*
  - *Shops that specialize in Cornish goods.*
  - *Used as a marketing tool.*
  - *More emphasis now.*
  - *Most Cornish people I know would like to bring it back.*
  - *People talk about it a lot but little seems to come of it.*

- **Neutral attitude:**
  - *Cornish culture is heavily diluted and of little interest to the majority of the population.*
  - *Most people don't care. (2)*
  - *Most people don't give a shit.*
  - *But there is a small committed minority.*
  - *Some people want to revive the language.*
  - *Only a minority of people place a high value on it.*
  - *Don't think that the Cornish people will just speak English and give up the old language.*
  - *It's not something I have taken an interest in, so I am not sure.*
  - *Seems to have just died over the years with more English-speaking people residing in the county.*
  - *General lethargy! Plus many residents are not Cornish.*
  - *Cornwall is being overwhelmed by people from other parts of the country.*
  - *There are quite a lot of 'emmets' that live in Cornwall that don't care for the Cornish identity.*
  - *It is not promoted or spoken enough.*
  - *But getting better.*
  - *Does not seem logical to put more languages in schools.*

    Cornish traditional enthusiasts are keen, but it does not reflect general overall attitude.

- *Not really discussed the Cornish language with anyone.* (born in Cornwall)
- *I haven't met anyone with an opinion on the promotion of Cornish.*
- *The Cornish language is there to learn and facilities are available if people wish to study it.*
- *There is little encouragement/incentive to learn.*
- *Only 45% of people in Cornwall are Cornish, there are not enough to have a strong influence.*
- *Some people in Cornwall are not aware of the Cornish language.*
- *For most people it would not be useful in everyday life.*

- **Negative attitude:**
  - *As it is not prevalent in everyday life, the general attitude is unfavourable - why could we bring something back that has been buried for hundreds of years!*
  - *Very few people seem motivated to learn it as it is not "useful".*
  - *Not used enough.*
  - *Not necessary*
  - *Cornish in general very favourable; Cornish as a language unfavourable.*
  - *Nobody seems interested.*
  - *I don't think the interest is there.*
  - *Most cannot be bothered.*
  - *It is regarded as a bizarre minority pastime.*
  - *It's a dead language.*

Conclusion: The comparison of figures has shown that despite strongly differing views Cornish speakers and non-Cornish speakers perceive the general attitude in Cornwall in a very similar way.

9.12 Recognition of Cornish as an official minority language within Britain in the European Charter for Regional or Minority Languages in 2002

This question was intended to find out whether informants were aware of the fact that the British Government officially recognized Cornish as a minority language in 2002 by signing the European Charter. However, only a minority of 30.7% have heard about this "breakthrough" which may raise the status of Cornish considerably in the long run.

9.13 Associations with 'Cornishness'

Participants were asked to write down spontaneous associations with 'Cornishness'. Quite interestingly, a culinary speciality was ranked first (frequencies in brackets, no number means 'mentioned once'):

- *Cornish pasties* (42; see Appendix 14.3)

- *Tin mining (history, mine engine houses)* (17)

- *Beaches, surfing/sailing, coastline; sea, sand, harbours* (16)

- *Clotted cream* (13)

- *Great scenic beauty, scenery* (7)

- *Laid back lifestyle; slow pace of life* (6)

- *Fishing; fishing boats (6)*

- *The black and white flag; St. Piran's flag* (4)[94]

- *Ruggedness; shipwrecks; cliffs full of mystery and legends* (4)

- *Seagulls* (4)

- *Farming* (3)

- *Tourism* (3)

- *Celtic/Gaelic* (3)

- *Piskies* (particular to Cornish folklore and legend, little people who live on the downs and moors of Cornwall) (3)

- *Independence* (3)

- *Friendly people* (3)

- *Home, family, community; we always come home to Cornwall* (3)

- *Distinct dialect; accent* (3)

- *St. Piran* (2)

- *Feast days and saints; festivals* (2)

- *Cornish bard with their kilts and druids* (2)

- *Ancient land/times* (2)

- *Pride in local culture and history* (3)

- *A Celtic identity, clearly different from 'English', which people are very aware of; a huge sense of identity and pride* (2)

---

[94] Saint Piran's Flag, a vertical white cross on a black background, is regarded as the "national" flag of Cornwall and a symbol of the Cornish people. Saint Piran, the patron saint of tin-miners, is considered to be the patron saint of Cornwall, although Saint Michael and Saint Petroc are also associated with this title. The two colours are said to originate from Saint Piran's discovery of tin as Piran saw the white tin in the black coals and ashes (see http://en.wikipedia.org/wiki/Saint_Piran's_Flag and http://www.encyclopedia.thefreedictionary.com).

- *Warmth* (2)
- *Pubs* (2)
- *Ice cream* (2)
- *Racism, xenophobia, unfriendliness; trying to reject people from outside Cornwall* (2)
- *Moor*
- *Daffodils and primroses*
- *Cider*
- *Countrified*
- *Cottages*
- *Wet weather*
- *Rugby*
- *Ancestors*
- *Celtic cross*
- *Cornish kilt*
- *Local traditions*
- *Unused language, died a long time ago*
- *Wonderful place names and people's names*
- *Place names like Polzeath and Tredragon, Kernow*
- *Culture*
- *Sayings*
- *Classlessness*
- *Patriotism of the people even if they move away. We will always be Cornish.*
- *Pride of a beautiful county*
- *The character of its people*
- *Honest*
- *Hard-working*
- *Elderly generation*
- *Reluctance to change*
- *Helpful, funny, strange*
- *Open, poor, backwards, vulnerable but beautiful with potential investment in tourism to sustain the natural heritage*
- *Old-fashioned shops*
- *Friendly, healthy, outdoors*

- *Lifestyle*
- *Easy-going, shrewd*
- *Mentality and attitude to life: easy lane, carefree, unrushed (has its good and bad points)*
- *Laziness, living off past glories*
- *Something that comes from Cornwall*
- *Knowledge of Cornwall*
- *Local people doing local things in a local way.*
- *People's appearance, i.e. dark hair (Celtic looking)*

Conclusion: People living in Cornwall are aware of their county's distinctive culture and identity which seems dominated by beautiful scenery, the sea, tin mining and culinary delights. In order to define 'Cornishness', the language only plays a minor role (mentioned in place names twice, referred to as a dead language once and as a distinct dialect/accent three times). Also Celtic "ingredients" such as bards or the Celtic cross were underrepresented, occurring 10 times. On the contrary, pubs, cottages, wet weather and rugby define English culture as well.

9.14 Support for the revival movement

Subjects were asked if they would be willing to support the Cornish revival movement. 6.9% did not answer the question, 9.9% were not sure and a majority of 53.5% said they would refuse to. Nevertheless, 29.7% of respondents would be willing to back up the movement. In the following, they describe how they would help:

- *Anyway I can* (2)
- *Through bookshop and publicity* (bookseller)
- *Through work* (Cornish Studies Library assistant)
- *By making people aware of Cornish history and culture*
- *Do what I could within reason.*
- *Going to meetings*
- *Not sure how*
- *I would be interested in Cornish musical events.*
- *Community events, local history study*
- *Would be willing to learn it at school.* (student)
- *If people are interested enough they will make the effort to learn the language. In schools it's the timetable – we need more hours in the day.*
- *Getting involved in Cornish lessons.*

- *By learning Cornish*
- *I am happy to learn Cornish names and place names and teach them to my children.*
- *By getting more people to learn it.*
- *By learning the language again and attending more events. (subject used to learn it 25 years ago)*
- *By learning it and encouraging others to do the same.*
- *By learning and using it daily, it will pass on to others automatically. Encourage more schools to hold classes. (from Scotland)*
- *I agree that Cornish should not be allowed to be forgotten, but that it should not be enforced.*
- *Open to suggestions*
- *Because I am Cornish.*
- *By being proud to be Cornish.*
- *Through children's local clubs*
- *Perhaps could ask questions at local schools.*
- *Buying things Cornish.*

More than half of the sample have given reasons explaining why they would not support the revival of Cornish:

- *Lack of time (7)*
- *Not interested, sorry! (5)*
- *Not enough interest to support it actively. (5)*
- *Dead language, if people want to learn a language there are plenty of that would be of more use in everyday use.*
- *British people need to do better at learning European languages rather than 'dead' languages.*
- *I can't see the language as an important factor.*
- *I am not from here and don't think there would be much interest from the younger generation.*
- *Reviving the language would segregate us even further from the rest of the UK; for Cornwall to succeed we must stop trying to be different.*
- *Never crossed my mind.*
- *I do not see a need to.*
- *No real use rather than as an interest.*
- *Do not see the value.*
- *Cornish is not my culture and I don't understand it.*

- *I am not against supporting it culturally but not for political reasons, we have to live in the British democracy system.*

- *The Cornish can be very racist.*

- *Because we should speak one language.*

- *Don't think it's worth it.*

- *Move to Spain*

- *I don't intend to live here when my course has finished.* (student)

- *Not a priority in my life at this time.*

- *Do not like parochial attitudes.*

- *It is counterproductive.*

- *Far more important things to worry about.*

- *No point*

- *Because the government don't care anyway.*

- *I can see no future in it.*

- *Youngsters have enough problems with English – don't confuse them.*

- *I would like to see it grow but personally I am not interested in learning another language.*

- *There are too many other movements that need support.*

- *It is more important to learn widely used languages like French.*

- *Not interested to actively support but can see why Cornish people born of Cornish parents may wish to cling on to it.*

Conclusion: Most respondents did not see themselves as providing active support for the revival. Time, interest and lack of use seem to prevent most of them. On the other hand, almost a third of the sample came up with a number of concrete suggestions which could indicate a growing potential of new learners. No correlation between Cornishness (born inside or outside, roots) and willingness to support could be found (χ^2 (6, N = 101) = 3.304, p = 0.770).

9.15 Future of the Cornish language

The final open question asked for predictions concerning the future of Cornish. Again, answers were manifold and, although sometimes overlapping, have been categorized:

- **Restricted future:**

  - *Restricted to research and academics*

  - *A few historians/linguists may learn the language but it will fade out, like many other languages.*

- *Moribund - esoteric interest with academics.*
- *Other than a hobby no real use; continue as a minority hobby.* (3)
- *That it will continue to be an interest for a minority of leisured eccentrics.*
- *It will only live on as a subject to be studied by professors rather than used every day.*
- *Enthusiasts will try to keep it a subject of study and thus alive.* (2)
- *Small groups of dedicated Cornish people keeping the language alive.* (2)
- *Only used in a minority of groups for hobby and historical interest/purposes.* (2)
- *Linguistically a curiosity*
- *A small minority only will continue the tradition and speak it.* (5)
- *It will continue to become a language used by fewer and fewer people as a second or third language.*
- *An increase in interest among a small percentage of the population.*
- *It will only exist in people that have the background, motivation and time to learn it.*
- *Limited take-up of the language*
- *It will be learnt by the minority not the majority; too many English living in Cornwall.*
- *It will probably be used less as time goes by apart from place names and street names.* (2)
- *Only as a relic of the past for recognizing why place names relate to areas.*
- *It will die out and become for 'tourists only' and road signs like in Scotland.*
- *It will fade even more and the only interest will be association of place names with meanings; won't bring it back to any effective extent.*
- *It will always remain a minority language that is taught at night school – but not a compulsory language in schools.*
- *A few (handful) able to speak. School children understanding basic, i.e. colours, place names.*
- *That it will be learnt and not die but won't become a 'must learn' in schools as the Welsh language is.*
- *Maintained by a minority. Schools should concentrate on mainstream European languages like French and German.*
- *The odd phrase will still be quoted, but no more than that.*

- **Positive prospects:**
  - *It seems to be gaining momentum with groups cropping up all over the place.*
  - *Positive*

– *Revival*

– *It's going to happen, I feel it! And I am proud of being Cornish.* (Cornish roots)

– *It gets bigger and more people enjoy learning it in the future.*

– *Hopefully more people will have the chance to learn it at school.*

– *Favourable, if young people are interested or keep interest ongoing.*

– *It may be considered to be dying out but I think we might see a revival of sorts.*

– *It may be used in schools as a second language and I would like to see it given the same recognition as others like Welsh.*

– *Would be good if people who wanted to learn the language had the opportunity.*

– *It would be nice if a few more people grew up knowing the language as once you get older it is harder to learn.*

– *It needs to be on offer at schools, colleges and be taught in connection with learning about the 'land' (i.e. history and where it can be found today).*

- **Uncertain future:**

  – *A revival could be possible (Welsh is undergoing a huge revival), although the language can be seen to be 'dead', which makes revival harder.*

  – *If schools don't introduce it then unfortunately it will die.* (2)

  – *Unless something is done, it will die out.*

  – *I hope it will grow in popularity – but perhaps only if they teach it more in school.*

  – *I would like to see it spoken more widely. However I think it may be a long tome before it attains the status of Welsh.*

  – *Probably nothing will be done about learning the language.*

  – *It will be a **very** slow process.*

  – *There will only be a small revival.*

  – *I don't know much about the subject, so maybe more awareness could be raised and taught in schools.*

  – *If promoted in primary schools soon, a revival could take place; if not promoted, then the drop in Cornish speakers will continue.*

  – *An uncertain future, needs to be enforced in schools to be successful.*

  – *Much the same as now.*

  – *I don't think that the revival of Cornish would be a success because people are more interested in learning other languages. However, it would be a really good thing if people were more aware of the language, maybe through translations on road signs.*

- **Negative prospects:**
  - *No future* (3)
  - *I do not foresee much.*
  - *Nothing hopefully.*
  - *It is a dying language because young people are not interested in it.*
  - *Like the Breton language in Brittany, I think it might die eventually due to no interest.* (from France)
  - *Probably death.*
  - *It will disappear eventually.* (3)
  - *Fading out.*
  - *Dying out completely.*
  - *Extinct*
  - *Lost*
  - *It will be used less and less.* (2)
  - *Not spoken aloud enough, therefore it will probably die out.*
  - *It will slowly die out unfortunately.*
  - *It will probably just die out like most other cultures. But it would be a shame.*
  - *It has been too long unspoken to revive into a spoken language in Cornwall.*
  - *Interest will die out as Cornwall is overrun with foreigners.*
  - *I personally cannot see the Cornish language becoming mainstream again – English is the main language Cornish people use. Very few (mainly the older generation) people use it and it isn't their first language.*
  - *Unfortunately the apathy that the Cornish mentality breeds will cause its decline. The Cornish population is getting more widespread whilst it gets more diluted within Cornwall itself.*
  - *Pushed aside for other issues.*
  - *Gradual decline except for a few supporters.*
  - *The future of Cornish is like a pasty: a load of old potatoes.* (14-year-old boy)

Conclusion: Although there are a few optimistic comments, broadly speaking respondents have mixed feelings. Most think that the Cornish will continue to be used in a limited way, mainly as an interest and hobby of a minority and generally visualized in the form of place names. Those who are uncertain mainly place their hopes in schools. A considerable number of informants are also very pessimistic about the future of Cornish, some with a hint of regret.

10 Overall Discussion

Researching the Cornish revival involves a certain risk. If you look out for the language, you tend to notice Cornish bits and pieces everywhere, in newspapers, on houses, in brand names etc. In addition, you get so enthusiastic about reporting on positive developments that you are tempted to present a somewhat distorted picture of the situation and forget about the fact that Cornish people speak English as their first language. Meeting a Cornish-speaking person on the street can be like looking for a needle in a haystack. To point out this contrast, the three samples were chosen accordingly.

Apart from reflecting opinions, attitudes and habits of Cornish speakers, pupils and non-Cornish-speaking inhabitants of Cornwall, the findings of the questionnaires have made clear again that Cornwall is still divided into a growing group of Cornish language enthusiasts and a majority who do not attach great importance to it.

10.1 Positive consequences of the recognition

Whereas more than two thirds of the non-Cornish-speaking sample have not even noticed an official recognition in 2002, perceptions of a change in status among Cornish speakers range from enthusiastic to pessimistic (cf. 7.8). Cornish speakers' wishes regarding concrete measures to promote Cornish have turned out to be realistic and correspond with Strategy provisions to a great extent.

Reactions of the pupils who have been given Cornish lessons as part of the curriculum are encouraging since a majority liked the Cornish lessons and are proud of knowing Cornish. A high percentage is also aware of the Cornish language as occurring in local place names.

Although it is too early to be able to notice any tangible effects of the implementation of the Charter, the Cornish language has extended its functional domains. For example, in a reference to an anti-war protest, *The Western Morning News*, Cornwall's only local daily newspaper with a weekly Cornish language column, showed some of the protestors with banners proclaiming "Peace – *Kres* – *Salam*". The paper explained that the words meant peace in English, *Kernewek* and Arabic. No further explanation was given of what *Kernewek* was, so it is assumed that the public know it is the Cornish language.

In 2002, the British supermarket chain ASDA was the first to introduce Cornish signage in its Cornish stores following a growing number of requests for bilingual information by customers. Showing that Cornwall's distinctiveness promotes commercial benefits, the event was even covered by Sky News, interviewing Cornish-speaking staff. This trend could be continued with little effort, giving customers the chance to pick up some Cornish phrases.

Shortly after the British Government announced that it would finally grant Cornish official status, a leading Cornish campaigner and teacher explained in *The Western Morning News* (23 July 2002), how both speakers and non-speakers could benefit without major financial hardship. The language could be easily taught as part of local studies lessons, timeworn road signs may just as well be replaced by bilingual ones and all existing Cornish language films are subtitled anyway.

However, these constructive suggestions were criticized heavily a month later in a letter to the editor by a fellow Cornishman (*The Western Morning News*, 20 August 2002). Different languages would only cause "civil unrest, violence and misunderstanding", as can be observed in many inner-city schools, so the reaction. Many children cannot even master English, therefore, any other "foreign language" is not necessary.

Convincing opponents and critics who have accused the Government of yielding to rising nationalism will be only one of the major challenges for the future.

10.2 Obstacles to overcome

Although Cornish, according to Jones (1998:343), has "become fashionable, especially among the middle classes" and is more often used for season's greetings (see Appendix 14.4, 14.5) and house names, "high-profile visual public manifestations" turn out to be "rather superficial" (ibid.). The following examples are supposed to support this claim.

On 3 March 2005, the weekly newspaper *The West Briton* (p.50) reported that Devon and Cornwall police had introduced a language service to assist residents with first languages other than English. The translation service includes 150 languages from Russian to Sorani, an Indo-European variant of Kurdi spoken mainly in Iraq, but excludes Cornish!

Vision 4 of the Strategy seeks to develop the economic value of Cornish in terms of marketing and in fact, Cornish phrases have been cropping up more frequently in advertisements. However, such basically positive initiatives may also be counterproductive, as the weekend lodge advertisement in the magazine *Cornwall Today* (December 2004, p.162, see Appendix 14.6) demonstrates. *Gwel an Mor* ('view of the sea', 'sea view') lodges in *Portreath* ('cove on the beach', a picturesque seaside village on the northern coast near St. Ives) invite city dwellers from outside Cornwall to escape the hectic pace of life. Tourists may enhance the general income and Cornwall's economy, which is largely dependent on tourism, but certainly not the use of Cornish as a community language.

One problem is that the circle of Cornish speakers is often associated in the public mind with a clique who prefer to stick to themselves. It is true that dedicated Cornish speakers tend to have mostly other Cornish-speaking friends because they spend most of their free time with language-related events where they always happen to meet the same people. These observations seem to fit with the questionnaire results that outside the classroom, the majority of Cornish speakers use Cornish with other Cornish-speaking friends (see 7.6).

In 2002, a Cornish publishing and translation service launched a badge with a black frog emblem so that Cornish speakers, previously limited in number, could identify each other in public.[95] Basically a good idea, this innovation was not generally accepted.

---

[95] The symbol was taken after Dolly Pentreath's favourite swearword when she was terribly angry at someone (*The Sunday Telegraph*, 17 November 2002).

10.2.1 Demography

The fact that 45% of the non-Cornish-speaking sample were born in Cornwall confirms current estimates about Cornwall's population structure.[96] Quite surprisingly, however, is that almost the same percentage also applies to Cornish speakers and that only about a quarter of those who were not born in Cornwall have Cornish roots (11% for the non-Cornish-speaking sample).

Only 66% of the Cornish speakers were actually living in Cornwall in March 2005. Although it could be interpreted as a very positive sign that the language attracts people from all over the UK and even as far as the USA or Australia, the real community does not benefit at all from this popularity which is certainly restricted to individuals. Often a sort of nostalgia for the homeland of one's forefathers is involved when people live abroad. Since 2002, a Cornish homecoming festival has witnessed thousands of Cornish descent return to trace their ancestors' history researching their family trees.

On the other hand, the close correlation between Cornish origin and residence in Cornwall (80%) shows that Cornish speakers tend to stay or return to their home county. The data concerning the length of stay of the non-Cornish-speaking sample indicate that people born outside Cornwall often regard their stay as temporary. For example, one purpose to establish Tremough Campus (see chapter 3) was to keep students within Cornwall, but the results of questionnaires suggest the opposite. Also adult children of Cornish speakers were reported to have moved away (see 7.7).

Further evidence of the prevalent population movement was given by a magazine's reader survey in 2004 (1,200 completed questionnaires). Only 11% of the readers of *Cornwall Today*, mostly female and 45 years and older, have lived in Cornwall all their lives, nearly 25% have moved into the county and 7% own holiday property here (*Cornwall Today*, January 2005, p.4).

It is difficult to interpret the situation objectively as the following percentages illustrate. Is the fact that 19% of the pupils and 35% of the non-Cornish-speaking population have Cornish speakers among their relatives or acquaintances positive because some do actually know somebody or are the percentages too low to be taken into consideration at all?

All in all, the present demographic status is not really encouraging for the prospects of the language. The fact that Cornish speakers do not exclusively reside in Cornwall and that a considerable part of Cornish society has been in a state of flux does not really promise a homogenous community.

10.2.2 Attitudes

According to Fishman (1991:383), the mainstream tend to regard committed RLSers with "fear" and "suspicion" and associate them with irrationality and mysticism, therefore they often reject them and their activities beforehand. Quite surprisingly, the general attitude towards promoting Cornish is perceived in a similar way by both speakers and non-speakers (cf. 7.9 and 9.11). On the other hand, individual reactions and attitudes differed considerably, even resulting in derision by some non-speakers.

---

[96] For comparative purposes, percentages are rounded off appropriately.

On the more positive side, almost half of the pupils from Hayle School find the Cornish language "cool". Children who have such positive attitudes are very likely to continue with language revival efforts once they are grown-up (Hinton 2001a:7). In comparison with English, however, Cornish is on the losing side (see 8.13).

When it comes to defining 'Cornishness', numerous kinds of adjectives and nouns have been associated by the non-Cornish speaking sample (see 9.13). For the majority, Cornwall's uniqueness springs from the beauty of the landscape, the sea, historical tin mining and local specialities. These qualities combined with a relaxed lifestyle are responsible for both the bulk of tourists and second home owners from England and abroad in the end. In the list of associations, the Cornish language and the Celtic identity only played a marginal role, which indicates widespread disregard and the absence of emotional links. Since Cornish is neither a "central unifying force in the community nor the hallmark of membership of that community", the incentive to maintain it is very low (cf. Jones 1998:244).

10.2.3   Education and motivation

The positive development of the steady growth in student numbers is also confirmed by 21% of the Cornish-speaking sample who have recently started studying the language. On the other hand, there are 22% who consider themselves not very fluent and 25% moderately fluent. Many of them seem to belong to the large category of semi-speakers who are unable to proceed further even after several years of study. In this context, the absence of Cornish language programmes on TV has been identified as an additional shortcoming.

On the more positive side, a vast majority (86%) are going to continue their studies after passing one or more CLB exams (65%) or with the option to take one in the future (20%). In addition, a slight growth in fluent speakers (by 3%) can be observed. Although almost half of the sample are generally pleased with their progress in Cornish, they also have to struggle with learning difficulties, worst of all the lack of opportunities to find others to speak to. In fact, 18% have nobody to talk to at all. Surprisingly, the difficulty of the language is regarded as a minor challenge.

Promoting education and teacher training starting from pre-school level is the biggest concern of Cornish speakers who also consider it to be the most difficult challenge. Also the teacher at Hayle School gave support to this impression as she seemed stressed and regretted not being able to spend more time with Cornish. Actually, a lot of project work was done in her free time. She also reported that the children preferred the modern CD-Rom because they did not very much like the Cornish books available which are more suitable for adults.

Unlike Welsh pupils, the majority of Hayle pupils do not see any advantages in speaking Cornish yet (see 8.9) and do not intend to carry on with Cornish (see 8.14). At the moment (beginning of 2006), it would still be difficult for pupils to continue with Cornish anyway since the implementation of concrete provisions for this target group does not happen overnight. At least, one can build on the infrastructure that is already there because "education is the key to the increase in the number of young speakers", so the Welsh Language Board chairman (Celtic League newsletter, 7 May 2003). However, the support of parents is crucial. On the model of Welsh, the Cornish Branch of the Celtic League has suggested creating residential non-formal learning centres for children in the school holidays and for adults during term time on a voluntary basis (see Hirner 1997:70).

Surprisingly, only 15% of the non-Cornish speakers are against the teaching of Cornish in schools. However, despite a considerable awareness of the Cornish language in everyday life and of the existence of a network of language classes throughout the region, only a minority of 18% of the non-Cornish-speaking inhabitants can imagine starting to learn Cornish in the future themselves. On the other hand, gaining 18% of the overall population (expressed in terms of 86,886 people) to study Cornish and winning the support of 30% (equivalent to 144,810 people; see 9.14) would imply a language "revolution". The data have shown that motivation could be increased if Cornish played a role in professional life. Basically, the initiative by ASDA would be the right approach to preferably employ Cornish-speaking staff (see above 10.1).

10.2.4   Fragmentation and spelling debate

Whereas the former investigation (Hirner 1997) included mostly speakers/learners of *Kernewek Kemmyn,* the present study has tried to consider all varieties with *Kemmyn* obviously dominating (65%). Almost 10% stated that they could speak/write more than one variety and for the first time, the Cornish Language Weekend 2005, was joined by learners who had previously studied a form different to *Kemmyn. C*hildren were not aware of the existence of different spellings at all. Also the spelling conflict seems to have lost much of its negative influence and several people even believe that it shows how passionate Cornish people are about their language.

On the other hand, while the translation of the Old Testament is not completed yet, two translated versions of the New Testament are in existence, which seems a waste of energy and resources. Rather more important is the need to produce attractive learning material for children and teenagers, which will more easily reach a sufficiently wide readership if there is one common standard (see Appendix 14.7). Moreover, the work load of teachers who may have prepared their own materials will be reduced if they can share more information.

10.2.5   Intergenerational transmission

Although 32% of Cornish speakers use Cornish with the partner and/or the family, no progress can be reported in terms of the number of "native" speakers (n = 2) when compared to the previous investigation (Hirner 1997), In fact, data show a downward trend as only 40% of those who have children speak some Cornish to them (1997: 65%). Reasons are manifold (see 7.7) but tend to be strongly linked to the dominant advanced age group of speakers and their adult children. On the other hand, the Cornish Language Weekend 2005 was attended by the highest number of young children ever (see 4.4.2.1). It is estimated that only ten households use Cornish as a first language and several parents of small children have been deploring the lack of support from outside and place their hopes in the establishment of Cornish nursery schools which have also proved successful in the Isle of Man and Israel.

Learning Cornish as a second or third language is certainly not enough to achieve intergenerational mother tongue transmission. The questionnaire findings reveal that outside the classroom, pupils from Hayle School are not really able to apply what they have learnt and what is more, not even a quarter of parents have supported the learning process. If Cornish becomes a regular subject at school, the profile of the language will have to be raised by the media and through attractive events, as the booming situation in Wales demonstrates.

Since 1988, when the Education Act made Welsh a core subject in the National Curriculum in all Welsh-medium schools and a foundation subject in the remaining schools, a whole generation of pupils has come into contact with the language for the first time ever. The benefits are obvious. In 2001/02, over 25% of children in Wales were attending Welsh-medium schools even though the majority of these pupils came from non-Welsh-speaking homes. For the third time in a row, census results in Wales have indicated an increase in the number of young speakers, from 1991 to 2001 of 9%, and over 26% of the population in Wales under the age of 35 are Welsh speakers (source: Welsh Language Board figures, May 2003; cf. also Aitchison and Carter 2000, Morgan 2001 and Williams 2001).

Every year, the largest youth festival in Europe, the *Urdd National Eisteddfod,* is a magnet for young Welsh speakers (cf. Hirner 1997:72f.). Moreover, a recent reality show with local celebrities learning Welsh has turned out to be highly popular among young viewers. The Cornish Branch of the Celtic League would also like to see an annual Cornish *Eisteddfod* in all Cornish primary schools, where awards should be given to pupils for achievements in the Cornish language.

According to MacKinnon (2002:277), there is still a "quantum leap" from the present position of Cornish to the Welsh level of promotion. Yet not all RLS methods work for all communities. In order to approach stage 6, a "complete change of lifestyle" and "lifetime commitment" would be demanded from parents when cooperating with Cornish-language pre-schools (Dauenhauer and Dauenhauer 1998:80f.). At this point, in the absence of a critical mass of native speakers, the goal is unrealistic and beyond the capacity and desire of most families.

10.2.6   The 'high power' stages

The difference between artificial language acquisition and natural language transmission cannot be ignored either in the light of the official status that opens up the door to the higher GIDS levels 1-3. Despite subventions, minority language media tend to be "pale imitations" of the dominant language, above all English, in terms of quantity and quality, only faking real community life (Fishman 2001b:473).

The *Kernewek* magazine *An Gannas* (see 4.3.1.1) and the quarterly bilingual *An Gowsva* ('The Talking Shop')[97] are considered high quality in terms of contents but due to limited means still amateurish in design.

Apart from *The Western Morning News* (see above 10.1), the coloured quarterly magazine of Cornwall, *Cornish World*, subtitled as *Bys* ('world') *Kernowyon* ('Cornishmen'; see Appendix 14.8), features many Cornish language related issues and advertisements (see 14.9). There is also a regular Cornish page written by the Grand Bard of the *Gorsedh* and all page numbers are in Cornish (see 14.10). Moreover, the

---

[97] *An Gowsva* is published by the Unified related organization *Agan Tavas* (see 2.7.1.1). Around 90 of its 200 members are subscribers of the magazine.

magazine presents reviews of Cornish books, CDs, DVDs, videos and web sites, such as *Pymp Gwel* ('Five Scenes'; in Cornish, nouns following numbers stay in the singular), a 15-minute collection of short episodes in Cornish with English subtitles, supported by Cornwall Film Fund and shown at the Cornwall Film Festival 2005. Although well filmed, it is not perfect technically.

The problem is that badly produced low-budget programmes often "turn off" rather than attract minority language speakers. So it is more effective and cheaper to invest in unspectacular neighbourhood activities such as sports clubs, choirs or youth groups because such small-scale community events are more likely to keep pace (cf. Fishman 2001b:473f.).

Figure 19, a simplified model of Fishman's GIDS (see 2.6.1), is represented in the form of a pyramid because the higher stages, especially 1 and 2, are rarely reached by minority language communities. Stages that have already been successfully targeted, such as 8 and 7 at the bottom and 5, 4 (partly) and 2, are written in bold type.[98]

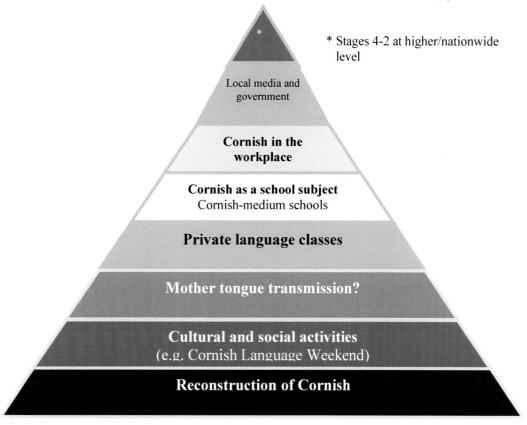

* Stages 4-2 at higher/nationwide level

Local media and government

Cornish in the workplace

Cornish as a school subject
Cornish-medium schools

Private language classes

Mother tongue transmission?

Cultural and social activities
(e.g. Cornish Language Weekend)

Reconstruction of Cornish

Figure 19: Fishman's GIDS model applied to Cornish

Although the base of the pyramid is rather solid and the use of Cornish even reaches stage 2 to some extent (see Kerrier Council below), stage 6 is the big question mark for the future. Fishman himself has made clear that keeping the order of stages is not necessary (2.6.2.7) but reversing the process of language shift can only succeed if all measures are linked to this ultimate goal. Otherwise, Cornish will remain to be used as a second language in "highly restricted circles" (Jones 1998:347).

---

[98] For an attempt to apply Fishman's model to all Celtic languages, cf. Ó Néill (2005).

11   Conclusion and Perspectives

> [...] we've had a good, but slow and sometimes painful start and we've made a number of mistakes along the way. We now need to learn from this experience and make the whole process of consultation and 'contracting' with the Government smoother and more open, whilst still keeping focus on our objectives. (Climo-Thompson 2005:5)

Unlike a majority of the world's 1,982 *Kleinsprachen* (see Table 1), Cornish, embedded in a comparably favourable European tradition of linguistic diversity and respect for minorities, is in a highly privileged position. In sum, the language has increased its use and prestige over the past ten years and further protectionist policies through Cornish local authorities will enhance its status. Even though language learning cannot be forced on people, there is a growing potential of new learners who do not belong to the formerly dominating intellectual middle-class elite. But will Cornish ever go beyond the status of a second language and become a community language?

The dynamics of language restoration are complex since language is a non-linear system whose evolution is influenced by both deterministic and indeterministic processes. Thus, future contributions may go deeper into this topic (see 1.4) and investigate it from a chaos theoretical approach.

Since spring 2005, a number of notable events, gains but also setbacks, have taken place which will be presented in chronological order:

- Andrew George, the MP for St. Ives in Cornwall who had taken an active part in the recognition of Cornish (see 3.6.1), affirmed his allegiance to the Queen in both English and Cornish. All MPs have to swear the oath before they can take their seat in the House of Commons. Much symbolic importance has been attached to this act (Eurolang newsletter, 13 May 2005).

- In May, a first direct consequence of the Strategy's implementation became known. The Council of Kerrier (one of Cornwall's six districts comprising the towns of Camborne, Redruth and Helston, see map 3) decided to have bilingual road signs, letterheads and a logo displaying both Cornish and English. This breakthrough was mainly due to the dedication of one of the councillors who is a fluent Cornish speaker (http://www.cornish-language-news.org, 23 May 2005).

- The Strategy was presented for anyone interested at Truro County Hall on 26 May. The public meeting had been announced in local papers, which shows that the whole population is supposed to be given a say in the process (http://www.cornish-language-news.org, 24 May 2005).

- In June, a new CD containing only *Kernewek* songs from the Cornish language rock band *Skwardya* ('to tear', 'to rip') was released (*Warlinenn* news, 5 June 2005). Provided the music is played by radio stations like Radio Cornwall, it will make Cornish accessible to a wider audience.

- The most encouraging news was also received in June, when the British Deputy Prime Minister announced that over the next three years, the Government would provide £240,000 of funding to support the reinvigoration of the Cornish language

(Celtic League newsletter, 11 July 2005). This means that for the first time ever the language receives an annual sum of money from Central Government that is 16 times higher than before. It is hoped that other sources, e.g. Objective One, will contribute another £120,000 a year. This major funding package is supposed to subsidize a Language Officer plus supporting team (*Warlinenn* news, 19 June 2005).

- In July, the UK had to submit its second report on the application of the European Charter, whose contents was heavily criticized as a "disorganized and misleading mishmash" by a Scottish Gaelic language expert.[99] He accused the UK Government of failing to fulfil many of its commitments concerning Scottish Gaelic (details in Eurolang newsletter, 28 July, 2005).

  Also Cornish language groups have disapproved of a lack of concrete commitments and the general character of the report's contents. Whereas "awareness about different cultures, heritage and the importance of language learning" are occasionally mentioned, measures for the teaching of Cornish at school are missing.

  Moreover, they criticize that the report completely ignores a possible inclusion of a Cornish question in the next UK census. In fact, it is very difficult to "plan ahead" in terms of "potential demand" if the exact number and ability of speakers is still based on estimates.

  The third critical comment concerns the disregard for Cornish NGOs' reactions to the UK's first report, which was specifically aimed at Part II, Article 7.1.b (see 3.5.1). According to this paragraph, the geographical and administrative boundaries of the area where the RM is spoken should be respected. However, financial decisions are often made outside Cornwall as part of the South West Region, which may "constitute an obstacle to the promotion" of Cornish and as such violates Article 7.1.b of the Charter.

  Both the evaluation report of the expert committee, which is not expected to visit the UK before February 2006, and the recommendation of the CoE's Committee of Ministers are not published yet.

- In July, a trendy bilingual *Kernewek – Sowsnek* ('English') / English-Cornish mini-dictionary containing 8,000 words was published (George 2005), which can be purchased in most bookshops in Cornwall. Now that the language has development money, further attractive publications will be expected.
    (source: *Warlinenn* news, 29 July 2005)

---

[99] The 85 page report can be looked up on the CoE website under 'monitoring'. NGOs can submit comments at least until February 2006.

- Although the British Government finally rejected the petition for a Cornish Assembly in July 2005 (see 4.1.1), claiming that Cornwall was too small to be a region and thus would not qualify for devolution, the campaigning for a referendum to establish a devolved directly-elected Regional Assembly in Cornwall continues with even stronger public support (http://www.cornish-language-news.org, 19 July, 12 August 2005).

- The presenter of the weekly news in Cornish on BBC Radio Cornwall '*An Newodhow*', the Grand Bard of the Cornish *Gorsedh*, can be viewed on the BBC homepage talking about the future of the Cornish language (8 August 2005, http://www.bbc.co.uk/videonation/articles/c/cornwall_cornishbard.shtml).

- The Cornish language has increasingly become an issue in the local press. After the Government had promised to promote Cornish, a Packet newspaper started attacking the Cornish language. First the question was raised whether money should not be spent more urgently on other services. But later on, a journalist went as far as to compare Cornish speakers with terrorists (http://www.cornish-language-news.org, 17 August 2005).

- Striving for uniformity involves the risk of imposing a standard and denying personal choice in a pluralistic system. In September, a Welsh speaker sent a message to the 'Cornish Language Fellowship', encouraging Cornish speakers on the issue of standardization. The letter was published on the organization's homepage (http://www.cornish-language-news.org, 1 September 2005):

Dear Cornish Speakers,

Please send on to whoever this concerns. I have read recent articles in the English newspapers describing the arguments going on between the three separate groups of Cornish speakers as to which form should be the 'true' descendant of your ancient spoken language. While I understand your need to make a successful re-launch of your Celtic speech, why not take a lead from your cousins across the Bristol Channel? Welsh is a largely phonetically written language which has many regional variations. In this it is far more flexible than English. In Wales, like the three Cornish varieties, everyone understands everyone else. To say 'How are you'?

*In Welsh it can be '*Sut dach chi, Sut dech chi *or* Sut dych chi*' and that's just in the North! Go further south and the 's' thickens to 'sh' while the 'u' is no longer an 'ee' sound but said as in English with an 'oo'. But nobody's bothered.*

I hope I'm not being patronising when I say that if you look upon the three forms of Cornish as resplendent regional forms, for instance, what is the problem? Like the Welsh, you all seem to be able to speak to each other so go forward together and continue to bring Cornish back to life. Pob lwc *and good luck to all of you.*

Sincerely from Mark Abraham.

- The same month, an online campaign was launched by four Cornish speakers in order to agree on one Standard Written Form of Revived Cornish by consensus (http://www.cswf.org.uk).

- The Strategy Conference on 17th September 2005 provided a forum for speakers and was enriched by guest speakers from Wales, Scotland and the Isle of Man (see above 4.3.5). In the afternoon, various topics for discussion were offered, e.g. education or orthography. Over half of the conference participants attended the orthography session where they were split into three groups. The discussion seemed to be restricted along pre-determined lines so that no free debate was possible. According to a representative of *Kernewek Kemmyn,* the subsequent summing-up was selective and unrepresentative so that many left the conference "with a nasty taste in their mouths". The Cornish speaker believes that the fall-out from this meeting will go on for months (source: e-mail communication, 13 November 2005).

- In November, a first report on the progress of the Strategy in the district of Kerrier was delivered by a local council representative.

  Experts from various Cornish organizations have agreed on a single Cornish spelling for new bilingual street signs and have also assisted in translating names of Kerrier district council services, which is clearly a step towards realizing vision 3 (cf. 4.5.2).

  All six district councils are part of the Cornish Language Partnership, a Cornwall-wide committee, which is responsible for driving forward the Strategy for the next three years and supervising the finances and their distribution. The next task will be to appoint language development staff who will be paid and employed by the CCC (http://www.cornish-language-news.org, 15 November 2005).

  At the moment, the Partnership is busy preparing a detailed work programme. Its next meetings are scheduled for 20 February and 17 March 2006 whose agendas and minutes will be published on the CCC website (http://www.cornwall.gov.uk).

- On 11 February 2006, a *Dydh Lowender* (see 4.4.2.1) will be organized by the Cornish Language Fellowship. Everybody, from beginner to fluent speaker, is welcome to spend a day meeting other speakers and practising Cornish in an informal atmosphere.

- The Cornish Language Weekend 2006 will again take place at Duporth Holiday Village near St. Austell from 7 to 9 April.

There is no doubt that the Cornish language has been granted a comeback and for the first time ever, a comparably huge amount of money can be invested just for the sake of promotion. This offers a great chance to gain more supporters but the public will watch carefully how their tax money is going to be spent, eager to monitor any progress. Once the language is stronger, revivalists will push for it to be included under Part III of the Charter.

Eight years ago, Jones (1998:348) estimated that Revived Cornish was very likely to "share the fate of its predecessor", namely to die out again eventually. This view must certainly be revised given the fact how much has already been "achieved with so little by so few" (MacKinnon 2002:276). Against all odds, the language has survived into the 21st century but it remains to be seen whether the highly complex process of reversing language shift will be able to re-establish Cornish as a community language. To conclude, the words of a Cornish speaker are supposed to express an optimistic spirit:

> We have a highly exciting time ahead of us. The time for our language is come. The next ten years will see a revival our parents and grandparents could never have imagined. (Climo-Thompson 2005:5)

12 Summary

This book deals with the phenomenon of language death which is currently being observed to occur in all parts of the world at an unprecedented pace. In particular, some 30% of the world's estimated 6,000 languages, defined as *Kleinsprachen* (Haarmann 2001) because they have fewer than 1,000 speakers, are seriously threatened by extinction.

The forces which lead to language obsolescence have certainly changed over the centuries but they have always been related to socioeconomic and political rather than purely linguistic causes. According to Sasse's model (1992a), external factors primarily trigger a community's shift in speech behaviour and attitude.

In Europe, the Celtic language group represents a special case as all the surviving languages are minority languages and, with the exception of Breton, endangered by the dominant global language English. Cornish, one of the six Celtic languages, was completely replaced by English in the 18th century and after lying dormant for more than 100 years, it witnessed a remarkable revival at the beginning of the 20th century. Since then, interest in and efforts to revive the language have grown considerably in Cornwall, the county situated in the southwest corner of the British Isles. The number of people learning Cornish as a second language is continuously rising and even a few parents have taught their children Cornish from birth, a fact that implies some guarded hope since Cornwall has the first native speakers of Cornish for 200 years. However, those families who are scattered all over Cornwall have frequently deplored the lack of pre-school playgroups which would obviously bring bilingual children together outside home. Moreover, it is difficult to determine the exact number of speakers because no such question has ever been asked in a national census. Estimates range from 2,000 to 3,500 speakers with varying communicative competence, which is not even equivalent to 1% of the overall population. Out of these, around 300 are considered to be fluent speakers.

Apart from a general growing awareness internationally, the protection of minority languages has become an important concern of language ecology, a subfield of the relatively new scientific discipline ecolinguistics. In order to arrive at a prognosis concerning a language's process of recovery, if that is possible at all, Fishman's model of 'Reversing Language Shift' (RLS, 1991) has proved a useful theoretical framework. The theory is based on eight targets or obstacles that a language has to aim at or surmount to count as fully restored. Some languages, including Cornish, may even have to start from scratch, which means that they have to be reconstructed because of the absence of native speakers or grammars and dictionaries. The further up the 'Graded Intergenerational Disruption Scale' (GIDS) the obsolescent language is able to climb, the more official and educational status it gains. A shortcoming of the model is the early third position of the most crucial stage where intergenerational mother tongue transmission is supposed to be achieved. As this ultimate goal is most difficult to attain for many obsolescent languages, Fishman (2001) later on amends that the order of stages can be adapted to special circumstances.

Although globalization and advanced communicative technology have frequently been held responsible for the decline of indigenous languages, it is obvious that electronic dissemination of information has facilitated cooperation between international organizations and moribund language communities in their RLS efforts. Also Cornish speakers and learners who often have to travel long distances to meet other speakers have definitely benefited from interactive learning materials and the various opportunities the Internet offers. On the other hand, it cannot be denied that a virtual community can never make up for a real community.

When it comes to promoting linguistic and cultural diversity and protecting minority rights, the European Union and related institutions such as the European Bureau for Lesser Used Languages and the Council of Europe are playing an important role and have actively contributed to the official recognition of Cornish. In 2002, the British Government eventually recognized Cornish as a minority language by signing Part II of the legally binding 'European Charter for Regional or Minority Languages'. Although this step was enthusiastically celebrated as a great success for the Cornish language movement, provisions for institutional promotion under Part II are rather general in nature, allowing room for interpretation. If a minority language qualifies for Part III, such as Welsh, Scottish Gaelic and Irish Gaelic (in Northern Ireland), it will automatically acquire more specific measures of protection. Still, for Cornish, which had up to then mainly depended on private initiatives not being able to expect any regular funding, it has marked the beginning of a more promising future.

Despite a clearly demonstrable distinctive historical status (the Duchy of Cornwall), culture and identity which also find expression in an abundance of Celtic place names, the Cornish people have so far been deprived of treatment as a separate ethnic minority. Cornwall, together with several other counties, forms part of the South West Region, a fact that more than 10% of the Cornish population (over 50,000 people) would have liked to change by signing a petition for a Cornish Assembly on the model of Wales.

However, neither the population of Cornwall nor the Cornish-speaking minority are homogenous. In fact, Cornwall's beautiful landscape combined with a healthier lifestyle, reasonable living costs and booming business has attracted people from all parts of the United Kingdom and abroad, so that only 30-50% of the inhabitants are estimated to have been born in Cornwall.

When the language was reconstructed in the 20th century, no native speakers of Cornish had been available to act as authorities. Consequently, the spelling and pronunciation of Revived Cornish has been subject to repeated criticism and resulted in the creation of four different varieties whose proponents have founded their own organizations. Obviously, this situation implies a waste of energy and confuses (potential) learners. In order to implement the objectives of the Charter and to integrate Cornish into the regular school system, agreement on a standard version is considered to be absolutely necessary. Concerning grammar and lexicon, Revived Cornish is already complex enough to express modern concepts.

Up to now, Cornish has predominantly been taught as an extracurricular activity in lunchtime or after-school clubs and is currently absent from pre-school education. Two specialist language colleges offer Cornish as part of their curriculum for 11-12-year olds. However, a lack of funding and the shortage of resources have so far made it impossible to obtain a special teaching qualification and to establish a network of peripatetic teachers. The majority of learners are adults who study the language in evening classes both in- and outside Cornwall and who also have the opportunity to take examinations held by the Cornish Language Board. Apart from the classes and organized events, occasions for speaking Cornish are still rare, which partly explains the low motivation and failing of many learners to become fluent.

Great hopes are being placed in the implementation of the first official document, a 'Strategy for the Cornish Language', which was published by Cornwall County Council in 2005. Its long-term aim, the vision to re-establish Cornish as a widely-spoken community language, includes several target measures. A top priority is to increase provisions for learning Cornish from pre-school to adult education so that everybody who wishes to learn Cornish can do so. Especially Cornish language nursery schools for the very young on the successful models of Hebrew, Welsh and Manx should be reinforced. Another goal is to raise the media profile and the public visibility of Cornish by prolifically displaying bilingual signs, promotional materials and letterheads. In the long run, it should be common practice to have official documents translated into Cornish. In addition, the economic value of Cornish should be advanced, e.g. as a marketing tool for local products. To realize all those visions, Cornish orthography must be standardized first. Another immediate aim is to employ a Language Development Manager who should coordinate projects and assist language groups in fund-raising and establishing contacts.

The aim of this paper was to assess the sociolinguistic status of Cornish in terms of possible consequences and obstacles to the implementation of the European Charter.

The hypotheses derived from the account given so far can be divided into positive expectations and further challenges:

1. The recognition of Cornish has strengthened the status of Cornish and will raise its position on Fishman's scale.

2. Still, there are a number of inherent obstacles to overcome on the way towards successfully reversing language shift:

    2.1 The weak demographic basis of the language

    2.2 Passive or negative attitude of the non-Cornish-speaking population

    2.3 Lack of pre-school playgroups, learners' motivation and funding for teachers, absence of Cornish on TV, few opportunities for daily use

    2.4 Fragmentation – spelling debate

    2.5 Intergenerational transmission will remain the exception in a virtual rather than real community.

The data were collected by means of questionnaires, local newspapers and interviews in the course of several stays in Cornwall over a nine year period of observation. An empirical survey of language attitudes, habits and motivational factors, carried out in March 2005, involved three groups of subjects:

a.   Cornish speakers (including learners): n = 100

b.   11-12-year old pupils who have been instructed in Cornish as part of the curriculum in a pilot school: n = 64

c.   A sample from the non-Cornish-speaking population: n = 101

Here, only the most important findings of the questionnaire investigation which also elicited detailed individual comments can be summarized according to the hypotheses established:

1.   Whereas more than two thirds of the non-Cornish-speaking sample are not even aware of an official recognition, perceptions of a change in status among Cornish speakers range from enthusiastic to pessimistic. Cornish speakers' wishes regarding concrete measures to promote Cornish largely coincide with Strategy provisions which are even supposed to extend as far as the second highest level on the GIDS scale.

2.1   The fact that 18% of Cornish speakers do not have anyone to talk to in their everyday lives must be attributed to the scattered distribution of speakers. At least 19% of the pupils and 35% of the non-Cornish-speaking population have Cornish speakers, mostly one, among their relatives or acquaintances. 55% of the non-Cornish-speaking sample were born outside Cornwall, which confirms current estimates about Cornwall's demographic trends. Quite surprisingly, a similar percentage also relates to Cornish speakers and only about a quarter of those who were not born in Cornwall have Cornish roots (11% for the non-Cornish-speaking sample). Only 66% of the Cornish speakers were actually living in Cornwall in March 2005. The close correlation between Cornish origin and residence in Cornwall (80%) shows that Cornish speakers tend to stay or return to their home county. The data concerning the length of stay of the non-Cornish-speaking sample indicate that people born outside Cornwall often regard their stay as temporary. All in all, the present demographic conditions do not really reflect a homogenous community.

2.2   Quite surprisingly, the general attitude towards promoting Cornish is perceived in a similar way by both speakers and non-speakers (21%/18% favourable, 56%/64% neutral, 10%/12% unfavourable). Yet individual comments differed considerably, even giving rise to ridicule by some non-speakers. When it comes to defining 'Cornishness', the Cornish language has been ignored by most non-Cornish speakers who seem to be more ready to identify with their county's beautiful scenery and traditional dishes. Yet 32% appreciate the language's function as a symbol of national identity and more than 90% are aware of Cornish place names (pupils 66%). The pupils' reactions are encouraging since a majority liked the Cornish lessons and are proud of knowing Cornish, almost half of them find the Cornish language "cool". In comparison with English, however, Cornish is on the losing side since 61% prefer English.

2.3   Although an encouraging 21% of the Cornish-speaking sample are beginners and fluent speakers account for 32% (1997: 29%), some 40% seem to belong to the large category of semi-speakers who are unable to improve their skills even after several years of study. In this context, the call for Cornish language programmes on TV has been evident. Almost half of the sample are generally satisfied with their advancement in Cornish, but even fluent speakers have mentioned learning difficulties, worst of all the limited opportunities to speak Cornish regularly, motivation and lack of time. Still, 86% intend to carry on with Cornish, 65% have already passed one or more Cornish Language Board exams and 20% would not exclude the possibility of taking one in the future. Education including pre-school level is regarded as the most important field to promote and at the same time the biggest challenge for the future. Only a quarter of the pupils are convinced that being able to speak Cornish has advantages and 63% would not be prepared to continue studying. Surprisingly, only 15% of the non-Cornish speakers would oppose the teaching of Cornish in schools. However, only a minority of 18% can imagine starting to learn Cornish in the future themselves.

2.4 Even if one variety is dominant (65%), 9% of the Cornish speakers claimed to know two forms of Cornish. The pupils were not aware of the existence of different spellings at all. All in all, the spelling conflict, ranked 7th out of 12 challenges, seems to have lost much of its negative influence.

2.5 Although 32% of Cornish speakers use Cornish with the partner and/or the family, no progress can be reported in terms of the number of native speakers (n = 2). In fact, data suggest a downward trend as only 40% of those who have children speak some Cornish to them (1997: 65%). Reasons tend to be strongly linked to the dominant advanced age group of speakers (over 50) and their adult children. The questionnaire findings have revealed that outside the classroom, pupils are not really able to apply what they have learnt and what is more, not even a quarter of parents have supported the learning process. Learning Cornish as a foreign language is certainly not enough to achieve intergenerational mother tongue transmission.

Concluding from the investigation, the Cornish population is still divided into a growing minority of Cornish language supporters and a majority whose lives have remained unaffected by the language. In June 2005, the British Government promised to provide £240,000 of funding over a three year period, so for the first time ever a large sum of money can be invested just for the sake of the language and additional protectionist measures are likely to enhance its status. Yet it will be years, if ever, before the transition from a deliberately learnt to a natural community language takes place. Further research will be needed to examine this complex development.

13 Bibliography

Ahlqvist, Anders (2002). "Irish and Finland Swedish." In: Bradley and Bradley, eds. (2002). 40-58.

Aikhenvald, Alexandra Y. (2002a). "Traditional Multilingualism and Language Endangerment." In: Bradley and Bradley, eds. (2002). 24-33.

Aikhenvald, Alexandra Y. (2002b). "Language Obsolescence: Progress or Decay? The emergence of new grammatical categories in 'language death'." In: Bradley and Bradley, eds. (2002). 144-156.

Aitchison, Jean (1993). *Language Change: Progress or Decay?* 2nd ed. Cambridge: Cambridge University Press.

Aitchison, John and Harold Carter (2000). *Language, Economy and Society. The changing fortunes of the Welsh language in the 20th century.* Cardiff: University of Wales Press.

Amery, Heather, Stephen Cartwright and Graham Sandercock, eds. (2003). *The First Thousand Words in Cornish. An Kynsa Mil er yn Kernewek.* New rev. ed. Redruth, Cornwall: Cornish Language Board.

Anderson, A.B. (1990). "Comparative Analysis of Language Minorities: A Sociopolitical Framework." In: Gorter et al., eds. (1990). 119-136.

Azurmendi, Maria-Jose, E. Bachoc and F. Zabaleta (2001). "Reversing Language Shift: The Case of Basque." In. Fishman, ed. (2001). 234-259.

Baker, Colin (1988). *Key Issues in Bilingualism and Bilingual Education.* Clevedon, Avon: Multilingual Matters.

Baker, Colin (1993). *Foundations of Bilingual Education and Bilingualism.* Clevedon, Avon: Multilingual Matters.

Ball, Martin J., ed. (1993). *The Celtic Languages.* London and New York: Routledge.

Bartens, Angela (2001). "Review of *Can Threatened Languages be Saved? Reversing Language Shift, Revisited: A 21st Century Perspective.* (Fishman, ed. (2001))." Linguist List. University of Helsinki.

Becker, Kathleen (2003). "Back to its roots." *Spotlight* September 2003: 20f.

Berlitz, Charles (1982). *Die wunderbare Welt der Sprachen, Fakten, Kuriosa, Geheimnisse.* Vienna and Hamburg: Zsolnay.

Berresford Ellis, Peter (1974). *The Cornish Language and its Literature.* London and Boston: Routledge and Kegan Paul.

Berresford Ellis, Peter (1985). *The Celtic Revolution. A Study in Anti-Imperialism.* Talybont, Wales: Y Lolfa.

Berresford Ellis, Peter (1998). *The Story of the Cornish Language.* 3rd ed. Redruth, Cornwall: Tor Mark Press.

Blumenwitz, Dieter (1996). "Das Recht auf Gebrauch der Minderheitensprache. Gegenwärtiger Stand und Entwicklungstendenzen im europäischen Völkerrecht." In: Bott-Bodenhausen, ed. (1996). 159-202.

Bodmer, Frederick (1955). *Die Sprachen der Welt. Geschichte – Grammatik – Wortschatz in vergleichender Darstellung.* Cologne: Kiepenheuer & Witsch.

Bott-Bodenhausen, Karin, ed. (1996). *Unterdrückte Sprachen. Sprachverbote und das Recht auf Gebrauch der Minderheitensprachen.* Frankfort et al.: Peter Lang.

Bott-Bodenhausen, Karin (1996b). "Sprachliche Dominanz am Beispiel der deutsch-sorbischen Beziehung." In: Bott-Bodenhausen, ed. (1996). 117-158.

Bowden, John (2002). "The Impact of Malay on Taba: A Type of Incipient Language Death or Incipient Death of a Language Type?." In: Bradley and Bradley, eds. (2002). 114-143.

Bradley, David and Maya Bradley, eds. (2002). *Language Endangerment and Language Maintenance.* London and New York: RoutledgeCurzon.

Bradley, David (2002). "Language Attitudes: The Key Factor in Language Maintenance." In: Bradley and Bradley, eds. (2002). 1-10.

Bradley, David and Maya Bradley (2002a). "Conclusion: Resources for Language Maintenance." In: Bradley and Bradley, eds. (2002). 348-353.

Brenzinger, Matthias, ed. (1992). *Language death: Factual and Theoretical Explorations with Special Reference to East Africa.* Berlin and New York: Mouton de Gruyter.

Brenzinger, Matthias and Gerrit J. Dimmendaal (1992). "Social Contexts of Language Death." In: Brenzinger, ed. (1992). 3-5.

Broderick, George (1999). *Language Death in the Isle of Man.* Tübingen: Niemeyer.

Brown, Wella (²1993). *A Grammar of Modern Cornish.* Callington: Cornish Language Board.

Brown, Wella (1996). *Skeul an Yeth – The Language Ladder* I. Cornish Language Board.

Brown, Wella (1997). *Skeul an Yeth – The Language Ladder* II. Cornish Language Board.

Brown, Wella (1998). *Skeul an Yeth – The Language Ladder* III. Cornish Language Board.

Brown, Wella and Graham Sandercock (1994). *The Cornish Language Board: A Policy Statement.* Cornish Language Board.

Buszard-Welcher, Laura (2001). "Can the Web Help Save My Language?." In: Hinton and Hale, eds. (2001). 331-345.

Campbell, Lyle and M.C. Muntzel (1989). "The Structural Consequences of Language Death." In: Dorian, ed. (1989). 181-196.

Cavalli-Sforza, Luigi Luca (2001). *Gene, Völker und Sprachen. Die biologischen Grundlagen unserer Zivilisation.* Munich: Deutscher Taschenbuch Verlag.

Cenoz, Jasone (2001). "Basque in Spain and France." In: Extra and Gorter, eds. (2001). 45-57.

Chubb, Ray, ed. (2003). *Cornish is Fun – an Informal Course in Living Cornish.* Talybont, Wales:Y Lolfa.

Climo, Laurie (2002). "Why does Cornish matter?." *An Gowsva*: 4-6.

Climo-Thompson, Andrew (2001). *Kernuak Es. Cornish the Easy Way. A Beginner's Course in Everyday Cornish.* Truro: Kernuak Es.

Climo-Thompson, Andrew (2005). "The Cornish Language Strategy Heralds Revolution for Cornish Speakers." *An Gowsva*: 4f.

Cooper, R.L. and B. Spolsky, eds. (1991). *The Influence of Language on Culture and Thought: Essays in Honor of Joshua A. Fishman's Sixty-fifth Birthday.* Berlin: Mouton.

Cornish Language Board, ed. (1999). *Agan Yeth – Cornish Language Studies* 1. Saltash: Cornish Language Board.

Cornwall County Council, ed. (2004). *Strategy for the Cornish Language.* Truro: Cornwall County Council.

Coronel-Molina, S. (1999). "Functional Domains of the Quechua Language in Peru: Issues of Status Planning." *International Journal of Bilingual Education and Bilingualism* 2(3). 166-180.

Council of Europe (1992). *European Charter for Regional or Minority Languages.* Charter No. 148. Strasbourg: Council of Europe.

Crystal, David (1995). *Die Cambridge Enzyklopädie der Sprache.* Frankfort and New York: Campus.

Crystal, David (2000). *Language Death.* Cambridge: Cambridge University Press.

Crystal, David (2001). *Language and the Internet.* Cambridge: Cambridge University Press.

Crystal, David (2004). *The Language Revolution.* Cambridge: Polity Press.

Dalby, Andrew (2002). *Language in Danger. How language loss threatens our future.* London: Penguin.

Dauenhauer, Nora Marks and Richard Dauenhauer (1998). "Technical, Emotional, and Ideological Issues in Reversing Language Shift: Examples from Southeast Alaska." In: Grenoble and Whaley, eds. (1998). 57-98.

Deacon, Bernard, Dick Cole and Garry Tregidga (2003). *Mebyon Kernow and Cornish Nationalism.* Cardiff: Welsh Academic Press.

Deere, Andrew and Daniel J. Cunliffe (2005). "Bilingual Websites in Jurisdictions Requiring Minority Language Use: Effective Implementation of Policies and Guidelines." Conference paper presented at the 10th ICML in Trieste, Italy.

Denison, Norman (1982). "A Linguistic Ecology for Europe?" *Folia Linguistica* 16: 1-16.

Dixon, Robert Malcolm Ward, W.S. Ramson and Mandy Thomas (1990). *Australian Aboriginal Words in English. Their origin and meaning.* Oxford: Oxford University Press.

Dixon, Robert Malcolm Ward (1997). *The Rise and Fall of Languages.* Cambridge: Cambridge University Press.

Dorian, Nancy C. (1981). *Language Death: The Life Cycle of a Scottish Gaelic Dialect.* Philadelphia: University of Pennsylvania Press.

Dorian, Nancy C., ed. (1989). *Investigating Obsolescence.* Cambridge: Cambridge University Press.

Dorian, Nancy C. (1998). "Western Language Ideologies and Small-language Prospects." In: Grenoble and Whaley, eds. (1998). 3-21.

Dorian, Nancy C. (1994). "Purism versus Compromise in Language Revitalization and Language Revival." *Language in Society* 23: 474-494.

Dressler, Wolfgang (1972a). "Allegroregeln rechtfertigen Lentoregeln. Sekundäre Phoneme des Bretonischen." *IBS* 9: 9f.

Dressler, Wolfgang (1972b). "On the Phonology of Language Death." Papers from the Eighth Regional Meeting of the Chicago Linguistics Society: 448-457.

Dressler, Wolfgang and Ruth Wodak-Leodolter, eds. (1977). *Language Death. International Journal of the Sociology of Language* 12.

Dressler, Wolfgang and Ruth Wodak-Leodolter (1977). "Language Preservation and Language Death in Brittany." In: Dressler and Wodak-Leodolter, eds. (1977). 33-44.

Dressler, Wolfgang (1981). "Language Shift and Language Death – a Protean Challenge for the Linguist." *Folia Linguistica* 15: 5-27.

Dumitrescu, Anca (2003). "Romania's Policy on its Minority Languages." Conference paper presented at the 9th ICML in Kiruna, Sweden.

Edwards, John (1991). "Gaelic in Nova Scotia." In: Williams, ed. (1991). 269-297.

Edwards, John (1992). "Sociopolitical Aspects of Language Maintenence and Loss: Towards a Typology of Minority Language Situations." In: Fase, Jaspaert and Kroon, eds. (1992). 37-54.

Edwards, John (1994). *Multilingualism.* London and New York: Routledge.

Extra, Guus and Durk Gorter, eds. (2001). *The Other Languages of Europe.* Clevedon: Multilingual Matters.

Extra, Guus and Durk Gorter (2001a). "Comparative Perspectives on Regional and Immigrant Minority Languages in Multicultural Europe." In: Extra and Gorter, eds. (2001). 1-41.

Fase, Willem, Koen Jaspaert and Sjaak Kroon, eds. (1992). *Maintenance and Loss of Minority Languages.* Amsterdam: Benjamins.

Fettes, Mark (1997). "Stabilizing what? An ecological approach to language renewal." In: Reyhner, ed. (1997). 301-318.

Fill, Alwin (1993). *Ökolinguistik: Eine Einführung.* Tübingen: Narr.

Fill, Alwin (1998). "Ecolinguistics: State of the Art 1998." *Arbeiten aus Anglistik und Amerikanistik* 23/1, 3-16.

Fill, Alwin and Peter Mühlhäusler, eds. (2001). *The Ecolinguistic Reader. Language, Ecology and Environment.* London and New York: Continuum.

Fill, Alwin (1998/2001). "Ecolinguistics: State of the Art 1998." In: Fill and Mühlhäusler, eds. (2001). 43-53.

Finke, Peter (1996/2001). "Identity and Manifoldness: New Perspectives in Science, Language and Politics." In: Fill and Mühlhäusler, eds. (2001). 84-90.

Fishman, Joshua A. (1991). *Reversing Language Shift. Theoretical and empirical foundations of assistance to threatened languages.* Clevedon: Multilingual Matters.

Fishman, Joshua A., ed. (2001). *Can Threatened Languages be Saved? Reversing Language Shift, Revisited: A 21ˢᵗ Century Perspective.* Clevedon: Multilingual Matters.

Fishman, Joshua A. (2001a). "Why is it so Hard to Save a Threatened Language?." In: Fishman, ed. (2001). 1-22.

Fishman, Joshua A. (2001b). "From Theory to Practice (and vice versa): Review, Reconsideration and Reiteration." In: Fishman, ed. (2001). 451-483.

Fromkin, Victoria and Robert Rodman (1998). *An Introduction to Language.* 6ᵗʰ ed. Fort Worth et al.: Harcourt Brace.

Gendall, Richard (1991). *A Student's Grammar of Modern Cornish.* Liskeard: The Cornish Language Council.

George, Ken (1986). *The Pronunciation and Spelling of Revived Cornish.* Saltash: Cornish Language Board.

George, Ken (1993a). "Cornish." In: Ball, ed. (1993). 410-468.

George, Ken (1993b). "The Revived Languages: Modern Cornish." In: Ball, ed. (1993). 644-654.

George, Ken (1993c). *Gerlyver Kernewek Kemmyn. A modern and scholarly Cornish-English Dictionary.* Callington: Cornish Language Board.

George, Ken (1995). "Which Base for Revived Cornish?." In: Payton, ed. (1995). 104-124.

George, Ken and Paul Dunbar (1997). *Cornish for the 21ˢᵗ Century.* Cornish Language Board.

George, Ken (1998). *An Gerlyver Kres. The New Standard Cornish Dictionary.* Cornish Language Board.

George, Ken (2005). *Gerlyvrik. Mini-Dictionary.* Callington, Cornwall and Fouenant, Brittany: The Cornish Language Board and Yoran Embanner.

Gibbs, W.Wayt (2002). "Saving Dying Languages." *Scientific American*: 62-69.

Gonthier, Nathalie, Jean-Paul van Bendegem and Diderik Aerts, eds. (2006). *Evolutionary Epistemology, Language and Culture.* Berlin and New York: Springer (forthcoming).

Gorter, Durk et al., eds. (1990). *Fourth International Conference on Minority Languages. Vol. I: General Papers.* Clevedon: Multilingual Matters.

Gorter, Durk (2001). "A Frisian Update of Reversing Language Shift." In: Fishman, ed. (2001). 215-233.

Gorter, Durk, Alex Riemersma and Jehannes Ytsma (2001). "Frisian in the Netherlands." In Extra and Gorter, eds. (2001). 103-118.

Gould, Stephen Jay (1993). *Eight Little Piggies: Reflections in Natural History.* New York: Norton.

Görlach, Manfred (1995). *New Studies in the History of English.* Heidelberg: Universitätsverlag Winter.

Grenoble, Lenore A. and Lindsay J. Whaley, eds. (1998). *Endangered Languages. Current issues and future prospects.* Cambridge: Cambridge University Press.

Grenoble, Lenore A. and Lindsay J. Whaley (1998a). "Toward a Typology of Language Endangerment." In: Grenoble and Whaley, eds. (1998). 22-54.

Grenoble, Lenore A. and Lindsay J. Whaley (2006). *Saving Languages. An introduction to language revitalization.* Cambridge: Cambridge University Press.

Grimes, Barbara F., ed. (1996). *Ethnologue: Languages of the World.* 13th ed. Dallas: Summer Institute of Linguistics.

Grimes, Barbara F., ed. (2000). *Ethnologue: Languages of the World.* 14th ed. Dallas: Summer Institute of Linguistics.

Grin, François (1999). "Market Forces, Language Spread and Linguistic Diversity." In: Kontra et al., eds. (1999). 169-186.

Grinevald, Colette (1998). "Language Endangerment in South America: A Programmatic Approach." In: Grenoble and Whaley, eds. (1998). 124-159.

Haarmann, Harald (1993). *Die Sprachenwelt Europas. Geschichte und Zukunft der Sprachnationen zwischen Atlantik und Ural.* Frankfort and New York: Campus Verlag.

Haarmann, Harald (2001). *Die Kleinsprachen der Welt – Existenzbedrohung und Überlebenschancen.* Duisburger Arbeiten zur Sprach- und Kulturwissenschaft. Band 41. Frankfort et al.: Peter Lang Europäischer Verlag der Wissenschaften.

Haarmann, Harald (2002a). *Kleines Lexikon der Sprachen. Von Albanisch bis Zulu.* 2nd ed. Munich: Beck.

Haarmann, Harald (2002b). *Lexikon der untergegangenen Sprachen.* München: Beck.

Hagen, Anton M. and Kees de Bot (1990). "Structural Loss and Levelling in Minority Languages and Dialects." *Sociolinguistica* 4: 136-149.

Hale, Amy and Philip Payton, eds. (2000). *New Directions in Celtic Studies.* Exeter: University of Exeter Press.

Hale, Ken (1998). "On Endangered Languages and the Importance of Linguistic Diversity." In: Grenoble and whaley, eds. (1998). 192-216.

Haugen, Einar (1971). "The Ecology of Language." *Linguistic Reporter*, supplement 25 to vol.13 (1): 25.

Haugen, Einar (1972). *An Ecology of Language.* Stanford, California: Stanford University Press.

Highfield, A. and A. Valdman, eds. (1980). *Theoretical Orientations in Creole Studies.* New York and London: Academic Press.

Hindley, Reg (1990). *The Death of the Irish Language.* London and New York: Routledge.

Hinton, Leanne and Kenneth Hale, eds. (2001). *The Green Book of Language Revitalization in Practice.* San Diego et al.: Academic Press.

Hinton, Leanne (2001a). "Language Revitalization: An Overview." In: Hinton and Hale, eds. (2001). 3-18.

Hinton, Leanne (2001b). "Sleeping Languages – Can they be awakened?" In: Hinton and Hale, eds. (2001). 413-417.

Hinton, Leanne, Matt Vera and Nancy Steele (2002). *How to Keep Your Language Alive.* Berkeley, California: Heyday Books.

Hirner, Ute (1997). *Language Death and Revival: A Sociolinguistic Investigation of Cornish and Welsh.* Unpublished Master's thesis. University of Graz.

Hirner, Ute (1999). "Language Death and Revival: A Sociolinguistic Comparison between Cornish and Welsh." In: Cornish Language Board, ed. (1999). 16-41.

Hirner, Ute (2004). "Revived Cornish at its Centenary: The End of the Struggle?" (translated into Estonian). In: Pajusalu and Rahman, eds. (2004). 51-66.

Holmes, Julyan (2000). *1000 Cornish Place Names Explained.* Truro: Dyllansow Truran.

Holmes, Julyan (2003). "On the Track of Cornish in a Bilingual Country." In: Payton, ed. (2003). 270-290.

Hornberger, Nancy and Kendall King (2001). "Reversing Quechua Language Shift in South America." In: Fishman, ed. (2001). 166-194.

Huebner, Patricia Bowden (2001). *The Revival of the Cornish Language.* Unpublished Master's thesis. Idaho State University, Department of Anthropology.

Hymes, Dell (1974). *Foundations in Sociolinguistics: An Ethnographic Approach.* Philadelphia: University of Pennsylvania Press.

Janich, Nina and Albrecht Greule, eds. (2002). *Sprachkulturen in Europa. Ein internationales Handbuch.* Tübingen: Gunter Narr.

Janse, Mark and Sijmen Tol, eds. (2003). *Language Death and Language Maintenance. Theoretical, practical and descriptive approaches.* Amsterdam and Philadelphia: John Benjamins.

Jenner, Henry (1904). *A Handbook of the Cornish Language.* London.

Jones, Mari C. (1998). *Language Obsolescence and Revitalization. Linguistic Change in Two Sociolinguistically Contrasting Welsh Communities.* Oxford: Clarendon Press.

Joseph, John E. (2004). *Language and Identity. National, Ethnic, Religious.* Basingstoke and New York: Palgrave Macmillan.

Kennedy, Neil (2002). "Fatel era ny a keel? Revived Cornish: Taking Stock." In: Payton, ed. (2002). 283-302.

Kimura, Goro Christoph (2002). *Perspektiven menschlicher Eingriffe bei Spracherhalt und -revitalisierung von Minderheitensprachen.* PhD diss. University Hitotubasi, Tokyo.

Kincade, M. Dale (1991)."The Decline of Native Languages in Canada." In: Robins and Uhlenbeck, eds. (1991). 157-176.

Kloss, Heinz (1969). *Grundfragen der Ehnopolitik im 20. Jahrhundert. Die Sprachgemeinschaften zwischen Recht und Gewalt.* Vienna and Stuttgart: Braumüller.

Koerner, E.F.Konrad, ed. (1865). *Linguistics and Evolutionary Theory.* Amsterdam and Philadelphia: John Benjamins Publishing.

Kontra, Miklos, Robert Phillipson, Tove Skutnabb-Kangas and Tibor Varady, eds. (1999). *Language: A Right and a Resource: Approaches to Linguistic Human Rights.* Budapest: Central European University Press.

Krauss, Michael (1992). "The World's Languages in Crisis." *Language* 68/1: 4-10.

Krauss, Michael (1997). "The Indigenous Languages of the North: A Report on their Present State." In: Skoji and Janhunen, eds. (1997). 1-34.

Kronenthal, Melissa (2003). "The EU and Minority Languages: Real or Perceived Failure?" Conference paper presented at the 9th ICML in Kiruna, Sweden.

Kulick, Don (1992). *Language Shift and Cultural Reproduction.* Studies in the social and cultural foundations of language 14. New York: Cambridge University Press.

Ladefoged, Peter (1992). "Another View of Endangered Languages." *Language* 68: 809-811.

Lee, Adrian (2003). Review article: "Mebyon Kernow" of *Mebyon Kernow and Cornish Nationalism* (Deacon et al. (2003)). In Payton, ed. (2003). 305-311.

Lightfoot, David (1999). *The Development of Language: Acquisition, Change and Evolution.* Malden: Blackwell.

Lyon, Rod Trevelyan (2001). *Cornish. The Struggle for Survival.* Tavas an Weryn.

MacAulay, Donald, ed. (1992). *The Celtic Languages.* Cambridge: Cambridge University Press.

Mackey, William F. and Jacob Ornstein, eds. (1979). *Sociolinguistic Studies in Language Contact.* The Hague et al.: Mouton Publishers.

Mackey, William F. (1980). "The Ecology of Language Shift." In: Nelde, ed. (1980). 35-41.

Mackey, William F. (1980/2001). "The Ecology of Language Shift." In: Fill and Mühlhäusler, eds. (2001). 67-74.

MacKinnon, Kenneth (1991). "Language-retreat and Regeneration in the Present-day Scottish Gàidhealtachd." In: Williams, ed. (1991). 121-149.

MacKinnon, Kenneth (2000). *An Independent Academic Study on Cornish.* SGRÙD Research.

MacKinnon, Kenneth (2002). "Cornish at its Millennium: An Independent Study of the Language Undertaken in 2000." In: Payton, ed. (2002). 266-282.

MacKinnon, Kenneth (2004). " 'As Cornish as Possible' – 'Not an Outcast anymore': Speakers' and Learners' Opinions on Cornish ." In: Payton, ed. (2004). 268-287.

Matsumura, Kazuto, ed. (1998). *Studies in Endangered Languages.* Papers from the international symposium on endangered languages, Tokyo, 18-20 November 1995. Tokyo: Hituzi Syobo.

McLeod, Wilson (2005). "A New Multilingual UK? The impact of the European Charter." Conference paper presented at the 10th ICML in Trieste, Italy.

Menn, Lise (1989). "Some People who don't Talk Right: Universal and Particular in Child Language, Aphasia and Language Obsolescence." In: Dorian, ed. (1989). 335-346.

Mercator-Education, ed. (2001). *The Cornish Language in Education in the UK.* Ljouwert/Leeuwarden: Mercator-Education.

Mithun, Marianne (1998). "The Significance of Diversity in Language Endangerment and Preservation." In: Grenoble and Whaley, eds. (1998). 163-191.

Morgan, Gerald (2001). "Welsh – A European Case of Language Maintenance." In. Hinton and Hale, eds. (2001). 107-113.

Mougeon, Raymond and Edouard Beniak (1991). *Linguistic Consequences of Language Contact and Restriction: The Case of French in Ontario, Canada.* Oxford: Clarendon Press.

Mufwene, Salikoko S. (2001). *The Ecology of Language Evolution.* Cambridge: Cambridge University Press.

Mühlhäusler, Peter (1980). "Structural Expansion and the Process of Creolization." In: Highfield and Valdmann, eds. (1980). 19-55.

Mühlhäusler, Peter (1994). "Babel Revisited." *UNESCO Courier:*16-21.

Mühlhäusler, Peter (1994/2001). "Babel Revisited." In: Fill and Mühlhäusler, eds. (2001). 159-164.

Mühlhäusler, Peter (2002a). "Why one cannot Preserve Languages (but can preserve language ecologies)." In: Bradley and Bradley, eds. (2002). 34-39.

Mühlhäusler, Peter (2002b). "A Language Plan for Norfolk Island." In: Bradley and Bradley, eds. (2002). 167-181.

Munske, Horst Haider, ed. (2001). *Handbuch des Friesischen.* Tübingen: Max Niemeyer Verlag.

Nelde, Peter H., ed. (1980). *Sprachkontakt und Sprachkonflikt.* Wiesbaden: Franz Steiner.

Nelde, Peter, M. Strubell and G. Williams (1996). *Euromosaic: Production and Reproduction of Minority Language Communities in the European Union.* Luxembourg: Commission of the European Communiities.

Nettle, Daniel and Suzanne Romaine (2000). *Vanishing Voices. The extinction of the world's languages.* New York: Oxford University Press.

Ó hIfearnáin, Tadhg (2005). "Orthography as Ideology: Manx Speakers and their Gaelic Literacy." Conference paper presented at the 10th ICML in Trieste, Italy.

Ó Muirthile, Liam (1999). "An Peann Coitianta [The Common Pen]." *Irish Times* 25/9/1999: 28.

Ó Murchú, Máirtín (1993). "Aspects of the Societal Status of Modern Irish." In: Ball, ed. (1993). 471-490.

Ó Néill, Diarmuid, ed. (2005). *Rebuilding the Celtic Languages: Reversing Language Shift in the Celtic Countries.* Talybont, Wales: Y Lolfa.

Ó Riagáin, Padráig (2001). "Irish Language Production and Reproduction 1981-1996." In: Fishman, ed. (2001). 195-214.

Ozolins, U. (1999). "Between Russian and European Hegemony: Current Language Policy in the Baltic States." *Current Issues in Language and Society* 6(1): 6-47.

Page, John (1993a). *Grammar for the First Grade.* 5th rev. ed. Cornish Language Board.

Page, John (1993b). *Grammar beyond the First Grade.* 4th rev. ed. Cornish Language Board.

Pajusalu, Karl and Jan Rahman, eds. (2004). *Kiil ja Hindätiidmine (Language and Identity).* Conference papers. Voru, Estonia: Voro Institute.

Pan, Christoph and Beate Sibylle Pfeil (2000). *Die Volksgruppen in Europa: Ein Handbuch.* Vienna: Braumüller.

Pan, Christoph and Beate Sibylle Pfeil (2002). *Minderheitenrechte in Europa. Handbuch der europäischen Volksgruppen.* Band 2. Vienna: Braumüller.

Pan, Christoph and Beate Sibylle Pfeil (2003). *National Minorities in Europe.* Vienna: Braumüller.

Pap, Leo (1979). "Language Attitudes and Minority Status." In: Mackey and Ornstein, eds. (1979). 197-207.

Payton, Philip, ed. (1995). *Cornish Studies 3.* Exeter: University of Exeter Press.

Payton, Philip, ed. (2000a). *Cornwall for Ever! Kernow Bys Vyken!* Truro: Cornwall Heritage Trust.

Payton, Philip (2000b). "Cornish." In: Price, ed. (2000). 109-119.

Payton, Philip, ed. (2002a). *Cornish Studies 10.* Exeter: University of Exeter Press.

Payton, Philip (2002b). *A Vision of Cornwall.* Fowey, Cornwall: Alexander Associates.

Payton, Philip (2002c). *Cornwall's History. An Introduction.* Redruth, Cornwall: Tor Mark.

Payton, Philip, ed. (2003). *Cornish Studies 11.* Exeter: University of Exeter Press.

Payton, Philip (2004a). *Cornwall: A History.* Fowey, Cornwall: Cornwall Editions Limited.

Payton, Philip, ed. (2004b). *Cornish Studies 12.* Exeter: University of Exeter Press.

Peltzer-Karpf, Annemarie (2006). "The Self-organization of Dynamic Systems: Modularity under Scrutiny." In: Gonthier, van Bendegem and Aerts, eds. (2006). forthcoming.

Phillipson, Robert (2003). *English-Only Europe? Challenging Language Policy.* London and New York: Routledge.

Pinker, Steven (1994). *The Language Instinct.* London: Penguin.

Pinker, Steven (1999). *Words and Rules. The Ingredients of Language.* London: Phoenix.

Pool, P.A.S. (^{2}1982). *The Death of Cornish (1600-1800).* Saltash: Cornish Language Board.

Price, Glanville (1984). *The Languages of Britain.* London: Arnold .

Price, Glanville, ed. (2000). *Languages in Britain and Ireland.* Oxford: Blackwell.

Reyhner, John, ed. (1997). *Teaching Indigenous Languages.* Flagstaff: Northern Arizona University.

Robertson, Boyd (2001). "Gaelic in Scotland." In: Extra and Gorter, eds. (2001). 83-101.

Robins, Robert H. and Eugenius M. Uhlenbeck, eds. (1991). *Endangered languages.* Oxford and New York: Berg.

Romaine, Suzanne (1989). *Bilingualism.* Oxford: Blackwell.

Rottland, F. and Okombo, D.O. (1992). "Language Shift among the Suba of Kenya." In: Brenzinger, ed. (1992). 273-283.

Rupp, Christian (2004). "Sprachen sterben aus." *Salzburger Nachrichten* 7/9/2004: 11.

Sandercock, Graham (2004). *Cornish This Way. A Beginner's Course in Cornish.* 3rd ed. Cornish Language Board.

Sandford, Mark (2003). "A Cornish Assembly? Prospects for Devolution in the Duchy." In: Payton, ed. (2003). 40-56.

Sapir, Edward (1921). *Language*. New York: Harcourt Brace.

Sasse, Hans-Jürgen (1992a). "Theory of Language Death." In: Brenzinger, ed. (1992). 7-30.

Sasse, Hans-Jürgen (1992b). "Language Decay and Contact-Induced Change: Similarities and Differences." In: Brenzinger, ed. (1992). 59-80.

Schleicher, August (1865). "On the Significance of Language for the Natural History of Man." In: Koerner, ed. (1865). 73-82.

Senior Secondary Assessment Board (1996). *Australia's Indigenous Language Framework*. Adelaide: Senior Secondary Assessment Board of South Australia.

Sim, Ronald J. (1995). "Review of *Language death: factual and theoretical explorations with special reference to East Africa* (Brenzinger, ed. (1992))." *Journal of Linguistics 31*: 469-470.

Skoji, H. and J. Janhunen, eds. (1997). *Northern Minority Languages. Problems of survival*. Osaka.

Skutnabb-Kangas, Tove and Robert Phillipson, eds. (1994). *Linguistic Human Rights. Overcoming linguistic discrimination*. Berlin and New York.

Skutnabb-Kangas, Tove (2000). *Linguistic Genocide in Education – or Worldwide Diversity and Human Rights?* Mahwah, NJ: Lawrence Erlbaum.

Spolsky, Bernard (1989). "Review of *Key Issues in Bilingualism and Bilingual Education* (Baker 1988)." *Applied Linguistics 10* (4): 449-451.

Spolsky, Bernard (1991). "Hebrew Language Revitalization within a General Theory of Second Language Learning." In: Cooper and Spolsky, eds. (1991). 137-155.

Spolsky, Bernard (1996). "Conditions for Language Revitalization: A Comparison of the Cases of Hebrew and Maori." In: Wright, ed. (1996). 5-50.

Spolsky, Bernard and Elana Shoamy (2001). "Hebrew after a Century of RLS Efforts." In: Fishman, ed. (2001). 350-363.

Spriggs, Matthew (2003). "Where Cornish was Spoken and When: A Provisional Synthesis." In Payton, ed. (2003). 228-269.

Stiles, Michelle (2004). "Mother Tongue." *Cornwall Today* December 2004: 56-61.

Stowell, Brian (2000). "Provision of Manx Language Tuition in Schools in the Isle of Man." In: Payton and Hale, eds. (2000). 141-151.

Strubell, Miquel (2001). "Catalan a Decade Later." In: Fishman, ed. (2001). 260-283.

Swadesh, Morris (1948). "Sociologic Notes on Obsolescent Languages." *International Journal of Linguistics 14*: 226-235.

Thieberger, Nicholas (2002). "Extinction in Whose Terms? Which parts of a language constitute a target for language maintenance programmes?." In: Bradley and Bradley, eds. (2002). 310-328.

Thomas, Alan R. (1992). "The Cornish Language." In: MacAulay, ed. (1992). 346-370.

Thomas, Ned (2000). "How Much IT can Minority Languages Afford?" *Contact* 16 (3): 2.

Trudgill, Peter (1976). "Creolization in Reverse: Reduction and Simplification in the Albanian Dialects of Greece." *Transactions of the Philological Society* 7: 32-50.

Trudgill, Peter (2000). *Sociolinguistics. An Introduction to Language and Society.* 4th ed. London: Penguin.

Tsitsipis, D. (1989). "Skewed Performance and Full Performance in Language Obsolescence: The Case of an Albanian Variety." In Dorian, ed. (1989). 117-138.

Tsunoda, Tasaku (2005). *Language Endangerment and Language Revitalization.* Trends in Linguistics. Studies and Monographs 148. Berlin: Mouton de Gruyter.

Viereck, Wolfgang, Karin Viereck and Heinrich Ramisch (2002). *DTV-Atlas Englische Sprache.* Munich: Deutscher Taschenbuch Verlag.

Wardhaugh, Ronald (1987). *Languages in Competition. Dominance, Diversity, and Decline.* Oxford and New York: Blackwell.

Weatherhill, Craig (2005). *Place Names in Cornwall and Scilly.* Launceston: Wessex and Westcountry Books.

Weinreich, Uriel (1968). *Languages in Contact: Findings and Problems.* The Hague: Mouton.

White, Paul (1991). "Geographical Aspects of Minority Language Situations in Italy." In: Williams, ed. (1991). 44-65.

Williams, Colin H., ed. (1991). *Linguistic Minorities, Society and Territory.* Clevedon: Multilingual Matters.

Williams, Colin H. (1991a). "Linguistic Minorities: West European and Canadian Perspectives." In: Williams, ed. (1991). 1-43.

Williams, Colin H. (2000). "Making Good Boundaries. An interview with Joshua A. Fishman by Xabier Erize." *Planet 140*: 66-75.

Williams, Colin (2001). "Welsh in Great Britain." In: Extra and Gorter, eds. (2001). 59-81.

Willmann, Urs (2002). "Leben und sterben lassen." *Die Zeit* 10 28/2/2002.

Winkler, Eike and Josef Schweikhardt (1982). *Expedition Mensch. Streifzug durch die Anthropologie.* Vienna and Heidelberg: Ueberreuter.

Wright, S., ed. (1996). *Language and the State: Revitalization and Revival in Israel and Eire.* Clevedon: Multilingual Matters.

Wuketits, Franz M. (2003). *Ausgerottet – ausgestorben: Über den Untergang von Arten, Völkern und Sprachen.* Stuttgart: Hirzel.

Wurm, Stephen A. (1998). "Methods of Language Maintenance and Revival, with Selected Cases of Language Endangerment in the World." In: Matsumura, ed. (1998). 191-211.

Wurm, Stephen A. (2001). *Atlas of the World's Languages in Danger of Disappearing.* 2nd rev. ed. Paris: UNESCO.

Wurm, Stephen A. (2002). "Strategies for Language Maintenance and Revival." In: Bradley and Bradley, eds. (2002). 11-23.

Yule, George (1996). *The Study of Language.* 2nd ed. Cambridge: Cambridge University Press.

14 Appendix

14.1 Extract from the 'Strategy for the Cornish Language'

In: English
Kernewek Kemmyn
Unified Cornish
Unified Cornish Revised (UCR)
Late Cornish (Dewedhas)

Where are we now?

This chapter highlights some of the main findings of an independent report for the Government Office for the South West in early 2000 and more recent developments. The full report can be found on GOSW's website at http://www.gosw.gov.uk/.

Ple'th eson ni lemmyn?

An chaptra ma a boeslev nebes sywyans a-dhiworth derivas anserghek rag Soedhva an Governans rag an Soth West a-varr y'n vlydhen 2000 ha'n displegyans moy a-dhiwedhes. Y hyllir kavoes an derivas leun war wiasva Soedhva an Governans rag an Soth West http://www.gosw.gov.uk.

```
Pleth eson ny lemmyn?

An trogh ma a dhelynyas re a'n determynyans bras a'n deryvas
anserhek rag Sothva a'n Government rag an Sothwest (SGSW) yn
2000 avar ha dysplegyans moy agensow. An deryvas cowal a yl bos
kefys war'n wyasva SGSW dhe http://www.gosw.gov.uk.
```

```
Ple theron ny lemmyn?

An trogh ma a dhelynyas re a'n determynyans bras a'n deryvas
anserhak rag Sodhva a'n Government rag an Sothwest (SGSW) yn
2000 avar ha dysplegyans moy agensow. An deryvas cowal a yl bos
kefys war'n wyasva SGSW dhe http://www.gosw.gov.uk.
```

Peleah era ny lebmen?

Ma an chaptra'ma poeza war nebas an kensa determianjow en daryvas fre a ve gwres rag Sodhva SW an Governans en vledhan arvis 2000, keveris ha'n peath a rig displegia ouja hedna. An daryvas lean a veath keves war wiasva an Sodhva Governans ort http://www.gosw.gov.uk.

The report estimated there might be around 300 effective speakers of Cornish with around 750 people learning the language through adult education classes and correspondence learning. The number of speakers continues to grow. There was some form of teaching the language in 12 primary and 4 secondary schools. More recently language colleges began teaching Cornish as part of the curriculum. New interactive CD Rom learning tools have been published. 100 pupils from primary schools piloting Cornwall Education Authority's 'Sense of Place' initiative performed songs in Cornish on St Piran's Day in March 2003.

An derivas a dhismygriv bos a-dro dhe 300 kowser freth a gernewek gans a-dro dhe 750 den ow kewsel an yeth gans klasow adhyskans tevisogyon ha dre lyther. Niver a gowsoryon a bes dhe devi. Yth esa neb furv a dhyskans a'n yeth yn 12 skol gynsa ha 4 skol nessa. Moy a-gynsow Kolljiow Yethow a dhallathas dyski Kernewek avel rann an Stus. Plasennow arghans nowydh re beu dyllys. 100 skoler a-dhiworth skolyow kynsa a ganas kanow rag Goel Pyran mis Meurth 2003, henn o dhe lywya urdhyans Awtorita Adhyskans Kernow 'Sense of Place'.

An deryvas a estematys y fo adro 300 cowsor effethus a Gernewek gans adro dhe 750 person ow tysky an tavas dre glassow dyscans tevysek ha dyscans dre lyther. An nyver a gowsoryon a besy dhe yncressya. Yth esa re form a dhyscans an tavas yn 12 scol kensa ha 4 scol nessa. Moy agensow coljyow tavas a dhallatha dhe dhysky Kernewek kepar ha ran an curriculum. Platten Gompact toul dyscans ynteractyf noweth a ve dyllys gans Eurotalk. 100 studhyer dyworth scolyow kensa ow lewyas an devysyans 'Sense of Place' a'n Auctoryta Dyscans Kernow a berformys canow yn Kernewek Degol Peran yn Merth 2003.

An deryvas a estematys y fo adro 300 cowsor effethus a Gernuak gans adro dhe 750 person ow tesky an tavas dre glassow deskans tevysak ha deskans dre lyther. An nyver a gowsoryon a besy dhe encressya. Theja re neb form a dheskans an tavas yn 12 scol kensa ha 4 scol secund. Moy agensow coljyow tavas a dhallatha dhe dhesky Kernuak kepar ha ran an curryculum. Platten Gompact toul deskans ynteractyf noweth a ve dyllys gans Eurotalk. 100 studhyer dheworth scolyow kensa ow lewyas an devysyans 'Sense of Place' a'n Auctoryta Deskans Kernow a berformys canow yn Kernuak Degol Peran yn Merth 2003.

An daryvas a judgias dr'alja boaz dro dha 300 clappier freth ha dro dha 750 a deez ez a tesky an tavas en deskajow rag teez cowldeves po durt kesscreffa. Ma mens an clappiers whath cressia. Ma menak a deskans war neb coor en 12 scoll kensa ha 4 scoll an nessa degre. Coljyow tavas a dhallathas alerh dha desky Kernuak herweth go towl-deskans. CD Roms interactiv noweth a ve dylles vel towyles rag diskiblon. Cans diskibel a gomeras radn an trial cries 'Sens Plas' gen Radn Deskans Kernow ha'ngy a ganas en Kernuak rag Gol-Peran en 2003.

The language is important for Cornish identity in terms of regional development and cultural heritage, with an increasing demand for weddings and other public ceremonies in Cornish taking it beyond the effective language speaking community. The New Testament was added in 2002 to the number of religious texts translated into Cornish.

An yeth yw a vern rag an hevelepter kernewek rag displegyans rannvroek ha'n ertach gonisogethek, yma gorholedh owth ynkressya rag demmedhyans ha solempnytys poblek erell, henn a ystynn dres an gemmynieth a Gernowegoryon. An Testament Nowydh a veu keworrys yn 2002 dhe'n niver a dekstow kryjyk treylys yn Kernewek.

Mur a vry yu an tavas rag gnas Kernewek yn form a dhysplegyans ranvroek hag ertach culturek, gans demond owth yncressya rag demedhyansow ha solempnytys poblek aral yn Kernewek orth y gemeres yn hans kemeneth a'n tavas effethus. An Testament Noweth a ve keworrys yn 2002 dhe'n nyver a dextennow crysyk trelys dhe'n Kernewek.

Muer a vry yw an tavas rag gnas Kernuak yn form a dhysplegyans ranvroak hag ertaj culturek, gans demond owth encressya rag demedhyansow ha solempnytys poblek aral yn Kernuak orth y gemeres yn hans kemeneth a'n tavas effethus. An Testament Noweth a ve keworrys yn 2002 dhe'n nyver a dextennow cryjyk trelys dhe'n Kernuak.

Besy ew an tavas rag gon haze Kernuak rag mava tuchia cressians economik an pow ha gon heynes. Dreth an deziria ez rag demidhianjow ha solempnyta arall an bobel, mava ystena pelha vel kescowethians an deez a gowz freth an Kernuak. Trellies ve an Testament Noweth en 2002 ha junes dha'n scripturs eroll a ve gwres kens.

Music, song and dance of all kinds has brought Cornish to a wider and more popular audience. Many choirs now include Cornish language items in their repertoire and there is an annual Song for Cornwall event sponsored by Pirate FM radio. The annual Gorsedh Kernow has become an important institution in Cornwall's cultural and civic life.

Ilow, kan ha dons a bup sort re dhros Kernewek dhe woslowysi ledanna ha kerys yn ta. Meur a geuryow a gyv taklennow y'n yeth Kernewek y'ga rol hag yma darvos blydhenyek Kan rag Kernow restrys gans Pirate FM. Gorseth Kernow res eth ha bos fondyans dhe les yn bywnans gonisogethek ha sivek.

Musek, can ha dons a pub sort a ve drys Kernewek dhe'n goslowysy efanna ha moy a gerys. Lyes cor lemmyn a wra yncludya defnythyow a'n tavas Kernewek y'ga raglennow ha yma wharfos Can rag Kernow pub bledhen scodhyes gans radyo Pirate FM. An Orseth a Gernow bledhennek re dheth ha bos ynstytucyon mur dhe les yn bewnans burjesek ha culturek a Gernow.

Musek, can ha dons a pub sort re dhrow Kernuak dhe'n goslowysy efanna ha moy a gerys. Lyes cor lemmyn a wra yncludya defnythyow a'n tavas Kernuak y'ga raglennow ha thera wharfos Can rag Kernow pub bledhen scodhyes gans radyo Pirate FM. An Orseth a Gernow bledhennek re dheth ha bos ynstytucyon mur dhe les yn bewnans burjesek ha culturek a Gernow.

Diffrans sortow meusek, cana ha downssia a dhroaz Kernuk deraag presens moy a deez a lias ehan. Ma lias coer cana en Kernuak ha ma'n radio Pirate FM provia gool pub bledhan henwes 'Caon rag Kernow.' An Orseth Kernow bledhednak ew devedhes institucion mear en bounas gonedhegethak ha civik Pow Kernow.

A number of short film dramas, documentaries and a full-length feature film have been produced in Cornish, some of which have won awards. The broadcast media coverage is limited to a brief news programme on Radio Cornwall on Sundays and, in print, the Western Morning News has a weekly Cornish language column. There is, however, an active specialist press publishing Cornish language material, including full-length novels, and new books continue to be published each year. There are periodicals, comic books and other publications for children.

Niver a fylmow dramatek berr, skrifennow ha fylm leunhys a veu gwrys, nebes anedha re waynyas piwasow. An media tavethliys yw finweythys dhe dowlenn verr a nowodhow war Radyo Kernow pub dy' Sul hag yma kolovenn yn yeth Kernewek yn Western Morning News. Yma, byttegyns, gwask arbennik bywek a dhyllo taklow y'n yeth Kernewek, hwedhlow leunhys ha lyvrow nowydh yw dyllys pub blydhen. Yma lyvrow-termyn, lyvrow gwari ha dyllansow erell rag fleghes.

Nyver a waryow fylm ber, deryvadow ha fylm fytur a hyder lun re be gwres, re anodha re waynys rohow. An coveraj mayn darlesans yu constrynys dhe raglen newodhow ber war Radio Cornwall Dedhyow Sul, hag yn prynt, dhe'n Western Morning News yma coloven seythennek yn Kernewek. Yma, bytygans, gwask specyalst hag actyf ow tyllo defnydhyow y'n tavas Kernewek, owth yncludya novels a hyrder lun, ha lyvrow noweth pesya dhe vos dyllys pub bledhen oll. Yma magasyns, lyvrow comyk ha dyllansow aral rag fleghes.

Nyver a waryow fylm ber, deryvadow ha fylm fytur a hyder luen re be gwres, re anodhanjy re waynys rohow. An coveraj mayn darlejans yw constrynys dhe raglen newodhow ber der Radio Cornwall Dedhyow Sul, hag yn prynt, dhe'n Western Morning News thera coloven seythennek yn Kernuak. Thera, bytegans, gwask specyalst hag actyf ow tyllo defnydhyow y'n tavas Kernuak, owth yncludya novels a hyrder luen, ha lyvrow noweth pesya dhe vos dyllys pub bledhen oll. Thera magazyns, lyvrow comyk ha dyllansow aral rag flehes.

Nebas gwariow-film ber ha daryvadow ve gwres, keveris ha cine-film heer ha radn 'nodhans a waynas poesow. Gen an television ha'n radio, ema bes edn dowlan nawodhow ber gen BBC Radio Kernow war an Zeel ha en paperiow-nawodhis ma artickell pub seithan en Western Morning News. Bettedhewetha, ma gwasg special bewak igge asdereval peath an tavas pecarra daralles heer, rag sompel, ha ma levrow noweth 'tisquedhas pub bledhan. Ma levrow-termen, papyriow wharthis ha dyllianjow eroll ew dha plegadow flehas.

Cornwall County Council, all the District Councils and 38 Town and Parish Councils in Cornwall have so far adopted a policy statement of support for the language. The Heritage Lottery Fund now has a policy on heritage languages, which includes Cornish.

Konsel Kernow, oll an Konselow Ranndiryel hag 38 Konsel an Dre ha Plyw re assentyas dhe'n lavar ambos a skoedhyans rag an yeth. Yma ambos rag yethow ertach dhe'n Heritage Lottery Fund, ha kernewek synsys ena.

```
Consel Conteth Kernow, oll a'n Consellyow Randyr ha 38
Consellyow Dre ha Plu yn Kernow re adoptys deryvas a polycy dhe
scodhya an tavas re bell. Dhe'n Fundyans gwary dall ertach yma
lemmyn polycy yn kever tavasow ertach owth yncludya Kernewek.
```

```
Consel Conteth Kernow, oll a'n Consellyow Randyr ha 38
Consellyow Dre ha Plu yn Kernow re adoptys deryvas a bolycy dhe
scodhya an tavas pelha. Dhe'n Fundyans gwary dall ertaj 'ma
lemmyn polycy yn kever tavasow ertaj owth yncludya Kernuak.
```

Betanurma, Cussel Pow Kernow ha oll an cossyljow tereath ha 38 an cossyljow trea po pleaw a gomeras aman screef polycy dha skoodhia an tavas. Ma polycy en kever tavosow eh'tas dha'n 'Heritage Lottery Fund' lebmen ha Kernuak ew comprehendes.

In addition to the place-names themselves, Cornish has a growing public presence. Many towns have a Cornish welcome in their name-boards and some now have place name signs in historic form at their main route entrances. Carrick District Council has a policy on designating Cornish language names for new streets and public buildings and there are a number of examples of Cornish names as well as Anglicised names in signage and pamphlets. A pamphlet produced for Bodmin Moor uses some Cornish.

Kekeffrys ha'n henwyn-tylleryow aga honan, yma presens poblek ow kressya. Yma dynnargh Kernewek dhe lies tre war'n arwoedhyow hag yma henwyn-tylleryow yn furv istorek a borthow an trevow. Yma ambos dhe Gonsel Karrek dhe gavoes henwyn Kernewek dhe'n stretow nowydh ha'n drehevyansow poblek hag yma meur a ensamplow a henwyn Kernewek kekeffrys ha'n re sowsnekhes yn arwoedhyow ha lyvrigow. Y kevir Kernewek ynwedh skrifys yn lyvrik rag Hal Fowydh.

Marnas hynwyn tyllerow aga honen, dhe'n Kernewek yma presens poblek ow thevy. Dhe'n lyes dre yma dynergh Kernewek y'ga bordys henwel ha lemmyn yma arwedhow hynwyn tyller yn form ystorek dhe'n forth entrans bras. Dhe'n Consel Randyr Carrek yma polycy dhe henwel hynwyn y'n tavas Kernewek rag stretys noweth ha chyow poblek hag yma nyver ensomplow a hynwyn Kernewek kepar ha hynwyn Sawsnakhes war arwedhow ha folennygow. Folennek a bryntyas rag Hal Falwyth usya nebes Kernewek.

Marnas henwyn tyllerow aga honen, dhe'n Kernuak 'ma presens poblek ow thevy. Dhe'n lyes dre 'ma dynergh Kernuak y'ga bordys henwel ha lemmyn 'ma arwedhow henwyn tyller yn form ystorek dhe'n forth entrans bras. Dhe'n Consel Randyr Carrak 'ma bolycy dhe henwel henwyn y'n tavas Kernuak rag stretys noweth ha chyow poblek hag yma nyver ensomplow a henwyn Kernuak kepar ha henwyn Sawsnakhes war arwedhow ha folennygow. Folennek a bryntyas rag Gun Bren usya nebes Kernuak.

Moy vel gon henwyn tellyriow a veath nevra spladn, ma presens an Kernuak cressia deraag an bobel. Ma lias trea 'tisquedhas welcum Kernuak ort ago seenes ha ma radn dodhans henwyn-tellyriow ort porthow ago forrow broaz. Ma war towl Cussel an Tereath Carrak ry henwyn Kernuak dha staites noweth ha derevianjow poblak ha nebas henwyn Kernuak ew keves orth seenes eroll ha folednow-pleges warbarha'n formes Sowsneghes. Ma folen rag an Oon Bren dodhy tabm Kernuak, rag sompel.

(Source: http://www.cornwall.gov.uk/index.cfm?articleid=6080)

14.2 The questionnaires

14.2.1   QUESTIONNAIRE on CORNISH (March 2005)

*I am a PhD student at the University of Graz in Austria and my thesis deals with minority languages, with particular reference to the revival of Cornish. In order to obtain authentic data from **speakers/learners** of Cornish, I would be most grateful if you could kindly spare a few minutes of your time to fill in this questionnaire and return it to me personally or send it to:*

Ms Ute Wimmer
Zaglausiedlung 16
A-5600 St. Johann im Pongau

Thank you very much for your cooperation!

1.   **Age:**

☐ Under 20   ☐ 20-29   ☐ 30-39   ☐ 40-49   ☐ 50-59   ☐ Over 60

2.   **Sex:**   ☐ Male   ☐ Female

3.   What is your **occupation?** _____

4.   **Where are you from (birthplace/origin)?**

☐ Cornwall   Where exactly? _____

☐ Outside Cornwall   Where exactly? _____

5.   **Where do you live now?**

☐ In Cornwall   Where exactly? _____

☐ Outside Cornwall   Where exactly? _____

6.   Only for those who are not from Cornwall: **Do you have Cornish roots (ancestors)?**

☐ Yes   ☐ No   If yes, please specify: _____

7.   **What have been your motives for speaking/learning Cornish?** You can tick more than one box.

☐ Cornish was the language of my ancestors so it's important to keep it alive.

☐ Cornwall has a rich culture and the Cornish language is a key to it.

☐ The Cornish language is a symbol of our national identity.

☐ By speaking Cornish, I feel more a part of the community in which I live.

☐ I can take part in Celtic festivals and the Gorsedh.

☐ I am generally interested in languages.

☐ The more languages you speak the easier it is to learn another.

☐ It's useful to have a 'secret' language.

☐ Other motives: _____

8.   How would you rate your fluency in Cornish?

☐ Beginner   ☐ Not very fluent   ☐ Moderately fluent   ☐ Fluent   ☐ Very fluent

9.   Which variety of Cornish do you learn/speak?

☐ Kemmyn   ☐ Unified   ☐ Late/Modern (Dewedhas)   ☐ Unified Cornish Revised

10.   a. How long have you been learning (did you learn) Cornish? _____

   b.   For how many hours per week? _____

   c.   Using which method? ☐ Evening class   ☐ Autodidactically

      ☐ Correspondence course   ☐ Other (please specify) _____

   d.   Are you going to continue your studies? ☐ Yes   ☐ No Why not?

   _____

11.   Have you taken and passed a Cornish Language Board exam?

   ☐ Yes   When and which grade(s)? _____

   ☐ No   Do you intend to take an exam? When? _____

12.   Are you pleased with your progress in the language? What are the main difficulties?

   _____

13.   Outside the classroom, to whom do you speak Cornish and in which settings (home, work, pub...)?

   _____

14.   Do you have children? ☐ Yes (Ages: _____) ☐ No

   If yes, do you speak Cornish to them?

   ☐ Yes→How often? _____

   ☐ No→ Why not? _____

15. **Do you feel that since the recognition of Cornish under part 2 of the European Charter for Regional or Minority Languages in 2002, the status of the Cornish language has improved considerably?**

☐ Yes   ☐ No   Please give reasons for your answer:

_____

16. **How would you rate the general attitude in Cornwall with regard to promoting Cornish?**

☐ Very favourable   ☐ Neither favourable nor disfavourable   ☐ Unfavourable

Explain:

_____

_____

17. **Which concrete measures to further develop Cornish would you like to see implemented in the near future?**

_____

_____

18. **What do you regard as the most difficult challenges to overcome?** Please rank the following challenges by writing numbers from 1-12 in each of the boxes next to the listed challenges, where **1 represents the most difficult challenge and 12 = the least difficult challenge/obstacle.**

☐ Lack of pre-school playgroups

☐ Cornish is no proper subject at school.

☐ Fragmentation-spelling debate

☐ Few opportunities for daily use

☐ No concentrated area of speakers

☐ Cornish is not useful for social advancement.

☐ Private costs to pay classes

☐ Lack of funding and resources for teacher training

☐ Difficult grammar (e.g. mutations)

☐ Lack of interactive teaching materials

☐ Absence of Cornish on TV

☐ Growing number of 2nd home owners from outside Cornwall

14.2.2 QUESTIONNAIRE on CORNISH – Pupils (March 2005)

*My name is Ute Wimmer and I am a PhD student at the University of Graz in Austria. My thesis deals with minority languages, with particular reference to the revival of Cornish. In order to obtain authentic data from **pupils**, I would be most grateful if you could kindly spare a few minutes of your time to fill in this questionnaire.*

1. **Age:** _____

2. **Sex:**   ☐ Male   ☐ Female

3. **Parents' occupation:** _____

4. **For how long did you learn Cornish?** _____

5. **How often did the lessons take place and how long did they last** (e.g. once a week, 1 hour)**?** _____

6. **Did you like the lessons?**   ☐ Yes   ☐ No   Why (not)?

7. **Rate your ability to speak Cornish on a five-point-scale by marking the appropriate box:**

    ☐ I understand a bit of Cornish but can't speak it.

    ☐ I know a few phrases.

    ☐ I can manage a simple conversation.

    ☐ I can take part in most conversations.

    ☐ I am fluent in Cornish.

8. **What has made learning Cornish hardest? Grammar, vocabulary or the pronunciation?**

    Explain:

9. **Have you used Cornish outside the classroom? On what occasions? With whom?**

10. **Have you used Cornish in writing? When?**

11. **Do you learn/speak any other foreign language?**

    ☐ Yes→ Which one? _____ ☐ No

12. **a. If yes, do you prefer the other language to Cornish? Give reasons.**

    b. If not, would you prefer learning another language to learning Cornish? Which one and why?

13. **Are you proud of knowing Cornish?** ☐ Yes ☐ No

14. **Did your parents encourage you to learn Cornish?** ☐ Yes ☐ No

15. **Do you think being able to speak Cornish has advantages?** Give reasons.

16. **Apart from school, do you know anybody who speaks Cornish?**

    ☐ Yes→Please specify: _____

    ☐ No

17. **How is the Cornish language noticeable in everyday life?** You can tick more than one box.

    ☐ Place names   ☐ Shop and building names   ☐ Tourist attractions

    ☐ Street signs   ☐ Advertising

    ☐ Other: _____

18. **a. Do you think the Cornish language is cool?** ☐ Yes ☐ No Why (not)?

    b. Do you think English is cooler? ☐ Yes ☐ No **Why (not)?**

19.   Are you going to continue to learn Cornish? ☐ Yes   ☐ No **Why (not)?**

20.   Which variety of Cornish do you learn/speak?

☐ Kemmyn   ☐ Unified   ☐ Late/Modern (Dewedhas)   ☐ Unified Cornish Revised

☺   Thank you very much for your cooperation! ☺

14.2.3   QUESTIONNAIRE on the CORNISH LANGUAGE (March 2005)

I am a PhD student at the University of Graz in Austria and my thesis deals with minority languages, with particular reference to the revival of Cornish. In order to obtain authentic data, I would be most grateful if you could kindly spare a few minutes of your time to fill in this questionnaire and return it to me personally or send it to:

Ms Ute Wimmer   Thank you very much for your
Zaglausiedlung 16   cooperation!
A-5600 St. Johann im Pongau

1.   **Age:**

☐ Under 20   ☐ 20-29   ☐ 30-39   ☐ 40-49   ☐ 50-59   ☐ Over 60

2.   **Sex:**   ☐ Male   ☐ Female

3.   What is your **occupation?** _____

4.   **Where are you from (birthplace/origin)?**

☐ Cornwall   Where exactly? _____

☐ Outside Cornwall   Where exactly? _____

5.   **Where do you live now? Since when?**

_____

6.   **Only for those who are not from Cornwall: Do you have Cornish roots (ancestors)?**

☐ Yes   ☐ No   If yes, please specify: _____

7.   **The Cornish language belongs to the Celtic language group. Do you know any other Celtic languages?**

☐ Yes → Which ones? _____ ☐ No

8.   **Do you know any Cornish words that are still used in your area?**

☐ Yes→Give examples: _____
☐ No

9.   **Do you know anybody who speaks Cornish?**

☐ Yes→Please specify: _____
☐ No

10. **How is the Cornish language noticeable in everyday life?** You can tick more than one box.

   ☐ Place names   ☐ Shop and building names   ☐ Tourist attractions

   ☐ Street signs   ☐ Advertising

   ☐ Other: _____

11. **Have you got the feeling that the media (newspapers, TV, radio) are raising the public awareness of Cornish?**

   ☐ Yes   ☐ No

   If yes, please specify: _____

   _____

12. **Could it be possible that you start learning Cornish in the future?**

   ☐ Yes   ☐ No Why (not)?

   _____

13. **Have you heard of any Cornish language evening classes that are offered in your area?**

   ☐ Yes→Where? _____

   ☐ No

14. **Motivation for learning Cornish:** Tick the statements you agree with.

   ☐ Cornish was the language of my ancestors so it's important to keep it alive.

   ☐ Cornwall has a rich culture and the Cornish language is a key to it.

   ☐ The Cornish language is a symbol of our national identity.

   ☐ By speaking Cornish, I would feel more a part of the community in which I live.

   ☐ I am generally interested in languages.

   ☐ Other: _____

15. **Apart from English, do you speak any other languages?**

   ☐ Yes   ☐ No

   If yes, which one(s) and how fluently?

   _____

16. **How do you think Cornish should be taught in schools in Cornwall?**

  ☐ not at all

  ☐ as an extra/voluntary subject outside the normal timetable

  ☐ as a compulsory subject

  ☐ as a 2nd language on a par with languages such as French or German

17. **How would you rate the general attitude in Cornwall with regard to promoting Cornish?**

  ☐ Very favourable ☐ Neither favourable nor disfavourable ☐ Unfavourable

  Explain:_____

  _____

18. **Did you know that the British Government recognized Cornish as an official minority language within Britain by signing the European Charter for Regional or Minority Languages in 2002?**

  ☐ Yes ☐ No

19. **What do you associate with 'Cornishness'?** Write down whatever comes to your mind immediately.

  _____

  _____

20. **Would you be willing to support the revival movement?**

  ☐ Yes ☐ No

  If yes, how? _____

  If no, why not? _____

21. **What do you foresee regarding the future of the Cornish language?**

  _____

  _____

  _____

14.3 Advertisement for Cornish pasties

(*Cornish World*, issue 40, winter 2004, p.49)

14.4 Cornish language Christmas cards

Literal translation: 'Christmas happy and year new good'

14.5 Cornish language postcards

Gorhemmynnadow A'n Gwella Diworth Kernow
Best wishes from Cornwall

Kernewek   Sowsnek

Nebes geryow a Gernewek   A few words of Cornish

Fatla genes?   How are you?
Yn poynt da, meur ras   Very well thank you
My a gar Kernow   I love Cornwall
An mor   The sea
Nans   Valley
Meyn   Stones or rocks
Dowr   Water
Eglos   Church
Chi   House
Bos   Home
Bre   Hill

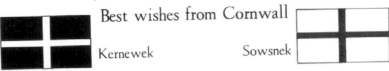

"By Tre, Ros, Poll, Lann and Penn,
You shall know the Cornishmen"
Settlement, Moor, Pool, Enclosure, Headland or Peak

14.6 Holiday lodge advertisement

(*Cornwall Today*, December 2004, p.163)

14.7 Course books in Kernewek

Skeul an Yeth ('The Language Ladder') is a 3-part course (Brown 1996,1997, 1998) covering all 4 Grades of the Cornish Language Board's Exams.

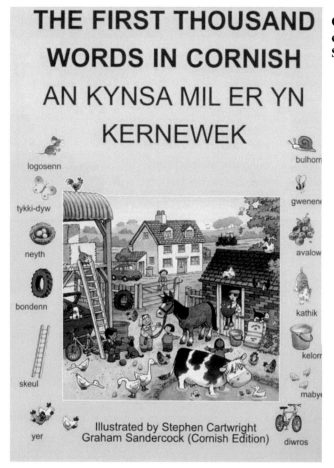

One of the few attractive books for children by Amery, Cartwright and Sandercock (2003)

14.8 Cover picture of the magazine *Cornish World*

14.9 Cornish language/products advertisements

(*Cornish World*, issue 40, winter 2004, pp.40, 73)

(*Cornwall Today*, December 2004, p.24)

14.10 Cornish language section in the *Cornish World*

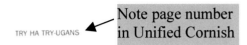

TRY HA TRY-UGANS

Note page number in Unified Cornish

CORNISH WORLD | **FEATURE** | **63**

An Pennti Kernewek y'n 'dydhyow koth da'

Y'n jydh hedhyw ni a breder a bennti Kernewek avel neb chi byghan romansek, desedhys yn kres an pow a-dro, afinys gans pub gorlanwes a'n bys arnowydh, ha kerghynnys gans lowarthow teg po glesin kempenn fylghys. War fos an pennti – mars yw onan piwys gans estrenyon dhe Gernow – y fyth kregis ros-kert, nowydh pentys, hag a-dherag an chi, yn le may hyll pub huni y weles, gravath-ros koth, ynwedh nowydh pentys, ha lenwys gans bleujennow.

Mes y'n termyn eus passys – y'n 18ves kansblydhen po a-varr y'n 19ves – yth o skeusenn dhyffrans. An pennti y'n dydhyow na – yn hwir, krowji a via ger gwell – o truan, yeyn, tewl ha glyb. Yth o pur vyghan, isel, gans fosow a gobb ha leur a weres troes-stankys. An daras o yn dew hanter, an hanter a-wartha gwithys yn ygerys dhe asa nebes golow a-ji, ha'n hanter a-woeles gwithys yn deges dhe dhifenna an fleghes rag mos yn-mes ha rag an yer ha'n mogh rag dos a-ji. Yth esa unn fenester vyghan, a-dro dhe dhew droes-hys pedrak, gans an gweder – y'n re na a's teva gweder – kammformys gans 'lagasow' po kolmow. Mars esa kwarel byghan terrys, an toll a via gwalghys gans pil po kudhys gans tamm leghenn koth. Ny wrug fenestri y'n penntiow ma gasa golow a-ji, mes difenna keun ha kathes rag entra.

An unn stevell y'n pennti a servya pub porpos oll marnas koska. Yth o kegin, floghva, golghva hag 'esedhva' oll warbarth. Y'n chymbla igor yth esa tan a dowargh po kyfys eythin hag a asa moy a doemmder diank warvan an chymbla es mos y'n stevell. Ow kregi y'n chymbla war drybedh yth esa pot-horn po chekk bras.

Yn kever mebyl, hemm o skant dhe leverel an lyha. Yth esa moes arow – moy kepar ha bynk ser prenn, ha dhe esedha orti hi, skown hir ha skavell teyr-gar. An re ma o rag tus a oes – res o dhe'n fleghes esedha war stokk a brenn. Nebes hanavow a gloam, padelligow ha basons, niver boghes lowr a blatys a brenn po a sten, ha'n pot-horn po chekk a gampoellis vy a-ugh, a gomprehendya an daffar y'n stevell.

Nyns esa chambour po chambours. Yth esa neppyth henwys 'talfat', nag o yn hwir travydh marnas leur igor yn dann an to hag ystynna dres hanter an stevell a-woeles. Gwrys a blenkys kentrynnys warbarth, ef a worwedhas war gopel a geberyow settys y'n fosow. Dhe lettya tus rag koedha diworth an talfat, yth esa kledhrenn kentrynnys dhe'n amal. May hylli an teylu yskynna dhe'n talfat diworth an leur a-woeles, yth esa skeul.

Mars esa an 'mebyl' skantlowr a-woeles, yth o gweth y'n talfat. Ny vern braster an teylu, nyns esa marnas unn gweli. An gour ha'y wreg a goski yn kres an gweli, an dhew flogh an yowynka gansa war emlow a-ves, fleghes erell war golghes war leur an talfat, ha'n baban yn kostenn. An gweli y honan o gwrys a brenn, gans lovanow ystynnys ynter an dhew du dhe synsi an kolpes. Drefenn bos fowt a vona dhe'n teylu, nyns esa meur yn maner a ballennow war an gweli, hag y'n yeynder Gwav, kotas, powsyow po seghyer a veu devnydhys dhe assaya gwitha an annedhysi toemm.

To an pennti o gwrys a gala, ha wosa y vos nebes koth hag yn kewer wynsek ha glyb, a wre sygera kepar ha kroder, ow cul an gweli a-woeles glyb ynwedh. Gwra dismygi an gour ow tehweles tre wosa jorna fest hir y'n parkow po y'n bal, yeyn gans dillas glyb, ha wosa dybri neb kowl po iskell gwann, assaya

omsygha a-dherag tan a dowargh, hag ena heb dillas sygh ewn, mos dhe'n gweli, le may hwre ev unnweyth arta assaya dos ha bos toemm ha cafos nebes kosk.

Der aga boghosognedh, yth o anpossybyl rag an teylu prena dillas lowr – heb prederi a-dro dhe wellheans dhe'n pennti. Res o dhe bub esel an teylu mos y'n parkow po y'n bal dhe oberi – fleghes ynwedh. An fleghes ogas dhe gettup penn a wodhevis dre fowt a dhillas ewn, yn fenowgh heb eskisyow ha lostennow po treylyans vydholl a dhillas. Y'n Gwav, yn kewer rewek po pan esa yrgh, nyns o anusadow gweles mebyon naw po deg bloedh y'n parkow owth oela yn hwerow awos an yeynder, gans aga diwla mar las ha marow na yllens i skantlowr dalghenna an ervin rewys dh'aga tenna 'mes an dor.

Gans bywnans mar uthek – fowt a dhillas lowr, ha'n dillas esa gansa yn fenowgh glyb, penntiow yeyn ha glyb, boes drog – yth yw marthys y tevis dhe oes an fleghes ma. Mes rem o klavder yn pub tyller yn mysk an boghosek ma. Pan dhrehedhas ev 50, den o yn hwir koth, skantlowr kerdhes heb diw lorgh, ha re wrussa dos ha bos mar dhiwedhen yn yn gevalsyow, pan wrussa esedha, yth o gans kaletter meur yth ylli omsevel arta. An dydhyow koth da! *Rod Lyon Grand Bard of the Cornish Gorsedd.*

Today we think of a Cornish cottage as some romantic haven in the country, surrounded by pretty gardens and provided with all the luxuries of modern-day life. In the eighteenth and early nineteenth centuries this was certainly not the case. General poverty realised cottages that were small, wet, cold and generally wretched, as this narrative reveals.